Prosecution among Friends

I0091100

Joseph V. Hughes Jr. and Holly O. Hughes Series on the Presidency and Leadership

Prosecution among Friends

**PRESIDENTS, ATTORNEYS GENERAL,
AND EXECUTIVE BRANCH WRONGDOING**

David Alistair Yalof

TEXAS A&M UNIVERSITY PRESS • COLLEGE STATION

This paper meets the requirements

of ANSI/NISO Z39.48-1992 (Permanence of Paper).

Binding materials have been chosen for durability.

⊗ ♻

LIBRARY OF CONGRESS CATALOGING-IN-PUBLICATION DATA

Yalof, David Alistair.
  Prosecution among friends : presidents, attorneys general, and executive branch wrongdoing / David Alistair Yalof. — 1st ed.
      p. cm. — (Joseph V. Hughes Jr. and Holly O. Hughes series on the presidency and leadership)
  Includes bibliographical references and index.
  ISBN-13: 978-1-60344-744-7 (cloth : alk. paper)
  ISBN-10: 1-60344-744-X (cloth : alk. paper)
  ISBN-13: 978-1-60344-745-4 (pbk. : alk. paper)
  ISBN-10: 1-60344-745-8 (pbk. : alk. paper)
  ISBN-13: 978-1-60344-759-1 (e-book)
  ISBN-10: 1-60344-759-8 (e-book)
  ISBN-13: 978-1-60344-766-9 (e-book)
  ISBN-10: 1-60344-766-0 (e-book)
  1. United States. Dept. of Justice—History.   2. Corruption investigation—United States—History.   3. Special prosecutors—United States—History.
  4. Criminal investigation—Political aspects—United States—History.
  I. Title.   II. Series: Joseph V. Hughes, Jr. and Holly O. Hughes series
on the presidency and leadership.
  KF5107.Y35   2012
  364.1'3230973—dc23
  2011050638

Contents

Preface

Moments after taking the presidential oath of office on August 9, 1974, the thirty-eighth president of the United States offered the above words of assurance about a constitutional system that had just survived the ordeal of a twice-elected president's being forced to resign in disgrace. In the case of the Watergate scandal that eventually paralyzed the White House and much of official Washington, President Nixon and other high-level officials had been identified and then held politically accountable for their actions. Yet to what end? The vast majority of citizens who had watched the Watergate scandal unfold over the previous two years might well have reached a conclusion opposite to President Ford's about the effectiveness of the constitutional system. After all, the Constitution Ford was celebrating had failed to prevent such high-level wrongdoing from occurring in the first place. Meanwhile, the challenge of ferreting out such corruption had consumed the attention of two US attorneys' offices, two (and eventually three) special prosecutors, three attorneys general, one acting attorney general, and numerous deputy and assistant attorneys general, as well as countless lawyers and staff. Moreover, just as Ford was assuming the presidency, there remained serious doubts as to whether the disgraced former president would ever be held criminally liable for his actions. President Ford ended that final piece of speculation when he controversially pardoned his predecessor less than a month later.

Perhaps the newly sworn-in president intended his words about the Constitution as a rhetorical flourish—an eloquent, Lincolnesque cover for his own personal despair at the dilemma that faces any republic seeking to hold its public officials accountable within the strictures of a formal separation-of-powers framework. Several crucial challenges recur in this context: (1) How can the president of the United States and other high-level executive-branch officials be held accountable for illegal or unethical conduct by prosecutors and other officials who must themselves report (either directly or indirectly) to the president? (2) How can Department of Justice officials in particular be held accountable by fellow prosecutors who work in that same department or by entities accountable to that same department? and (3) If absolute accountability is indeed not possible, how can the constitutional system maintain the public's faith in its legitimacy? In the wake of numerous scandals that have afflicted administrations in modern times, the public's frustration with the process has grown even more intense. When accountability for official wrongdoing is limited primarily to those officials who are already politically weak, or who are seen as expendable by higher-level officials, the public is rarely satisfied. And if perceptions that the process is rigged or unfair cannot be dispelled, the American political system is certain to suffer.

For the better part of two decades, the independent counsel provisions of the Ethics in Government Act of 1978 (the EGA)—both in its original form and as amended in subsequent years—provided the all-purpose panacea for what many considered one of the system's most glaring ills: its inability to hold high-level executives accountable under the law. Before passage of the EGA, a president or his attorney general, when facing a conflict of interest, occasionally vested an outside attorney with the power to investigate and prosecute public officials for wrongdoing. Ulysses Grant appointed a special prosecutor to investigate allegations of corruption leveled at Treasury Department officials as part of the "whiskey ring" scandal in the 1870s; Calvin Coolidge appointed two special prosecutors to investigate the "teapot dome" scandal of the 1920s. So long as the ends achieved (whether indictments, convictions, or perhaps resignations) prove satisfying to the public at large, and in particular to the president's political opposition, calls for reforming this ad hoc appointment process generally fell on deaf ears.

The Watergate scandal marked a dramatic turning point in the prospects for reform, as it shone the public spotlight ever more brightly on the prosecutorial appointment process itself. Richard Nixon had only himself to blame for this development, as he ordered the firing of the Watergate special prosecutor (Archibald Cox) in a drama that played out publicly on October 20, 1973. Nixon's own attorney general, Elliot Richardson, had originally hired Cox for his "impeccable integrity," and thus refused to follow Nixon's instructions. When Richardson (and his deputy, William Ruckelshaus) resigned in protest of the president's order to fire Cox, they all but guaranteed that the process for selecting special prosecutors would receive unprecedented attention for the foreseeable future. Though the two subsequent Watergate special prosecutors, Leon Jaworski and Charles Ruff, enjoyed the equivalent of near unlimited discretion to pursue various aspects of the Watergate affair, Congress could no longer take such discretion for granted. To no one's surprise, it initiated hearings in 1975 to consider legislation that would offer some form of statutory protection for special prosecutors in the future.

After several years of wrangling on Capitol Hill, Congress eventually passed the EGA, which empowered a special three-judge panel of the US Court of Appeals for the DC Circuit to appoint neutral special prosecutors (later termed "independent counsels") if the US attorney general submitted an application based on a possible conflict of interest in the matter of public corruption or official wrongdoing. Once a special prosecutor was approved, the attorney general could then remove him or her only for cause, and only with the consent of the three-judge panel. Twenty independent counsels were appointed during the life of these statutory provisions, which stretched over two different periods (between 1978 and 1994, and then again between 1996 and 1999). The US Supreme Court upheld the independent counsel provisions as constitutional in *Morrison v. Olson* (1988);[1] still, the legislative regime proved mostly ineffective at addressing the real issues of accountability that had sparked the law's passage in the first place. Because for political reasons neither the attorney general nor the special court could effectively rein in independent counsels, the EGA had essentially addressed a breakdown in political accountability on one front (the Justice Department) by creating an officer who was, for all practical purposes, accountable to no one.

The lone dissenter in *Morrison*, Justice Antonin Scalia, declared that "under our system of government, the primary check against prosecutorial abuse is a political one."[2] Political checks in this context are not just theoretical: under various conditions presidents suffer politically when investigations do not proceed aggressively, and they may benefit politically from being tough on corruption that occurs within their own administrations. In this book I consider the conditions that are most likely to undermine traditional Justice Department processes for investigating and prosecuting executive branch corruption. Those conditions include (1) when the targets are themselves within the White House or the vice president's office, or are family members of the president or vice president, (2) when the targets work for the Justice Department or other federal law enforcement authorities, (3) when the targets are associated with the current administration rather than a previous one, (4) when elections threaten to intervene at a critical time in the course of the investigation, and (5) when one party controls both the White House and the Congress at the same time.

When one or more of the factors listed above are present, the risk of biased investigations and prosecutions increases substantially, and the need for a special prosecutor of some type becomes more compelling. Yet even then the decision to abandon routine Justice Department processes may offer a close call. In all such instances, the presence of an attorney general well equipped to perform his responsibilities without obvious bias or self-interest becomes critical. As Justice Scalia again reminds us in *Morrison*, "the prosecutors who exercise this awesome discretion are selected and can be removed by a President, whom the people have trusted enough to elect. . . . When crimes are not investigated and prosecuted fairly, nonselectively, with a reasonable sense of proportion, the President pays the cost in political damage to his administration. . . . That is the system of justice the rest of us are entitled to."[3]

Indeed, the appointment of a qualified and unbiased attorney general provides the most important check that the system must rely upon.

Our modern-day obsession with choosing special prosecutors or counsels who cannot easily be fired has significant implications for the political process as a whole. By directing the attention of a polity frustrated with officials' abuses toward the appointment of those individuals, Congress effectively draws the public's attention away from efforts to secure and improve the quality of political checks that are already in place. If those checks are strong, and if the current attorney general does not intentionally or inadvertently undermine them, an autonomous special prosecutor who performs his duties free from executive branch meddling may be unnecessary and superfluous. Even the most stringent special prosecutor laws normally incorporate a significant role for the attorney general: he or she must conduct an initial investigation into the matter, and only the attorney general may apply for an outside prosecutor in the first place. In the alternative, it is the attorney general who must determine that no such special treatment is warranted.

Meanwhile, the process of nominating and confirming attorneys general has generated only limited attention from the public at large. Since the beginning of the republic, the US Senate has explicitly rejected just two of eighty-six nominees for attorney general (two other nominees to head the Department of Justice withdrew their names without a Senate vote on their merits). The most recent controversy over an attorney general's appointment occurred in 2009, when Pres. Barack Obama's nominee, Eric Holder, faced accusations that as deputy attorney general in January of 2001 he had circumvented standard procedures to support a controversial pardon petition from President Clinton for financier (and Clinton supporter) Marc Rich. Holder was still confirmed easily by a 75–21 vote, with sixteen Republican senators supporting his confirmation. Two formal rejections in 220 years hardly constitute intense scrutiny of a position whose independence is so critical.

What criteria should the president use to select his attorney general? How much independence must the attorney general enjoy to act in the best interests of the public? Can the president, and by extension his attorney general, terminate Justice Department lawyers who fail to effectively investigate their own administration's corrupt practices? Or does the willingness to limit (and if necessary, terminate) prosecutors extend only to those who are too successful? Our obsession with independent prosecutors has tended to relegate most of these questions to the backburner of American politics.

The imperial presidency of modern times can be directed to good as well as evil. The routine use of the appointment and removal power carries with it important implications that may not arise until later in a presidency, when allegations of public corruption first surface. This book offers evidence that the responsible exercise of those powers—whether through the appointment of qualified and unbiased attorneys general and deputy attorneys general or the removal of those officials whenever conflicts arise—often proves crucial to facilitating government efforts to address more serious official wrongdoing. Congress has a role to play in this context as well, taking more seriously its function of scrutinizing executive appointments for issues that may arise late in a presidency, rather than simply rehashing past incidents that are unlikely to arise again.

Justice Scalia's faith in political checks may be well placed, so long as those political checks are taken seriously from the outset. To assess this problem, this book examines twenty-six cases of public corruption (or alleged corruption) that occurred in the period beginning with the Nixon administration and extending up to and including the George W. Bush administration. All of these cases were identified and reported to varying degrees in the press and elsewhere. Some garnered significant attention; others drew only limited interest outside official circles. In all such cases, the attorney general and other prosecutorial authorities within the executive branch were charged with initially assessing the matter and determining the proper road for moving forward. Only a handful of the cases resulted in appointment of a special prosecutor or independent counsel. Thus the success or failure of the investigative process depended far more on the quality of those officials than on anything else. Nancy Baker, Cornell Clayton, and other social scientists have successfully identified and framed the conflicting loyalties of attorneys general when executive branch corruption is at issue.[4] How these conflicts are resolved, and the implications those conflicts have on the outcome of these cases, are the focus of this book and the case studies that support it.

The ultimate goal of these investigations and/or prosecutions should be a simple one: to ensure public faith in the system while safeguarding due process of law. The phrase "due process of law" has many different connotations in American law. The Fifth and Fourteenth Amendments guarantee it to all legal persons under the US Constitution, whether they are corporations or individuals. Some believe the concept ensures that all government proceedings feature the right to an opportunity to affect the judgment or result (whether through a trial, a hearing, or some other means). Others afford the concept far greater authority to challenge outcomes instead of just procedures. They would do so by, among other arguments, claiming the absence of a constitutionally protected liberty that is "deeply rooted" in American society. Regardless of how it is construed, due process of law is at its core a concept that compels "fundamental fairness."

Can the executive branch guarantee due process when it is charged with investigating and prosecuting executive branch corruption? Certainly it can do so when the public spotlight is not too glaring, since career prosecutors with more limited partisan biases can effectively treat each case like any other routine matter. Yet when the media and the public weigh in, the stakes usually rise. Fundamental questions of accountability haunt any political system that seeks to ensure public officials do not stand above the law. Often that issue becomes a matter of public passion only after significant damage has already been done.

A lot of people put up with the development of this book over many days, months, and years. They believed in the work but were never sure how exactly it would turn out (I include myself on that list). Mary Lenn Dixon of the Texas A&M University Press was enthusiastic from the moment she first learned of the project and never stopped encouraging me to make it a reality. Once the production of the book began in earnest, I benefited from a team of copy editors par excellence. Margret Kerbaugh's love for the English language is matched only by her god-given ability to help authors like me zero in on exactly what they want to communicate. If the final form of this book is accessible to the reader, it is only because Margret was so deeply committed to make it so. I am also indebted to Juliet Dickason for her diligent copy editing efforts and to managing editor Thom Lemmons for his fine contributions. Behind the scenes James Pfiffner, Nancy Kassop, and others supported my efforts, and I owe them much for their helpful comments and suggestions about the substance of the manuscript. Members of my family offered their unqualified support (and a willingness to let me run off on occasional weekends to get this done)—my wife, Andrea, and my three children, Rachel, Jane, and Ben, were cheerleaders when I needed them most. My colleagues at the University of Connecticut were always supportive, as were political scientists such as

Patrick Schmidt and Karen Hult, who allowed me to bounce ideas off them at various stages. Credit for what's right about this book belongs in large part to the people named above; its faults are entirely my own.

David Alistair Yalof
Storrs, CT
October 15, 2011

Prosecution among Friends

chapter 1

"Where There Is Smoke"

Investigating and Prosecuting Executive Branch Officials

When the Democrat-controlled Senate Judiciary Committee convened on January 15, 2009, to consider President-elect Barack Obama's nomination of Eric Holder to be the nation's eighty-second attorney general, those present in the Russell Building's Senate Caucus Room braced for what figured to be an uncomfortable tour of the Justice Department's recent troubles. True to form, Democratic senators questioned Holder repeatedly about his views of the controversies that had afflicted the department during the previous eight years under Pres. George W. Bush. Among those controversies were the role the department's leadership had played in seeking approval for warrantless surveillance, in drafting legal memoranda that defended the use of torture against detainees, and in dismissing US attorneys for partisan reasons following President Bush's 2004 re-election victory. Meanwhile, several Republican senators had their own bone to chew: Holder's controversial recommendation (issued during the waning days of the Clinton administration, when Holder was still deputy attorney general) that then-President Clinton should pardon the controversial financier Marc Rich.[1] The tenor and focus of the hearings was captured well by headlines from national news outlets, which emphasized the nominee's beliefs that "waterboarding amounts to torture"[2] and that the White House should act "within the dictates of wiretap law";[3] his belief that an "immediate review" of recent problems in the department's hiring practices was in order; and, of course, his willingness to offer the requisite mea culpa for his unfortunate role in the Marc Rich pardon.[4]

This focus on the department's past troubles consumed significant amounts of the Senate committee's time and energy. By contrast, the senators devoted comparatively little time to how Holder might fare going forward, in the administration that was about to be launched. In particular, how would he handle the challenge of balancing the position's dual role of neutral law enforcer and partisan advocate? What was Holder's personal relationship with the incoming president? Was he too close to President-elect Obama? Only Sen. Herb Kohl (D-Wis.) broached that subject directly, and he did so only during a lighter moment at the hearings. Knowing the two men frequently played basketball together, Kohl asked the nominee whether he could beat Obama at a game of one-on-one. "If you give me a little time and space to get back in shape," Holder responded, "I think I can hang with him."[5] So ended the Senate committee's inquiry into the personal relationship that may have existed between the next president of the United States and the man who appeared all but certain to serve as his administration's first attorney general.

The lack of a more systematic review of Holder's connections to Obama at the Senate confirmation hearings was surprising for several reasons. First, the close personal relationship between former Attorney General Alberto Gonzales and Pres. George W. Bush had been a source of ongoing difficulty for much of President Bush's second term in office. In fact, many of the same committee members now judging Holder had roundly criticized Gonzales for not showing enough independent judgment when he authorized the firing of several US attorneys following the 2004 election, and then later when he weakly defended the administration's efforts to secure legal authority to conduct controversial aspects of its war on terrorism. Second, there existed more than enough evidence in the public domain that Holder and Obama were not just passing acquaintances. Holder had originally met Obama at a dinner party in 2004. After years of contacts he then joined Obama's campaign as a senior advisor at its inception in 2007, and when candidate Obama had to make the all-important choice of a running mate, Holder was one of just three people Obama entrusted to help him with that task. And then there were the pickup basketball games they played together. While the Holder-Obama relationship perhaps stopped short of the close, long-standing Gonzales-Bush connection, the two men were hardly strangers. Indeed, a more searching inquiry into Holder's personal relationship with the president-elect was warranted, if only because it went to the core of the attorney general designate's ability to perform crucial responsibilities in investigating and prosecuting official wrongdoing in the post-Watergate era. As attorney general, Holder would face the same difficult decisions and dilemmas that had vexed so many of the nation's chief law enforcement officers in recent decades: What types of ethical violations warranted political remedies, and which ones warranted full-blown criminal inquiries? And in the case of the latter, which criminal allegations that implicated official conduct should be handled by routine Justice Department protocols, and which ones warranted the more extreme measure of appointing a "special prosecutor" or some other outside attorney?

Even Senate Republicans intensely critical of how Holder had handled the Rich matter eight years earlier conceded that his experience working in the Justice Department's Public Integrity Section for twelve years (from 1976 to 1988) made him uniquely qualified to pursue charges of corruption as attorney general. Still, if push came to shove, would he exercise his judgment to the detriment of Obama's political standing? More than any other cabinet official, the attorney general requires proper distance from the chief executive to make independent judgments. Yet despite all the issues surrounding Gonzales's troubled tenure at the Justice Department, Holder's hearings focused primarily on how he would have addressed past controversies and conflicts that did not involve the president-elect in any capacity. His hearings thus followed the same pattern as most previous confirmation hearings for attorney general nominees: absent the nominee's participation in some major scandal (on a scale beyond the affair of the Rich pardon) or some other embarrassing episode, the Senate would confirm the nominee easily. During the past half century presidents' close friends and personal counsels, and in one case a member of the president's own family, have coasted to confirmation as attorney general, and Holder's nomination followed that same predictable course. On February 2, 2009, the Senate confirmed Holder by a comfortable 75–21 vote.

Certainly the stakes for ensuring the attorney general's independence have never been higher. Congress allowed the Independent Counsel provisions of the Ethics in Government Act of 1978 to lapse between 1994 and 1996, and then permanently in 1999. More than a decade later, there exists little political will to revive the controversial measure. Thus in this post–independent counsel era, the attorney general retains the discretion to appoint a special counsel or prosecutor whenever it is in the "interest of the public" to do so,[6] and how the attorney general exercises that discretion can play a crucial role in determining whether the public views the Department of Justice as a bastion of integrity and fairness or as yet another political arm of the White House.

Within just six months of Holder's assuming office in February of 2009, several cases of alleged official misconduct were already testing the new attorney general's mettle in making decisions that might run counter to White House interests, including the appointment of a highly visible special prosecutor. Two matters in particular raised such questions. First, Holder had to decide whether federal interrogators who had allegedly tortured terrorism suspects during the Bush administration should be prosecuted, and if so, by whom. Senator Patrick Leahy (D-Vt.) and some members of the Democratic congressional leadership repeatedly called for a non-partisan legislative "truth and reconciliation panel" to investigate such charges during President Bush's final two years in office.[7] Yet the Bush administration had successfully countered those efforts, and little changed once Obama became president. The new president's oft-repeated statements that he wished to "look forward and not backward" effectively discouraged congressional leadership from embarking on a more formal legal investigation.[8] But calls for one grew more heated during the late spring of 2009 after the Department of Justice released several Bush administration memos that appeared to specifically authorize enhanced interrogation techniques such as water boarding and the use of temperature extremes.[9] Several CIA employees who participated in those interrogations during the period in question had already indicated they were prepared to testify that Bush administration attorneys had authorized such harsh conduct.[10]

The new attorney general was also wrestling with the possibility of naming a special prosecutor to investigate illegal acts by the CIA. On June 24, 2009, CIA Director Leon Panetta confirmed in two classified briefings to congressional intelligence committees that the Bush administration had established a CIA electronic surveillance program without giving notice to Congress or getting formal court approval; the goal of the program was ostensibly to capture or assassinate Al-Qaeda leadership.[11] Operating under this clandestine program, small teams of CIA operatives had allegedly been deployed in the mountain terrain of Afghanistan and Pakistan. Panetta terminated the program as soon as he discovered it, but given the evasion of congressional prerogatives, Democratic leaders were determined to hold investigations into the matter. In particular, Rep. Silvestre Reyes (D-Tex), chairman of the House Permanent Select Committee on Intelligence, had launched his own probe to explore how and when Congress needed to be briefed on intelligence matters for the foreseeable future. The 1947 law that first created the CIA included a provision mandating that the congressional committees be kept "fully and currently informed" of all intelligence issues, including covert actions; yet the law said such briefings should be conducted "to the extent consistent with due regard for the protection from unauthorized disclosure of classified information relating to sensitive intelligence sources and methods."[12]

The CIA inspector general's report in August of 2009 indicated that CIA interrogators had staged mock executions, among other controversial techniques, as part of their post–9/11 program. The report, authorized by CIA Director George Tenet in 2004, was transmitted to the Justice Department and congressional intelligence committee leaders shortly after it was written, but it was not shown to all members of the intelligence committees until September 2006, just as Pres. George W. Bush was publicly acknowledging the program's existence. Bush administration officials successfully lobbied Tenet to keep the report from being released to the public.

To make matters worse, by midsummer of 2009, Holder was under attack on various other fronts as well.[13] First, he had butted heads with Congress over national security matters after a bipartisan group of legislators blocked the Justice Department from bringing Guantanamo detainees onto American soil. He had also overruled Justice Department lawyers concerning the constitutionality of the DC voting rights bill; disagreeing with lawyers in his own Office of Legal Counsel, Holder believed the bill could be defended without an accompanying constitutional amendment.[14]

Given the onslaught of criticism coming his way for these other two blow-ups, appointing a special prosecutor to investigate abuses within the Bush administration offered Holder a tempting opportunity to hand off a politically explosive subject to an outside entity and possibly draw attention away from his own problems in the process. But, though a special prosecutor might have assisted Holder in the short term, the White House saw the matter quite differently. From its perspective, the dangers of authorizing a special prosecutor of any kind—even to investigate the abuses of a past administration headed by the opposing party—were significant for numerous reasons:

1. *Emphasizing the past.* President Obama, focusing on a host of legislative priorities during his first two years in office, repeated publicly throughout the spring of 2009 that he was "more interested in looking forward than looking backward." A special prosecutor dedicated to investigating and prosecuting either of the two controversies would be more likely to expand than to contract the size of such investigations.

2. *Losing control and/or accountability.* Although a special prosecutor does not enjoy the unfettered power of a statutorily protected independent counsel, such an officer is still vested with the "plenary authority" of an attorney general and is thus free from day-to-day supervision by officials of the Justice Department. And while some special prosecutors have been terminated,[15] the political ramifications of such a move tend to be damaging to the administration in power. Thus the appointment of a special prosecutor in effect authorizes an outsider to wield considerable discretion, mostly free from accountability to the Justice Department.

3. *Establishing an unwelcome precedent.* The appointment of special prosecutors to investigate past administrations' wrongdoing may well come back to bite the current administration when its own critics seek more special prosecutors appointed in the future.

4. *Threatening future intelligence activities.* The allegations against officials in the Bush administration addressed sensitive issues within the intelligence community, including the lengths to which CIA employees went to gather information, and the fragile state of relations between the intelligence

establishment and the Congress. Opening that relationship up to increased public scrutiny might chill the CIA's exercise of discretion to conduct legitimate intelligence activities in the future.

Moreover, unlike when a statutorily protected independent counsel statute was still in place, Obama's attorney general would enjoy virtually unlimited control over the initial selection of a person for the post. On the one hand, this might allay White House fears of a rogue prosecutor; on the other, White House officials understood that with that initial exercise of control by the administration would come subsequent loss of control over the media and the message going forward. President Clinton's strategy of stonewalling special prosecutors like Kenneth Starr—denying and withholding information as long as possible[16]— would be less effective if the special prosecutor making such requests was the attorney general's own hand-picked person.

The decision to appoint a special counsel or prosecutor, already laden with perils and the potential for unknown consequences, weighs even heavier when the Justice Department and the White House have conflicting interests. The political checks cited by Scalia and others in attacking the institution of an independent counsel are not nearly so effective when the attorney general is closely connected to the White House.

Holder's resolution of these two high-profile cases actually evinced a degree of independence from the White House. Deciding that the question of torture by CIA officials was too political an issue for routine protocols, on August 24, 2009, Holder announced that he would indeed appoint long-time prosecutor John H. Durham to investigate nearly a dozen cases of alleged detainee mistreatment at the hands of CIA interrogators.[17] As Durham was already an assistant US attorney in Connecticut, his appointment did not bespeak any desire by Holder to leave the department altogether in his search for objectivity. Still, Durham's experience working as a special prosecutor in past cases, and his newfound authority to pursue the inquiry free from the day-to-day supervision of the attorney general and Justice Department officials, promised a level of independence that exceeded White House preferences in the matter. On the other hand, Holder stood firm in his decision to discourage the prosecution of those who had followed the Bush administration's interrogation guidelines. In restating that position, Holder all but dismissed the possibility of appointing a special prosecutor to investigate CIA operatives, including military personnel and the lawyers who articulated and defended those same guidelines. With little explanation, he also dismissed calls to examine the CIA's surveillance program.

In all such cases the attorney general faced a classic tradeoff: either sacrifice prosecutorial accountability or take on the appearance of a conflict of interest that might threaten and undermine the legitimacy of the prosecution itself. How well Justice Department officials perform their duties in cases alleging executive-branch corruption—whether of past officials or of those in the current administration—is a critical element in the decision-making calculus. Accordingly, this book considers that factor explicitly as it relates to these questions:

1. What types of political conditions and checks render routine prosecutorial processes ineffective at addressing executive branch wrongdoing? Under what conditions are such risks to the exercise of legitimate prosecutorial discretion minimal?
2. When do conditions warrant the appointment of a special prosecutor or counsel who enjoys more independence in decision making than officials already in place?
3. What type of attorney general is best suited to exercise prosecutorial discretion most effectively, and in a manner consistent with the dictates of due process?

In this book I seek to link the type of attorney general chosen with the process by which the Department of Justice investigates executive branch wrongdoing. I contend that when this first critical step of attorney general recruitment is downplayed or given relatively short shrift, the administration often pays down the line in growing public frustrations, frequent calls for special prosecutors, and an overall undermining of routine investigative and prosecutorial functions. This is increasingly likely when circumstances make the attorney general's job that much more difficult, such as when presidents, vice presidents, members of their families, or members of the Justice Department are the targets of investigation. Other factors (united party government, looming election contests, whether the targeted official continues to hold the position in which he allegedly committed wrongdoing, etc.) may also play a role in the success or failure of the investigatory process. But everything begins with the choice of attorney general, one of the most important decisions that a new or returning president must make. The importance of that choice has only been compounded in recent decades by the role the attorney general must play in either invoking the independent counsel statute or choosing a non-statutory outside prosecutor in order to allay public fears.

The Rise and Fall of the Independent Counsel Statute

The Independent Counsel provisions of the original Ethics in Government Act of 1978, as modified by the Ethics in Government Act Amendments of

1982 and later reauthorized in 1987 and again in 1994,[18] authorized the attorney general to apply for the appointment of an outside prosecutor by a special court. The power to remove the independent counsel, once appointed, was duly limited. According to the statute, such a prosecutor could be dismissed only by the attorney general for "good cause" or by the special panel of the court.[19] During the spring of 1999 Congress held hearings to consider reauthorizing the statute once again.[20] Yet by then both sides of the political spectrum had grown weary of the office and its extensive powers; thus neither the Republicans who controlled both houses of Congress that year, nor the Democratic administration of Pres. Bill Clinton, had much desire to subject the next president to the albatross of yet another independent counsel statute.

The appointment of a "special prosecutor," even one who lacks statutory protections against removal, continues to raise many of the same issues and concerns. To be sure, special prosecutors are still nearly impossible to dismiss.[21] Even a modest amount of interference in the work of a special prosecutor by the attorney general responsible for the original appointment is likely to miscarry politically, inviting significant backlash against the Justice Department and/or the administration. And while special prosecutors who lack statutory protection tend to attract less day-to-day media attention than independent counsels, that fact may actually enhance their powers, as special prosecutors can fly under the public's radar with less regard for the political implications of their actions.

Meanwhile, the Justice Department and other investigative authorities have long possessed the capacity to maintain a suitable watch against most forms of executive branch corruption. In the two-decade history of the independent counsel law, only twenty independent counsels have actually been appointed; during that same period, the press has reported on hundreds of instances of alleged executive branch wrongdoing, ranging from officials accepting illegal gifts to their committing campaign finance violations, and in other ways betraying the trust of their offices. Some of the offenders were fired or otherwise dismissed from their duties. Others were formally prosecuted by either the Justice Department or some other authority.

Consider three different cases of executive branch corruption that have surfaced in the years since Watergate. The first offers what may be the ideal conditions for normal Justice Department prosecutions to prevail; the second offers a close and debatable case for the appointment of an outside or special prosecutor; and the third presents a set of circumstances under which the argument for appointing a special prosecutor who can advance the investigation in a fair and neutral way is especially compelling.

1. *When Political Checks Are Enough: Rita Lavelle*
and the Superfund Scandal (1982)

Chemical leaks during the Love Canal disaster in 1979 caused significant chromosomal damage among people living near Niagara Falls, New York. On December 11, 1980, the Democratic-controlled Congress consequently passed the Comprehensive Environmental Response, Compensation, and Liability Act (CERCLA).[22] CERCLA's provisions taxed the petroleum and chemical industries over a five-year period to the tune of $1.6 billion, which then entered into a trust fund for cleaning up abandoned or uncontrolled hazardous waste sites. More than fourteen months later, Pres. Ronald Reagan nominated Rita Lavelle, an official of an aerospace company in California, to the Environmental Protection Agency (EPA) as an assistant administrator for solid waste and emergency response, charged with supervising and controlling all of the new administration's efforts with Superfund, as the trust fund was called.

Within months of Lavelle's appointment, however, allegations of corruption and political manipulation began swirling around her management of Superfund. During a July 1982 meeting with White House aide James Medas, Lavelle allegedly discussed strategic use of Superfund monies for the benefit of political candidates favored by the White House. By one account, Lavelle targeted New Jersey toxic waste sites in a way that was designed to benefit Republican candidates for office in the immediate area, including Governor Thomas Kean.[23] At one point Lavelle and EPA head administrator Ann Gorsuch even met with White House counselor Edwin Meese, presumably to discuss the politics of Superfund.

Lavelle thus became swept up in what the press eventually labeled Sewergate, a scandal that led to the resignation or dismissal of twenty EPA officials for manipulating Superfund monies to help Republican candidates look good in their home districts. EPA's director of the cleanup of the dumps, William M. Hedemen Jr., testified to Congress that "the agency had an 'implicit policy' to curtail the superfund program and that Rita Lavelle . . . pushed him to finish a survey of the 15,000 hazardous sites while 'expressing concern' that they might provide a basis for expanding the superfund."[24]

Lavelle's problems mounted further: she was accused of testifying falsely in early 1983 before two congressional panels (one in the Republican-controlled Senate, and the other in the Democratic-controlled House) when she provided sworn testimony concerning the possible manipulation of Superfund in late 1982. Before her stint at EPA, Lavelle had managed programs at various divisions of Aerojet-General for over three years, including some that manufactured chemicals and chemical waste treatment systems. Testifying in February 1983, she told both legislative panels that she had been unaware before June 17, 1982, that Aerojet-General might be a responsible party in a toxic waste cleanup case. In fact, congressional investigators later confirmed that her staff had informed her nearly three weeks earlier (on May 28, 1982) of Aerojet-General's possible liability for hazardous wastes dumped near Glen Avon, California. Thus Lavelle could now be charged with the outright impeding of a congressional investigation into her former employer.

Lavelle's final undoing came as a result of a controversial internal memorandum she had written to the White House, which eventually became public. In it she accused a senior EPA official of "systematically alienating the business community."[25] One of the congressmen leading the investigation, Rep. John Dingell (D-Mich.), confirmed that Lavelle herself had written the memorandum in an attempt to politically manipulate the Superfund program. Bowing to the inevitable, President Reagan formally relieved Lavelle of her duties on February 7, 1983.

Lavelle's lack of candor led Democratic leadership in both houses to call for a Justice Department investigation of her conduct in all these matters. William French Smith's department moved quickly, and on December 1, 1983, Lavelle was convicted on three counts of lying to Congress about what she knew of her former employer's connection to Superfund, on one count of lying about the date she learned of that connection, and on one additional count of obstructing a congressional inquiry by sending Congress false statements. The jury ultimately acquitted her on just one of five counts: it believed Lavelle when she claimed her decisions were based not on the interests of Republican candidates, but only on public health grounds. On January 9, 1984, she was sentenced to six months in prison and fined $10,000 for lying to Congress.

Smith did not apply for an independent counsel to investigate Lavelle's transgressions. The case had partisan aspects (accusations of helping Republican candidates, etc.), but the same could be said for many cases of executive branch corruption. Though Lavelle's activities occurred against a political backdrop in which high-level administration officials (most notably EPA Administrator Ann Gorsuch and Interior Secretary James Watt) had been questioned for their commitment to environmental cleanup, Lavelle's lawyer was the only one asking whether Lavelle had been made a scapegoat by the Reagan administration.[26] Meanwhile, no evidence emerged to link high-level White House aides to Lavelle's fraudulent activities.

Consider several additional factors weighing heavily against the need for an outside appointment in this instance. The House at the time was controlled by the opposition party and was ideologically committed to follow up on all Superfund matters, eventually pressuring the upper chamber to join those efforts as well. Once hearings were held, the pressure on the Justice Department to follow with its own investigation grew intense. The only member of the White House with any record of contact with Lavelle during this period was Edwin Meese; meanwhile, Lavelle herself was a relatively low-level official whom the administration was unlikely to protect in any event. It was only in later phases of the congressional inquiry—when Gorsuch and Justice Department officials began battling with Congress over requests for documents—that the Sewergate matter compelled outside involvement in the form of independent counsel Alexia J. Morrison.

2. When Political Checks Are Limited: The Henry Cisneros Payoffs Scandal (1993–1995)

One cabinet secretary who ran into some hot water during Clinton's first term was Secretary of Housing and Urban Development Henry G. Cisneros. Cisneros's transgressions were initially of a personal nature; only when he sought to hide them from the Clinton administration at the time of his appointment did they become a matter of public trust. Finally, the bulk of the investigation of Cisneros's wrongdoing occurred when he was no longer an official of the Clinton administration. Those factors and more might have reduced the need for an independent counsel in this instance, had Clinton not involved himself directly in the matter. President Clinton's personal intercession in the case and the amount of turmoil it created within the Justice Department transformed an otherwise routine case for Justice Department control into at least an arguable case for appointing a special prosecutor.

Cisneros was the forty-four-year-old ex-mayor of San Antonio when he was tapped by President Clinton for a position in his new cabinet. During his tenure as mayor (1981–89), Cisneros had begun an affair with a constituent, Linda Medlar, that lasted at least until 1989.[27] Subsequently, between January 1990 and January 7, 1993, Cisneros paid Medlar about $189,000.[28] This came back to haunt him during the background check on his appointment to become the secretary of Housing and Urban Development (HUD) in 1993. Specifically, FBI agents wanted to investigate rumors that Cisneros had made payments of $250,000 to Medlar to keep the affair quiet. The affair itself was by then public knowledge, and Cisneros confirmed for FBI agents that he had indeed financially assisted Medlar. But Cisneros lied to the FBI about the amount of money he paid her, indicating that he "never paid her more than $10,000 in a single year or more than $2,500 at any one time."[29]

This discrepancy between Cisneros's answers and the truth became a public matter in July of 1994, when Medlar filed a civil suit against Cisneros in the District Court of Lubbock County, Texas, claiming that the HUD secretary in 1990 had promised that her monthly payments of $4,000 for "emotional distress" and "anguish" would continue at least until her sixteen-year-old daughter completed college.[30] According to the filed complaint, Cisneros breached that agreement when he stopped making payments in January of 1994.[31] Thus the total amount sought under the complaint was for an additional $250,000 in payments owed.

The first investigation into the matter originated from the White House itself. In September 1994, White House Counsel Leon Panetta instructed his office to review the allegations for purposes of making a recommendation to the president.[32] Meanwhile, the Department of Justice's Office of Public Integrity, led by division chief Lee Radek, began its own thirty-day initial inquiry into Cisneros on September 14, 1994.[33] Disagreements within the Justice Department were already starting to emerge; at a meeting on September 21, 1994, FBI agents still investigating Cisneros believed there was a need to further explore tapes Medlar had recorded of some of her conversations with Cisneros, while lawyers from the Public Integrity Section thought the tapes did not warrant further inquiry. Against this backdrop, on October 14, 1994, Attorney General Janet Reno launched a preliminary investigation into the Cisneros allegations.

The first woman appointed as attorney general, Reno was only Clinton's third choice to head the Justice Department. In fact, she was the beneficiary of what was later termed "Nannygate," disclosures that his first two candidates had employed illegal aliens to look after their children. Reno had no previous relationship with Clinton. Her extensive experience as the top prosecutor for fifteen years in Miami-Dade County, combined with her reputation for success in prosecuting violent crimes, ensured her an easy confirmation path before the Senate. More important, her capacity for independence from the White House was rarely at issue during her eight-year tenure in office.

Reno faced a split opinion within her own department on whether or not to appoint an independent counsel under the statute that had just recently been renewed. Radek's formal recommendation on February 27, 1995, opposed that measure on the ground that Cisneros had not been motivated in his actions by anything other than a real concern for the wellbeing of Medlar and her family, and that there had been no evidence that the false statements had any potential to affect the confirmation.[34] In short, he argued that while Cisneros might have knowingly made false statements in a matter within the jurisdiction of a federal department or agency, the statements were not material. The FBI, by contrast, believed that Cisneros's lies had greatly impeded its own work, and accordingly, FBI Director Louis Freeh pressed for the appointment of an independent counsel.[35] On March 13, 1995, notwithstanding the Office of Public Integrity's recommendation, the attorney general filed an application for the appointment of an independent counsel, and on May 24, 1995, the

Special Division obliged by appointing David Barrett. Cisneros's initial refusal to resign, and President Clinton's strong words of support for the HUD secretary, may have necessitated the use of an independent counsel when it could have otherwise been avoided. The case demanded significant attention from a public relations standpoint, lest future nominees fail to take FBI background checks seriously. At the same time, the allegations against Cisneros were quite limited, as Reno had found that the payments themselves were not technically illegal. Thus final charges against the HUD secretary were necessarily restricted to the single instance when he lied to the FBI, and then further restricted to his having lied only about the amount (Cisneros publicly conceded that he had made such payments and even publicly settled his lawsuit with Medlar for $49,000 on May 19, 1995.) Medlar herself was eventually sentenced to three and a half years in jail for participating in a bank fraud scheme—she had lied about the source of the payments when she purchased a home. By comparison, Cisneros pleaded guilty on September 8, 1999, to just a single misdemeanor count of lying to the FBI that carried a $10,000 fine but no jail time—and he did not resign from his office at the end of President Clinton's first term.

Clinton's decision to pardon Cisneros for the one misdemeanor account in January 2001 fueled suspicions that the president was never truly neutral in the matter. At the same time, given that the allegations themselves concerned lies made to FBI agents, it was difficult to characterize the FBI as completely neutral either. Janet Reno herself was less likely than Louis Freeh to bias her investigation of the matter, given the relatively low stakes for Cisneros, who was never in danger of facing serious criminal charges in the matter.

3. When Political Checks Fall Short: The Iran-Contra Scandal (1985–1987)

Once it became the source of congressional hearings during the summer of 1987, the so-called Iran-Contra affair became associated in the public's mind primarily with the misconduct of two Reagan administration officials: Lieutenant Colonel Oliver North and the national security advisor he reported to, Admiral John M. Poindexter. Yet just as critical a player in the affair was the former national security advisor Robert "Bud" McFarlane, who served the administration in that capacity from October 17, 1983, until his retirement in late 1985. As Reagan's national security advisor, McFarlane was an ardent supporter of the Strategic Defense Initiative (SDI), which he believed would serve as a key bargaining chip with the Soviets. Although the SDI was never completed, it did succeed in bringing the Soviets back to the bargaining table during Reagan's second term in office, a breakthrough for which McFarlane rightfully earned credit, as well as Reagan's personal trust.[36]

In mid-1985, McFarlane pressed the White House to sell arms to Iran (then in the midst of a nearly decade-long war with Iraq) in order to cultivate better relations between the United States and moderates in the regime.[37] Few question that during July President Reagan authorized McFarlane to make direct contact with Iran; McFarlane later claimed that by August, Reagan had actually approved the shipment of arms there through Israel.[38] Such a policy would have been controversial enough even without an additional wrinkle: the initiative was intertwined with efforts to rescue American hostages held in Lebanon by pro-Iranian terrorists. Subsequent news reports confirmed that White House officials implicitly approved this new policy toward Iran in part because it might lead to the release of the hostages. As the original arms deal essentially degenerated into a trade of arms for hostages, it contradicted a long-standing policy of the US government to refuse all such deals in order to protect the safety of American citizens traveling abroad in the future.[39]

The first sale culminated in an Israeli arms shipment to a moderate Iranian group in July 1985. Five months later, on December 5, 1985, Robert McFarlane resigned as national security advisor, claiming he wanted to spend more time with his family. Poindexter, then serving as deputy national security advisor, took over the program, with two changes going into effect immediately: First, all future weapons shipments to Iran would go to Iranian army leaders; and second, at the suggestion of Oliver North, an advisor to the US National Security Council, a portion of the proceeds from such arms sales would go to the Contras (Nicaraguan guerilla fighters opposed to communism) in support of their efforts. Though he had resigned, McFarlane continued to act as an envoy in the matter, assisting in the delivery of several planeloads of weapons parts to Iran. He even flew to London at one point to persuade the Iranians to release hostages before any further arms sales would occur.[40]

Direct military aid from the Reagan administration to the Contras had been prohibited by the so-called Boland Amendment passed by Congress in 1982. However, North viewed the use of third-party revenues (i.e., from military sales) as a loophole to be exploited. Aware that such actions were controversial, North kept them secret from almost all other officials in the Reagan administration.

In the spring of 1986, most of these activities became known to several Reagan administration officials, including Secretary of State George P. Schultz, Defense Secretary Caspar Weinberger, Attorney General Edwin Meese, CIA Director William Casey, and Vice President George H. W. Bush. Of those in that circle, Meese enjoyed perhaps the longest-running relationship with Reagan. A prosecutor in California, Meese had joined Governor Reagan's staff in 1967; he served as his executive assistant and chief of staff from 1969 through 1974.

Moreover, before his appointment as attorney general, Meese had served as counselor to the president. No one on the executive staff was closer to Reagan or better understood how he thought about these and other issues. Schultz and Weinberger reportedly opposed the sale, while Casey, Meese, and Bush endorsed it. At no time did Poindexter raise the question of whether proceeds from the sales should continue to be diverted to the Contras.[41]

The entire episode did not come to light for nearly a year. Finally, on November 3, 1986, an obscure magazine in Beirut (*Al Shiraa*) printed a story reporting that a "special envoy" from the White House (McFarlane) had flown into Tehran on a secret mission to sell US weapons to Khomeni's government.[42] Follow-up by major newspapers in the United States revealed that the purpose of the sales had been to secure the release of the American hostages in Lebanon, and that these activities had been carried out over the strong objections of Schultz and Weinberger. Angered by the flagrant violation of longstanding policy against trading arms for hostages and emboldened by their success in the recently concluded midterm elections, Democrats on Capitol Hill immediately called for a full congressional investigation, to be capped by public hearings. In this initial phase of the scandal, the "arms for hostages" trade was the only event at issue; the diversion of funds to the Contras was known to only a handful of officials, including Poindexter and North.

How did the Reagan administration and, in particular, Attorney General Meese respond to these new revelations? Meese's close involvement in the affair was no secret to many of its participants. Though hardly an architect of the plan, the attorney general had supported the policy when he learned of it the previous year. Undaunted by this clear conflict of interest, Meese assumed control of the matter with little hesitation. During the second week of November 1986, the Justice Department requested memos and information from the national security advisor and his staff about the arms deal. Then, on November 12, 1986, Meese asked Assistant Attorney General Charles Cooper to visit Poindexter and elicit details from him about the nature of the Iranian arms shipments. Among a host of documents, Cooper discovered a cover memo citing the opinion of a former attorney general that presidents could legally transfer arms and delay telling Congress about the transactions.[43] Meanwhile, President Reagan went on television on the evening of November 13 and indicated that while his "better judgment" told him this was not a trade of arms for hostages, the facts and the evidence now indicated otherwise.

Meese's half-hearted investigation of the matter continued. On November 17, 1986, Cooper received a chronology from the National Security Council indicating that a transfer of arms from Israel (acting as the intermediary) to Iran had occurred as early as September of 1985, even before the high-level discussions in which Meese had participated. According to one source, on November 21, four days after receiving the chronology, "Meese proposed conducting a series of interviews with all the principal participants in an effort to bring cohesion to all the facts. What he had in mind was not a formal inquiry, but just an attempt, as he put it, 'to get our arms around the problem.'"[44]

On that same day, the most curious moment of the crucial three-week period following the revelations occurred: Meese stressed to Cooper and his other coordinates that he would not be acting in his official capacity as attorney general, but rather as the president's personal troubleshooter, a role he had taken on many times in the past.[45] If Meese's comments are to be believed, he was now attempting to reprise his previous role as counselor to the president to help deal with the ongoing investigation into the Iran-Contra affair. Even if such a transformation were possible, Meese had an obligation at that point (if not earlier) to either recuse himself entirely from every aspect of the investigation, or take it up aggressively until a direct conflict presented itself. The route the attorney general chose instead was only the first in a series of many missteps he took during the Iran-Contra Affair.

On November 21, FBI Director William H. Webster offered Meese his assistance with the case. "Both agreed that it was a government administrative matter, probably not criminal; and that presidents in the past had been criticized for bringing in the FBI for purely political reasons."[46] So advised, Meese called Poindexter and asked him to make all relevant documents available for his aides to review. Cooper's interview of McFarlane revealed little; the former national security advisor was only partially forthcoming about the events surrounding the arms sales. Thus the documents Meese was seeking would have provided the bulk of the evidence for any initial investigation that might follow.

The next day, Saturday, November 22, 1986, the discovery of one document in particular brought the scandal to a head. That day, Assistant Attorney General William Bradford Reynolds and another of Meese's aides, John Richardson, were busy reviewing numerous documents at North's office in the Old Executive Office Building. The two men came across a five-page memorandum that mentioned the diversion of funds to the Contras. North had apparently authored the document sometime in April 1986, but surprisingly, he had failed to shred it before Meese's aides arrived. The first paragraph on the fifth page read as follows:

The residual funds from this transaction [a proposed April 1986 shipment of 3,000 TOWs and Hawk missile parts to Iran] are allocated as follows . . . $12m[illion] will be used to purchase critically needed supplies for the Nicaraguan Democratic Resistance Forces."[47]

After Reynolds discovered the document, he immediately alerted Meese, who—by Richardson's account—"visibly said something like, oh, a curse word." Meese then called North to set up an interview with him the following day at the Justice Department. With the stakes quickly rising, their interview could not be an intimate one-on-one affair; on that Sunday afternoon, numerous members of Meese's staff assembled at the Justice Department. According to author Ann Wroe, Meese began the interview with his "usual little speech underlining the importance of telling the truth," and then he handed North the memorandum, pointing out the paragraph about the diversion.[48] At that point Reynolds noticed a change in North's demeanor: his answers became halting; North did admit the diversion took place. He then telephoned Poindexter to tell him the memo had been found.[49] The document proved North and Poindexter's undoing: within just two days of its discovery, Poindexter was obliged to resign and North was summarily fired.

With Meese still formally heading the initial investigation, the central question was no longer whether North's actions could still be defended. The attorney general's focus now shifted to President Reagan and to whether the president himself had ever added his approval to the document. Discovery of such a fact might well endanger his presidency. Meese's transformation back to the role of White House counselor to the president was now complete.

On November 24, 1986, the attorney general directed Cooper to begin looking at criminal laws that might have been violated. Meese then held a series of short interviews with McFarlane, Poindexter, Bush, and Casey. The McFarlane interview lasted just two minutes, and in the last two interviews, Meese "took no notes."[50] On November 25, Cooper told Meese he had not found clear evidence of a law that had been broken. Yet Meese had not consulted with anyone from the Criminal Division of his own department during the first two weeks of the inquiry. Meese's foray into public relations fared no better than his internal investigation. He announced to the press (inaccurately) that (1) the transfer of arms through Israel was legal, (2) it went no higher than North and Poindexter, and (3) the money that was diverted to the Contras was not owed to the US government.

On November 26, 1986, the attorney general ordered Webster to begin his bureau's own formal investigation of the Iran-Contra episode. Meese also asked William Weld, head of the Department of Justice's Criminal Division, whether there was any basis for a criminal inquiry. Weld quickly identified several possible crimes: conspiracy to violate the Boland Amendment, mail fraud, wire fraud, tax violation, theft of government property, etc. He produced this list for Meese during the final week of November. Weld's analysis proved critical in Meese's decision to apply for an independent counsel just a few weeks later.

Cooper was correct that the diversion of funds might not have been technically illegal, as they were third-party proceeds. But the cover-up—the shredding of documents, refusal to comply, etc.—added up to a conspiracy to defraud. In fact, all the players in the National Security Council (including North) had been actively shredding documents at the exact same time that Meese was carrying out his inquiry.[51]

Meese's investigation was characterized by so much obfuscation that the Justice Department inquiry was doomed from the outset. Still, regular investigative processes continued to hum along during this period. Even before a decision had been reached on appointing an independent counsel, FBI agents assigned to the investigation secured and analyzed thousands of documents in National Security Council offices. They also conducted preliminary interviews with officials from the White House and the Justice, State, and Defense Departments, as well as with the CIA and the National Security Agency.[52] Despite this flowing of information, the most central operatives had refused to testify, and the current Justice Department structure headed by Meese was not in a position to compel their testimony.

Lawrence Walsh received his formal appointment as independent counsel in the matter on December 19, 1986. Instead of allowing the department's Criminal Division to proceed from the outset, Meese had treated the investigation as something to be handled with kid gloves. First, he had waited a full two weeks to seek documents from North after the arms sale to Iran became public. That proved an eternity in such an investigation, and it gave North and Poindexter more than enough time to destroy crucial papers.[53] Second, the interviews Meese conducted were "so casual that there was almost no written record . . . Meese's questions were less than penetrating."[54] No wonder Senator Warren Rudman (R-N.H.) would later refer to Meese's actions as nothing short of "gross incompetence."[55] Certainly advocates for an independent counsel were given considerable ammunition by Meese's behavior as attorney general during the latter part of 1986.

• • •

What do these three cases have in common? All involve allegations of misconduct by administration officials (Lavelle, Cisneros, and the North-Poindexter-McFarlane trio) acting to fulfill their own personal and/or political agendas. And in all three cases an opposition-controlled Congress stood ready in the wings to pounce at the mere appearance of impropriety by the president or his administration (the Congress in place during Lavelle's case was split between the two parties; in the other two cases, a newly emboldened opposition had only recently recaptured control of both houses of Congress). Finally, like most executive branch corruption, all these cases contributed to undermining confidence in public officials in general, and thus posed some threat to the administration in power on that basis alone.

Yet the three case studies also differ markedly in a number of critical respects, and thus considerations of due process demand that they be viewed separately and distinctly. Neither Lavelle nor Cisneros held a position within the Department of Justice or any other investigating entity, though Cisneros's most serious misconduct undermined FBI activities, so that agency maintained a stake in pursuing the claim against him. By contrast, the attorney general himself—the leading law enforcement officer in the federal government—had a personal stake in Iran-Contra, having signed off on the initial arms sale. And Meese was much closer to the president personally than either of the other two attorneys general (William French Smith and Janet Reno) had been to the presidents they served. Moreover, in the Iran-Contra affair at least one key official (McFarlane) had resigned from office before any formal investigation had been launched; by comparison, Lavelle, Cisneros, North, and Poindexter all left office as a result of the allegations lodged against them. Finally, while no presidential election was imminent in the case of Lavelle and Cisneros, the Iran-Contra scandal unfolded publicly with the specter of the 1988 election looming, and with one of the players in discussions over Iranian arms sales— Vice President George H. W. Bush—a likely frontrunner for the Republican nomination. In short, partisan politics may have played a role in disrupting normal Justice Department protocols in the third case, whereas it was limited or virtually a non-factor in the first two cases.

Executive branch corruption normally falls under the purview of the Justice Department. Public officials must justify their decision either to remove an investigation to a separate and more independent prosecutor within the Justice Department or to assign it to an attorney who sits outside the Justice Department altogether. Given the conflicting loyalties inherent in the position of attorney general, any investigation and prosecution of an executive branch official runs the risk of colliding with rigid conflict-of-interest standards. Yet if reassignment to a special prosecutor offers pitfalls as well, a key question remains: under what conditions does the conflict of interest require a response, and under what conditions can the conflict of interest be rightfully ignored in order to ensure that routine Justice Department protocols prevail?

Independent Counsels, Special Counsels, and Others

Strictly speaking, this is not a book about the independent counsel mechanism; I offer no polemic for or against the use of independent counsels as opposed to special prosecutors who lack statutory protection. The advantages and disadvantages of the independent counsel mechanism have certainly been well documented elsewhere.[56] That said, the role of an independent counsel who enjoys some form of statutory protection, and the effect of statutory protection on other investigatory mechanisms, was a critically important factor in the Justice Department's decision-making process, at least during the two periods, 1978–1992 and 1994–1999, when some form of that statute was in place.

Absent the availability of a statutorily established independent counsel mechanism, the choices on how to proceed are in fact many and varied. They include these possibilities:

1. Relying on congressional investigations (including hearings) that may (1) pressure officials accused of wrongdoing to quit or be fired or to take drastic steps to reform their agencies, etc., and/or (2) pressure the attorney general to launch his own inquiry or appoint a "special counsel"
2. Relying on internal auditors or inspectors general located within or normally assigned to the department where the wrongdoing is alleged to have occurred
3. Relying on executive branch law enforcement and prosecutors (the Justice Department, the FBI, etc.)
4. Initially appointing a member of the Justice Department to head a special or continuing investigation under the continued supervision of the attorney general
5. Initially appointing, in accordance with Department of Justice regulations, a "special counsel" with the "plenary authority" of an attorney general, who thus enjoys autonomy to proceed independent of day-to-day supervision by the Justice Department or the White House

With regard to this final category, regulations issued by the Justice Department (28 C.F.R. Part 600 et seq.) authorize the attorney general to appoint an individual to the US Office of the Special Counsel whenever he or she determines that criminal investigation is warranted and one of these conditions is present:

1. Investigation or prosecution by a US attorney's office or litigating division of the Department of Justice would present a conflict of interest; or
2. Under the circumstances, it would be in the public interest to appoint an outside special counsel to assume responsibility for the matter.

Technically, under 28 C.F.R. Part 600.3, the special counsel is to be selected from "outside government." However, this has not stopped the attorney general from appointing to the US Office of Special Counsel a US attorney from outside Washington, DC, or an attorney from another part of the Justice Department, such as the Criminal Division in Washington, DC, or the Solicitor General's Office. What advantage does a special prosecutor offer to the administration of justice as broadly defined?

Justice Department regulations provide that special prosecutors remain (at least technically speaking) within the structure of the Department of Justice itself. Although the provisions governing independent counsels authorize them to "request assistance from the Department of Justice in carrying out the function of the Independent Counsel," employees of the Department of Justice must thereafter be "detailed to the staff of the Independent Counsel."[57] By contrast, although the special counsel may receive staff assignments as well, it is presumed that "all personnel in the Department [of Justice] shall cooperate to the fullest extent possible with the Special Counsel."[58]

Although a special counsel is not subject to the day-to-day supervision of the attorney general or his delegates, he or she may still be forced to provide an explanation for any prosecutorial step or action.[59] Additionally, a special counsel is subject to discipline (including, under certain conditions, termination) by the attorney general just like any other Justice Department official under the attorney general's authority. The list of factors that justify outright removal include general misconduct, dereliction of duty, incapacity, conflict of interest, or other good cause, including violation of departmental policies.[60]

Still, the political power of such a mechanism remains significant. In the post-Watergate era, presidents and attorneys general have been increasingly reluctant to discipline and remove special prosecutors and counsels because of the public's negative reaction to such interference—and those who accept special prosecutor appointments are all too aware of this. Robert Fiske, the special counsel appointed to investigate the Clintons' Whitewater deal in 1993, was removed less than two years later, after President Clinton signed the Independent Counsel Authorization Act of 1994. Under the new law, a special division of the Court of Appeals received sole authority to appoint independent counsels. Although Attorney General Reno asked the Special Division to allow Fiske to continue his investigation, it ultimately declined, choosing instead to appoint Kenneth Starr under the revived statute. Reno's position confirms a fact that should have been obvious to many—that special prosecutors normally enjoy considerable job security, whether or not they enjoy the added protection that comes from an independent counsel statute. In the case of Whitewater, it took an act of Congress to remove Fiske from his position.

The last special prosecutor of any type to be summarily removed from office by the Justice Department and replaced with yet another non-independent special prosecutor was Archibald Cox, dismissed on October 20, 1973. As noted in the preface, neither Attorney General Elliott Richardson nor Deputy Attorney General William Ruckelshaus was willing to execute the removal order from President Nixon, who was then eager to terminate Cox because of his refusal to compromise on a request for a subpoena for presidential tapes. Both officials resigned their positions rather than dig in their heels and risk being accused of rank insubordination. Cox left only after Solicitor General Robert H. Bork, the highest ranked officer left in the Department of Justice, followed Nixon's order. As it turned out, what later became known as the "Saturday Night Massacre" did as much harm to Nixon in the short run as the tapes would have. Numerous bills of impeachment were introduced in Congress for the first time in the days following Cox's firing. For his part, Nixon replaced Cox within days with another special prosecutor (Leon Jaworski) who continued to sue the president for control of the tapes.

Congress passed the Ethics in Government Act of 1978 five years later, with the Cox firing still fresh in many legislators' minds. Unable to effectively address wrongdoing on its own under such circumstances, except by resorting to impeachment, Congress under the new act established the office of special prosecutor (later renamed an "independent counsel") to be appointed by a special panel of the federal District of Columbia appeals court. Once appointed, he or she could then investigate allegations of officials' misconduct with full subpoena power, on an unlimited budget, and with no deadline, and could be dismissed with cause only by the attorney general or a panel of three federal judges. Unfortunately, creating the new office exacerbated at least one problem: defendants targeted by special or independent counsels are not treated like other defendants. The near absolute independence of such prosecutors actually lies at the root of the problem. To the extent that special prosecutors or special counsels do their job free from political pressures, the judgments they make may be subject to the harshest criticism of all: that they are accountable to no one, and thus represent an amalgamation of all the prosecutors' natural biases and prejudices.

Central to the passage of the Ethics in Government Act in 1978 was the perceived need for "independent prosecutorial judgment." The fundamental decisions about whether to investigate, whether to prosecute, and what (if anything) to charge the accused with cannot be made based on partisan factors, or with the fear of ruining a political career. Thus, the argument went, a prosecutor who reports to the Justice Department run by an attorney general from one political party, who must then answer to a president from that same party, does not offer the judgment free of partisanship that is required to investigate executive branch corruption attributable to *either* party. Yet as it turns out, independent counsels tapped by a politically charged appointment process may be no more independent than anonymous assistant US attorneys, and mostly anonymous US attorneys. That is because membership in the pool of likely special counsel candidates generally requires a formal track record, whether as a prosecutor, a jurist, or as some type of legislative counsel. Naturally, those who fit such a description normally maintain strong affiliations with one of the two major political parties."[61]

On the face of it, appointing special prosecutors does not appear to separate prosecution from partisanship any better than using low-level, already-in-place federal prosecutors would.

The Relevance of Politics to Prosecution

Congress and the White House are inherently political institutions. The attorney general, who reports to the president within the executive branch, must also consider politics in his or her actions, albeit to a different degree. In describing his role as attorney general more than a half century ago, Robert H. Jackson noted that as "legal officer of the United States," he had a "responsibility to others than the president."[62] Describing the relationship between the Justice Department and the White House, Harvard Law professor and former Assistant Attorney General Jack Goldsmith rejected the analogy to either a private attorney beholden to the president, or a neutral court: "It is something inevitably, and uncomfortably, in between."[63]

Proponents of the now-defunct independent counsel law tend to make a more theoretical claim about the office: that it was necessary to instill public confidence. The trials and tribulations suffered by three modern attorneys general (John Mitchell, Edwin Meese, and Alberto Gonzales) provide clear examples of just what can happen when attorneys general are left to guard the henhouse.

Still traumatized by Watergate, the sponsors of the independent counsel law could not have foreseen that the statute itself would become a lightning rod for controversy. In the process of demonizing or glorifying the independent counsel, the media and the public have deflected attention from some of the real crimes committed. The risks are obvious. As Katy Harriger argued, "If the credibility of the independent counsel is undermined by political forces, then the main benefit of the statute—public confidence—is lost."[64]

Do traditional investigatory and prosecutorial mechanisms instill public confidence? That question is normally answered in the affirmative precisely because politics plays such a significant role in the process. Justice Antonin Scalia articulated this argument in *Morrison v. Olson.*[65] Scalia wrote: "If federal prosecutors 'pick people [to] get rather than cases that need to be prosecuted,' if they amass many more resources against a particular prominent individual, or against a particular class of political protesters, or against members of a particular political party, than the gravity of the alleged offenses or the record of successful prosecutions seems to warrant, the unfairness will come home to roost in the Oval Office."[66]

Politics may be an imperfect check on prosecutors, but it is still superior to any alternative set of controls one might impose. United party government tends to limit pressure on the executive branch, at least until it boils over into an extended controversy in the media. Yet if united party government shuts off public inquiry of minor incidents, divided party government tends to blow up even minor allegations into crimes that unnecessarily draw on special or independent counsel's energies and resources. Benjamin Ginsberg and Matthew Crenson argue in their book *Downsizing Democracy* that the growing use of criminal sanctions against public officials is "closely linked to struggles for political power in the United States."[67] The tactic of "revelation, investigation, and prosecution" (RIP) reached its height when the Democratic-controlled House of Representatives faced a Republican White House in the 1980s, and then again when a Republican-controlled House faced down the Clinton administration during the second half of the following decade. Not surprisingly, these periods coincided with the independent counsel's rising prominence on the American political scene.

Politics offers an imprecise and rough set of parameters within which the prosecution of public officials is normally cabined. Yet consider the dangers of a special prosecutor in a high profile political case: because no other cases compete for the special prosecutors' attention and resources, there exists a legitimate fear that the prosecution will be pursued more aggressively than it would have otherwise.

The triad of two adversaries and a neutral arbiter (the judge) remains sacred to the American system of law. In some inquisitorial systems, the prosecutor simply lays out the scope of the crimes for the judge and law enforcement officials to subsequently investigate. But prosecutors in the United States are expected to lead the inquiries themselves. American prosecutors alone enjoy the near absolute power to decide whether to charge a suspect with a crime. Included within that power are three underlying decisions. These concern (1) whether or not there is "sufficient probability of guilt to justify subjecting the suspect to a trial,[68] (2) what specific crime or crimes the defendant will be charged with, and (3) whether prosecution is in the community interest.[69] This final decision disrupts any theoretical notion of balance between the prosecution and the defense: the prosecution is under a strict obligation to care about more than simply getting the best deal it can on behalf of the government.

The requirement that prosecutors seek societal justice, however that may be defined, is obviously relevant to the debate over the merits of special prosecutors. The decision to appoint a special prosecutor is grounded in the belief that without such an outsider in place, societal justice will not be realized. Executive branch officials may lean on prosecutors to be less aggressive, potentially placing defendants "above the law." Yet placing them below the law instead is just as undesirable. Hoping to avoid even the appearance of impropriety, public officials are already under greater pressure than ordinary citizens *not* to invoke the privilege against self-incrimination. Add to that the threat of a special prosecutor's being unaccountable to normal political pressures and sporting a mandate to investigate backed by significant resources, and it is clear that fear of public officials' being cast below the law may be well founded.

Competing with the need to ensure that officials receive the exact same due process protections as everyone else is the need to instill public confidence in the system. Without a special prosecutor, law enforcement officials from the Department of Justice and the FBI are forced to investigate and prosecute individuals in other agencies reporting to the president. In cases where abuse is alleged to have occurred within the law enforcement agencies themselves, federal prosecutors might well be investigating wrongdoing in their own agencies. In the case of Watergate, before Archibald Cox's appointment as special prosecutor, officials in the Justice Department were investigating wrongdoing that pointed up the chain to the former attorney general, and perhaps further, to the White House staff and the president. In his analytical look at the concept, John Orth asks whether, consistent with notions of due process, a man can be made a judge in his own case.[70] In the American system of justice, the prosecutor renders judgment after judgment that goes a long way toward determining whether public officials will be convicted for violating the law. Failure to clearly separate the prosecutor from the prosecuted threatens a fundamental pillar of due process.

It is these two competing interests—the need for routine procedures and the need for procedural due process in which the judge and the judged are distinguished—that underlie debates about special prosecutors, independent counsels, and any other type of outside counsel used in this fashion.

Devising a Framework to Assess the Need for Special Prosecutors

There are times when an outside counsel is needed to ensure a comprehensive examination of alleged official misconduct. During Watergate, for example, the Justice Department was hamstrung by the fact that its former head, John

Mitchell, had been one of the officials implicated in campaign irregularities. Divided party rule does not always cure such difficulties. An opposition Congress may be more attentive to executive indiscretions and missteps, but the motive of congressional party leaders is notably different from that of prosecutors. Indeed, Independent Counsel Lawrence Walsh clashed frequently with Democratic congressional leaders during their respective investigations of the Iran-Contra scandal. Actions taken to investigate wrongdoing for purposes of considering possible arrests and indictments should not be confused with the search for embarrassing truths that may score important political points but few legal victories. More notably, in Watergate many congressional Democrats lost interest in the scandal once Richard Nixon resigned the presidency; by contrast, special prosecutor Leon Jaworski's work—along with that of his successor Charles Ruff—continued for years even after President Ford's pardon of the president.

Far more common are cases in which career Justice Department prosecutors investigate and prosecute from the beginning according to a reasonable timetable. Consider a central premise of law enforcement: that the circumvention of normal Justice Department protocols for investigating and prosecuting officials creates its own significant risk of abuse. Prosecution is by definition an act of discretion, as any evaluation of the chances of successful prosecution (based on the character and sufficiency of available evidence and testimony) opens up wide areas for legitimate judgment calls. Abnormal or unusual procedures for investigating official misconduct—while they may prove politically popular in the short run—vest discretion in officials who may be unconcerned about consistency between their own prosecutorial decisions and those rendered by the administration in power.

As the political theorist Otto Kirchheimer warned, procedures designed to "depoliticize" the process may be doomed to failure—instead of eliminating the necessary conflict between political goals and the values embodied in the constitutional and legal structure of the community, they "only shunt it to another location."[71] That alternative location—in this case the jurisdiction of an "independent" or "special" prosecutor—is problematic precisely because the special entity works under so few constraints. Consider the artificial economics of an independent prosecution: whereas issues of resource allocation among a high number of cases force traditional prosecutors to plea bargain an inordinate number of cases away, an independent counsel is not so constrained. As someone charged with assessing the case on its own merits, independent of any other criminal cases that might compete for the government's resources, the independent or special prosecutor has every incentive to pursue all targets to the greatest extent allowed under the law. Nor does the lapsing of the independent counsel statute—temporarily in 1994, and then more permanently in 1999—solve this problem. The appointment of so-called "special prosecutors" (chosen by and accountable to the attorney general) may diffuse some criticisms directed at political accountability, but it fails to address the larger problem of unusual prosecutorial incentives, as discussed above. The proliferation of such special counsels does not really restore the public trust much either: members of the public must have confidence in the routine as well as the extraordinary.

Few would challenge the basic premise that executive branch officials accused of criminal misconduct should be treated in the same way as targets subject to routine forms of investigation and prosecution.[72] When, if ever, should that premise be set aside? Under what circumstances, if any, should traditional law enforcement authorities (i.e., the inspector general, the Justice Department, or others in the administration) defer to special prosecutors? A number of considerations may arise in this context:

1. How is the Attorney General Identified and Perceived by the Public?
The attorney general's connections within the executive branch often determine the degree to which all the rest of the political checks work, and thus determine in many cases whether a special prosecutor may be needed:

- An "outer circle attorney general," who has no longstanding personal or professional ties to the president, sits in an especially strong position either to (1) conduct a neutral investigation and prosecution of executive branch wrongdoing or (2) investigate and subsequently offer a neutral viewpoint on the need for extraordinary investigatory measures in the public interest, including the possible appointment of a special prosecutor. If the latter route merits serious consideration, an outer circle attorney general can effectively exercise discretion to consider all appropriate factors in reaching such decisions.
- An "inner circle attorney general" who enjoys longstanding personal or professional ties to the White House may hamper the process in at least two ways. First, he or she cannot always conduct a neutral and fair investigation of executive branch corruption, and second, he or she cannot consistently render critical decisions about the appointment of a special prosecutor in an era when those decisions have become increasingly routine. An inner circle attorney general can overcome a perception of partiality by relying heavily on additional political checks that ensure some measure of his or her accountability. In the absence of such political checks—and considering an inner circle attorney general's connections to the president—more

extraordinary measures may be required, like using special prosecutors to maintain a degree of legitimacy with the public. Attorneys General John Mitchell and Griffin Bell both labored to create the required level of separation in the public's eyes, but in the long run their connections to the president proved too significant to overcome. Elliot Richardson and William French Smith, by contrast, were inner circle attorneys general who were by and large able to use political checks to protect their independence.

- An "Oval Office attorney general" is one who recently served the White House in an advisory or other personal capacity before becoming head of the Justice Department. Due process and impartiality are not just strained in such a case; fair investigation and prosecution of White House or other high-level administration officials, as well as neutral decision making about whether or not to appoint a special prosecutor, becomes a virtual impossibility. How can an attorney general sit in judgment of activities that he or she may well have participated in, approved of, or at least been aware of? How can that same attorney general now sit in judgment of people with whom he or she worked at the time of the activities in question?

The appointment of an attorney general lays a foundation for decision making, and this foundation determines whether the decision making is relatively straight-forward, strained, or perhaps altogether unworkable. An inner circle attorney general may be properly questioned concerning his or her exercise of discretion from the outset; an Oval Office attorney general is often compromised at the outset. By contrast, an outer circle attorney general can more confidently exercise discretion without inviting public skepticism. Thus the selection of an attorney general may later become the single most important consideration in determining whether or not to appoint a special prosecutor. And yet it is a process that is treated like any other executive branch appointment that receives considerable deference from the Senate and, to a degree, from the public at large.

Table 1.1

Impact of Attorney General Connections on Due Process in Executive Branch Misconduct Cases

Connections within the Executive Branch	Impact on Due Process
Outer circle	Maintained
Inner circle	Threatened
Oval Office	Compromised

Justice Scalia's faith in political checks may seem misplaced when circumstances make disinterested, objective prosecutorial discretion impossible. Considerations other than the attorney general's connections to the Oval Office can also affect the likelihood of bias on his or her part, and on the part of Justice Department attorneys under his or her charge.

2. Is the President or Vice President Implicated in the Alleged Misconduct?
The attorney general—as the chief law enforcement official and a cabinet-level officer—sits below only the president and the vice president in the executive branch hierarchy. The risk of a biased or unfair prosecution increases substantially when those two officials (or their close family members) are involved in the alleged misconduct under investigation. Allegations linked directly to these officials or their family members may offer a justification for circumventing routine Justice Department protocol.

3. Is the Official under Investigation Directly Connected to the
Justice Department or Other Prosecuting Authorities?
The risk of abuse and/or bias increases substantially whenever the Justice Department or FBI is called upon to investigate and prosecute someone from within its own agency. Can federal police and prosecutors be expected to police and prosecute officials from their own ranks with equal objectivity and determination? Misconduct within the Justice Department creates special snares for those who must investigate internally, depending on the nature of the misconduct and the officials who were most closely connected to the allegations.

4. Is the Official under Investigation Connected to the
Administration in Power?
Politically speaking, not all officials are connected in the same way to the administration. Some are holdovers from previous administrations and have more limited connections to the president himself. Some may not even be members of the president's political party. The revolving door of government makes it unlikely that an official under investigation still holds the same office as when a controversy first arose—if he or she even remains in the executive branch at all.[73] As a general matter, there exists no real or apparent conflict of interest when the Justice Department is charged with investigating incidents of alleged misconduct from previous administrations. Accordingly, there may be few reasons to circumvent routine Justice Department protocols. But if the official being targeted served the administration in power at some previous time, other questions may arise for consideration: (1) were the alleged offenses committed with the intention of advancing the administration's goals? and (2) did the alleged offenses actually undermine administration goals?

5. Are Elections Likely to Intervene in the Investigative or the Prosecutorial Process?

Federal prosecutors may believe that an upcoming election or other current political events have no influence on the way they conduct their work, but in fact public response to their investigations is greatly influenced by such events. When Independent Counsel Lawrence Walsh brought an indictment against high-level officials of the Reagan administration only four days before Republican George H.W. Bush faced the voters in November of 1992, many Republicans cried foul, claiming that the indictment's release was a calculated attempt to affect the election outcome. (Bush subsequently lost the election to Arkansas Governor Bill Clinton.)[74] Would Justice Department officials directly accountable to Bush's own attorney general at the time, William Barr, have waited until after election day to release such indictments? Should they have done so? A discretionary framework for assessing the need for special prosecutors must consider the timing of investigations in the calculus. Allegations that arise at a time when they may profoundly shape political events may compel the appointment of a more neutral special prosecutor.

6. Is Congress Controlled by the Opposition Party?

Does the opposition party to the president maintain the authority in Congress to exert an effective check through the exercise of oversight powers? The rise in power of the modern presidency has led to a diminished role for Congress during periods of united government. On the other hand, divided party government can provide a significant check on the chief executive, whether by shedding light on political corruption through congressional hearings or by placing added pressure on the executive branch to investigate on its own. The decision of whether or not to name a special prosecutor should not rest solely on this factor, but the role of Congress in this process cannot be ignored.

The categories listed in Table 2 provide a summary of the framework for analysis of individual cases that may confront the Justice Department.

The attorney general can investigate and prosecute alleged misconduct even by Justice Department officials, as Justice Scalia's dissent from *Morrison* (cited in the preface) suggests. Allegations of presidential misconduct might well draw enough media scrutiny that an attorney general with sufficient distance from the president would be hard-pressed to show undue favoritism towards his boss. This last countervailing influence should not be taken lightly. As one social scientist reminds us, "During the Watergate investigation, it was said that once an FBI investigation was started, it could not be stopped. Someone would leak the information, as 'Deep Throat' did. Perhaps the size of the federal law enforcement unit, perhaps the education and high salaries of the

Table 1.2

Potential Sources of Bias in Justice Department Handling of Executive Branch Misconduct Cases

	YES *Risk of bias:*	NO *Risk of bias:*
Is the president or vice president or one of their family members implicated in the alleged misconduct?	Significant	Low
Is the official targeted closely connected to the prosecuting authority or agency?	Significant	Low
Does the official maintain an ongoing relationship with the current administration?	Significant	Low
Is the investigation being held at a politically sensitive time (i.e., close to a presidential election)?	Significant	Low
Is congressional opposition empowered to check the prosecution?	Low	Significant

staff, perhaps the Washington publicity make it more difficult to *nolle prosequi* (drop prosecution) in federal cases."[75]

Among his many responsibilities as chief executive, the president's duty to address the outbreak of corruption is too often overlooked. Demanding special prosecutors, whether "independent" or not, becomes the fallback position for the administration under attack.

Book Organization and Case Selection Criteria

The political realities of investigating and prosecuting executive branch wrongdoing—and the factors that play into *how* an administration should address those realities—will be explored more fully in the chapters that follow. Chapter 2 briefly reviews the various special prosecutor provisions available to administrations in the past and then considers the individuals who have held the position of attorney general from Nixon's first term to the present. How were they selected? Can they be fairly characterized as inner circle, outer circle, or Oval Office attorneys general? How did their respective reputations bolster or undermine the administrations they were expected to serve? Did the political checks Justice Scalia referred to in his *Morrison* dissent actually work?

Chapters 3 through 5 then discuss the investigation and prosecution of executive branch officials dating back several decades, with a focus on the variables listed in Table 2. Counting the three presented earlier in this chapter, this book features twenty-six case studies in all, offering perspectives on the handling of alleged executive branch corruption by all the different attorney general types and—as shown by the chapter in which they are placed—the different factors that influence the success or failure of routine Justice Department procedures and protocols. As already noted, these 26 case studies hardly exhaust all the varieties of wrongdoing that the administrations in question were forced to address. We will never know the details of many of those cases, perhaps because they were handled quietly as internal matters or because they never resulted in any indictments or plea agreements that would have to be vetted in public court. Too little information may survive to render a judgment about such cases or to subject them to any form of systematic analysis. While these studies cannot be comprehensive, they still fill out a rich tableau of the choices facing attorneys general in the highly charged context of executive wrongdoing.

Obviously the availability of information (especially of primary sources) was a key factor in selecting cases for this study. Yet two other factors played a significant role as well: (1) case representativeness—every presidency from Nixon's through George W. Bush's was included to discern patterns of behavior by different administrations at different times; and (2) case significance—as evidenced by the active involvement of the attorney general and other high-level officials in the Department of Justice.

The second criterion, case significance, serves to eliminate instances of wrongdoing that are of little import or that implicate such low-level officials that no serious discussion of special prosecutors ever arose.

The first criterion, representativeness, must be qualified as well, because carefully addressing cases that occurred during all the different presidencies over a thirty-five-year span provides just one type of representativeness. Specifically, limiting the case selection to instances in which the invocation of a special prosecutor law or the appointment of a non-statutory special counsel is at least a relevant consideration for the key decision makers, creates a final pool of case studies that may tend to overemphasize the more conflictual and controversial cases—i.e., those in which the circumstances are less favorable for Justice Department lawyers to investigate executive branch officials free from unwanted biases or political pressures. Still, this book's approach of critically examining a political phenomenon falls into line with a long tradition of qualitative case studies in which the researcher tends to improve our understanding of the phenomenon in question by examining "various interests in the phenomenon, selecting a case [or cases] of some typicality, but leaning towards those cases that seem to offer *opportunity to learn*."[76] Recognizing up front that questions of representativeness cannot "ever be definitively settled in a case study format,"[77] the focus of case selection acknowledges, with the eminent social scientist Robert Stake, arguing that "potential for learning is a different and sometimes superior criterion to representativeness. Sometimes it is better to learn a lot from an atypical case than a little from a seemingly typical cases."[78]

To be sure, I have spent extensive time on what by any definition must be considered "special circumstances" cases, including some involving officials who are no longer in the administration, or who never had strong ties in the first place to the president or attorney general (see chapter 7). Additionally, this chapter's case studies include one in which divided government plays a significant role in policing administration officials (the Lavelle Superfund scandal) and another in which the targeted official (Henry Cisneros) lied to the FBI, thus requiring the Justice Department to either investigate aggressively or risk undermining its own agency. Both the Lavelle and the Cisneros cases provide circumstances favorable for maintaining Justice Department control. But of course, unfavorable circumstances create the most difficult (and interesting) dilemmas for the attorney general and the Justice Department lawyers and offer the best opportunity to study how the political process at issue works. Following traditional protocols for conducting qualitative case studies, this book relies solidly on a "purposive sample, building in variety and acknowledging opportunities for intensive study" here and elsewhere.[79]

To that end, chapter 3 considers cases in which presidents and vice presidents, or their family members, came under investigation for wrongdoing. Chapter 4 examines cases in which the Justice Department, the FBI, or other federal investigating entities were directly implicated in the actual wrongdoing. Chapter 5 looks at the investigation and prosecution of officials from past administrations, investigations that were politically sensitive to a high degree due to looming elections or other background political events, and investigations that occurred against a background of highly energized partisan opposition. Finally, in chapter 6, I draw on these many case studies to analyze relevant patterns in the decision-making process and their implications for government accountability and due process in a democracy.

chapter 2

Legal Regimes, Attorneys General, and Executive Accountability

The position of US attorney general, like that of many other chief law enforcement officers holding parallel positions in state governments, presents a contradiction of interests and purposes. As a presidential appointee and member of the cabinet, the attorney general plays a critical role in helping an administration formulate and implement legal policy in line with the president's overall goals. The attorney general's employment status within the federal government is unambiguous: as a cabinet-level executive officer and chief lawyer of the US government, he or she serves at the pleasure of the president of the United States, and can be removed by the chief executive at will.[1] At the same time, as the nation's chief law enforcement officer, the attorney general draws on his or her own independent base of power to act directly in the public's best interest. Since it was first established by Congress in 1870, the Department of Justice has served attorneys general in discharging their duties, which include investigating and prosecuting violators of federal law. And rarely does the attorney general face more intense cross-pressures than when his or her office must exercise its investigative and prosecutorial powers against members of the executive branch.

The implications of this conflict are profound. Even the proper and careful pursuit of allegations against executive branch officials may prove embarrassing or politically damaging to the president whom the attorney general must serve. Just as problematic, the White House may reap partisan political gains if alleged wrongdoing occurred while the opposition party was in control, inviting just the opposite form of pressure on Justice Department officials. And when the wrongdoing hits particularly close to home, such as when some of those targeted reside within the FBI or the Justice Department, the conflict of interest is most acute. The appointment of a special prosecutor (whether someone from within the Justice Department or outside it) offers one way out of the dilemma, but it brings with it an additional set of headaches, including the specter of an unaccountable or "rogue" prosecutor with no competing obligations or demands on his time and budget. The attorney general must weigh these and other considerations against the realities of a statutory regime that may encourage or discourage such special appointments by modifying the conditions that attach to them. The long history of special prosecutors in the United States offers some instruction on the limitations inherent in going this more controversial route.

Legal Structures and Executive Accountability, Past and Present

Until the early 1970s, special prosecutors appointed to investigate and prosecute high-profile cases were few and far between. In 1875, Pres. Ulysses Grant appointed John Brooks Henderson, a former Democratic representative and senator from Missouri, as a "special US Attorney" charged with indicting and trying the so-called "Whiskey Ring." A set of Midwest whiskey distillers based in St. Louis had allegedly conspired to funnel money to federal officials, including many federal tax collectors.[2] Grant's attorney general, Edward Pierrepoint, eventually fired Henderson for making impolitic comments, and the special prosecutor experiment appeared to stall for the half century to follow.

The next president to issue a formal call for a special prosecutor was Calvin Coolidge, who did so in response to the Teapot Dome scandal of the 1920s. Coolidge actually appointed *two* special counsels to investigate the bribery scandal involving Secretary of the Interior Albert Fall, accused of accepting cash gifts and no-interest loans in return for granting private companies leases to drill for oil on US government land in Wyoming and California during the Harding administration. Coolidge ordered his Justice Department to begin investigating the scandal in 1924; yet because deep concerns arose over Attorney General Harry Daugherty's close relationship with Fall, Coolidge appointed both Democrat Atlee Pomerene and Republican Owen Roberts to investigate the matter as "bipartisan counsel." President Coolidge had insisted that the two special counsels be vetted and confirmed by the Senate, and that meant going through several candidates before finding two who could survive Senate scrutiny and were willing to do the job. According to Burl Noggle's account of the process, "bitter and aggressive debate raged over confirmation," as some complained the two nominees did not know enough about public land law, while others complained about their training.[3]

According to Leslie Bennett of the Brookings Institute, history has largely judged the use of special prosecutors in the Teapot Dome scandal investigation a success: as the tale of corruption was unveiled, the oil leases were returned to the government, and "at least some of the perpetrators were successfully prosecuted."[4] Fall was the highest-ranked official swept up in the scandal, and he was successfully prosecuted and sentenced to prison in October of 1929. Pomerene and Roberts were successful, but their positions were not institutionalized, as the Justice Department continued to rely on special prosecutors only infrequently.

Watergate was a watershed moment in the on-again, off-again history of special prosecutors. Since the scandal that led to the downfall of Richard Nixon, calls for special prosecutors have become a routine part of the American political dialogue. By 1973, congressional leaders determined to root out corruption in the executive branch were no longer willing to rely exclusively on checks and balances in the form of congressional hearings. When Richard Nixon nominated Secretary of Defense Elliot Richardson to take over as attorney general for the publicly discredited Richard Kleindienst, Congress linked Richardson's confirmation to a willingness to name a special prosecutor suitable to congressional leaders.[5] At least seven candidates (mostly acting or semiretired judges) turned down the position of Watergate special prosecutor before it ultimately fell to Harvard law professor and former solicitor general Archibald Cox. As Cox's biographer notes, the relative scarcity of special prosecutors up to that point meant it was "an untested, risky job" with little opportunity for the officeholder to build a more prestigious name from taking it.[6]

Cox's investigation would eventually become a cause célèbre among those who believed the presidency had grown too powerful during the middle part of the twentieth century. His unceremonious firing by what remained of the Justice Department's leadership late during the evening of October 20, 1973,[7] cemented his place in history. Cox—who subpoenaed the president for copies of taped conversations recorded in the Oval Office—refused to accept a White House proposal that would later become known as the "Stennis compromise." Senator John Stennis (D- Miss.) had agreed to review and summarize the tapes for the special prosecutor's office in lieu of the White House's actually producing them. If Nixon intended Cox's dismissal to neutralize special prosecutors for the foreseeable future, he calculated badly. Cox's removal cleared the way for the appointment of a new special prosecutor, Leon Jaworski, just twelve days later. Jaworski proved just as relentless as Cox in pursuing the full contents of the tapes, successfully appealing all the way up to the Supreme Court to enforce his subpoena.

Cox's firing was one of several critical events during the Watergate affair that precipitated significant reform five years later through passage of the Ethics in Government Act of 1978. The road to passage of the independent counsel provisions was not smooth. During the summer of 1976, the Ford administration's attorney general, Edward H. Levi, actively opposed S. 495, the proposed Watergate Reorganization and Reform Act, on the ground that it would require appointment of far too many special prosecutors.[8] According to Levi, by the summer of 1976 the Justice Department's Criminal Division had already identified at least twelve current or recent cases that included "allegations of obstruction of justice, receipt of illegal campaign contributions, fraud, misuse of public funds and civil rights violations" on the part of officials of the executive branch."[9] Levi's determination to rebuild the Justice Department's reputation after Watergate did not square with the urgency of so many others to establish a special prosecutor on the assumption that the Justice Department could not be trusted to serve as an independent entity.

Eager to test alternatives, Levi's Department of Justice established the Office of Public Integrity (OPI) in early 1976, consolidating in one unit of the Criminal Division all of the Justice Department's oversight responsibilities with respect to the prosecution of criminal abuses of the public trust by government officials. Office of Public Integrity attorneys since that time have prosecuted selected cases involving federal, state, or local officials, and have also provided advice and assistance to prosecutors and agents in the field regarding the handling of public corruption cases. Over the following two decades, the OPI would indict almost 10,000 federal officials and secure more than 8,600 convictions.[10] In addition, it served throughout this period as the Justice Department's center for handling various issues regarding public corruption statutes and cases.

Levi also addressed the conflicts that occur when allegations of wrongdoing implicate officials within the Justice Department itself. To that end, he helped establish the Office of Professional Responsibility (OPR) within the Justice Department to investigate allegations of professional and criminal misconduct by department attorneys in Washington, DC, and in US attorneys' offices across the country. In practice, the OPR has served as the equivalent of an "ethics watchdog," an internal affairs unit made up of attorneys who could probe allegations of professional misconduct against department lawyers and oversee similar units at the FBI and the Drug Enforcement Agency.[11] To ensure its long-term success, Levi established the position of OPR counsel and lawyer-in-chief as a nonpolitical position separate from the rest of the department. And as it turned out, his initial appointment to that position, Michael E. Shaheen, went on to hold the job for more than two decades.[12] During the course of that time Shaheen's office would lead the investigation of several high-level Justice Department officials[13] in addition to performing its more common duties: following up on allegations of prosecutorial misconduct in all of the ninety-four US attorneys' offices around the country.

Levi was not opposed to the discretionary appointment of special prosecutors by the attorney general when circumstances warranted it. On one occasion during the summer of 1976, he agreed to expand the scope of inquiry of the latest Watergate special prosecutor, Charles Ruff, to include investigating possible campaign irregularities allegedly committed by Gerald Ford during his earlier races in Michigan for the House (see chapter 5). Still, Levi was not able to stem the tide of congressional support building for statutorily authorized special prosecutors, and the arrival of the Carter administration in 1977 would serve as the impetus in Congress to keep those efforts moving forward. In addition to backing so-called "sunshine laws" and other means of opening agency proceedings to the public, President Carter supported increased restrictions on lobbyists, expanded auditing of government officials' personal finances, and established commissions to recommend candidates for federal judicial offices. The new president also promised to support legislation that would not only give "full prerogatives and authority and independence" to special prosecutors, but would also immunize the attorney general from politics to a greater extent than in the past.[14]

With regard to the latter issue, one bill still weaving its way through Congress when Carter first took office focused on two key provisions: (1) a proposal to increase the independence of the attorney general by limiting the executive branch's power to terminate the office, and (2) a proposal to establish an Office of Government Crimes in the Justice Department. On February 18, 1977, Carter asked his newly minted attorney general, Griffin Bell, to prepare legislation immunizing the attorney general from dismissal by the president except in cases of "cause or malfeasance." Bell responded two months later with a formal opinion that such legislation might be unconstitutional given the Supreme Court's decision in *Myers v. US,* 272 US 52 (1926), which held that the basic underlying structure of the Constitution prevents any effort by Congress to restrict the discretionary right of the president to remove a "purely executive officer."[15] Robert Lipshutz, the White House counsel, echoed Bell's opinion about the proposal in his own memo dated June 23, 1977: Lipshutz urged the president to support both the Office of Government Crimes proposal (less controversial, given that a similar Office of Public Integrity had already been in place for a year) and legislation requiring the Justice Department to review violations of law or standards of conduct by department employees (another proposal to codify what had already been established by tradition, if nothing else).[16]

A proposal by some members of the House to further increase government accountability by establishing an Office of Inspector General in six different executive departments also attracted attention from the new administration. Sponsored by Reps. Lawrence Fountain (D-N.C.) and Jack Brooks (D-Tex.), H.R. 2819 aimed to reorganize the present internal audit and investigative units (then located in eleven separate agencies) into a single office. Some members of Bell's staff raised concerns with the proposed legislation. In a memo dated February 21, 1977, Acting Assistant Attorney General John Harmon offered Bell his opinion that the proposed new office would be subject to "divided and possibly inconsistent obligations to the Executive and Legislative Branches" in violation of the Constitution.[17] According to Harmon, the inspector general's obligation to keep Congress fully informed and to provide information requested by Congress without executive branch clearance or approval were "inconsistent with his status as an officer in the Executive Branch."[18] In Harmon's view, the bill could be saved only by having the inspectors general report to the head of the agency and not to Congress, with the president's power to remove them remaining intact. Bell passed these concerns on directly to the president.

Within a year, the bill was modified to meet most of the Carter administration's chief objections. The new bill, H.R. 8588, ensured that the president could remove an inspector general without reporting his reasons to Congress; it also softened several key reporting requirements and dropped the provision requiring the inspectors general to "inform Congress of any cuts in their budgets deemed to interfere with the adequate working of their offices."[19] The final bill passed by Congress ended up as a compromise between the two House resolutions.[20] Most critically, it established that "neither the head of the establishment nor the officer next in rank below such head shall prevent or prohibit the Inspector General from initiating, carrying out, or completing any audit or investigation, or from issuing any subpoena during the course of an audit or investigation."[21] The legislation became effective on October 1, 1978.

The final looming issue concerned the special prosecutor provisions of what would eventually be titled the Ethics in Government Act of 1978. Interest in creating such a mechanism was spurred by the belief that the Justice Department, answering directly to the president, might refuse to name a special prosecutor to investigate White House wrongdoing even under the most compelling of circumstances. It was also inspired by the desire to ensure that the individual named would enjoy a high level of bipartisan support. Richard Nixon named successive prosecutors to investigate the Watergate scandal even though their appointments did not remove either the threat of a congressional inquiry (it had already begun) or the threat of the Watergate case going to court (the criminal trial of the burglars had already taken place). More important, the offices of Archibald Cox and Leon Jaworski in turn moved the case forward and forced the issue of subpoenaing the Watergate tapes, which led directly to Nixon's resignation.

The Ethics in Government Act resolved this conflict by including a provision creating a special prosecutor (eventually renamed the "independent counsel" by amendments passed in 1982), who was authorized to investigate allegations of misconduct by individuals holding or formerly holding certain high positions in the federal government.[22] Appointed by a special panel of the federal appeals court in Washington, DC, upon application by the attorney general, the special prosecutor was subject to dismissal only by the attorney general for "good cause" or by a panel of three federal judges upon the completion of the special prosecutor's task. Of course, while the attorney general alone was authorized to "apply" for such an appointment, the judiciary committee of either house of Congress, or a majority of the members of either the majority or nonmajority party of those committees, could request that the attorney general make such an application. The attorney general then, within thirty days after receipt of the request, was required to report his decisions and provide reasons regarding each of the matters referred.

In early 1981 the newly organized, Republican-controlled Senate (the first in twenty-six years) began considering amendments to the new law. Senate leaders debated modifications that would increase the attorney general's discretion to initiate the process leading to the appointment of so-called "independent counsels."[23] Eventually, Congress put into law a proposal authorizing the attorney general to apply for a sixty-day extension to the original limit of ninety days for a preliminary investigation. Even more significant, the new changes provided the attorney general greater latitude in deciding whether to initiate a preliminary investigation in the first place. First, he or she would be able to consider the credibility of sources of information in deciding whether a preliminary investigation was warranted; second, the threshold for appointing independent counsels was raised to the equivalent of federal prosecutorial guidelines.[24] Rudolph Giuliani, an associate attorney general at the time, testified that simple fairness required prospective defendants in an independent counsel investigation to be judged by the same standards as any other defendant. All these changes were formalized in the 1982 amendments to the Ethics in Government Act, which became law on January 3, 1983.

Nearly a decade after the Watergate scandal had claimed a president, a former attorney general, a White House counsel, and many high-level White House aides, the independent counsel provisions of the Ethics in Government Act had evolved into a form of statutory authority that offered administrations an alternative means of pursuing executive branch corruption even at the higher levels of government. The 1987 amendments to the act went a step further in this direction, actually requiring the attorney general to open up a preliminary investigation under certain circumstances, and, even more telling, authorizing the special court (upon application) to expand the jurisdiction of the independent counsel to matters unrelated to those covered by the original grant.[25] Although the decision to apply for an independent counsel remained within the attorney general's discretion, he or she would be subject to intense scrutiny from Congress and the media when declining to make such an application under the statute, as the process of making a preliminary inquiry would become a matter of public record. Certainly the option to name a "nonindependent" special prosecutor remained available in theory. Yet it would be increasingly difficult for any attorneys general to justify the decision to take such an intermediate step without availing themselves of the statute's more substantial provisions.

The independent counsel law did more than just make available to the attorney general an option for a more independent prosecutor; it essentially closed off other options between routine Justice Department investigations and the more controversial appointments of high profile independent counsels. As Lloyd Cutler, the former White counsel under Carter (and later Clinton), testified at hearings over the 1983 amendments, "It's a matter of appearances to preserve faith in the system."[26] Cutler's comments go to the core of the real issue: that justice often requires a faith in due process that may not appeal to the public's imagination in the short run, but that might still offer significant dividends in the long run. The "all or nothing" regime created by the law placed considerable weight on the independent judgment of the attorney general. Yet, for all the attention paid to creating regimes that help or hinder attorneys general in performing their job, relatively little attention has been paid to questions concerning those placed in office in the first place. How well positioned are the individuals appointed to head the Department of Justice to carry out their responsibilities?

Attorneys General on the Hot Seat, 1972–2009

Since the 1960s, Congress has slowly extended federal jurisdiction to areas that were once the exclusive province of state law, including educational policy, juvenile justice, and gun control. With this dramatic expansion of federal jurisdiction has come increased reliance on the Department of Justice to meet its responsibility as the federal government's chief law enforcement agency. The expansion of federal law enforcement authorities after the September 11, 2001, attacks only added to the Department of Justice's powers.[27] And as if the Department of Justice were not busy enough, the succession of special prosecutor laws and amendments passed in the post-Watergate era has placed even more decision-making responsibility in the hands of the Department of Justice, which must determine in most instances whether to appoint special

Table 2.1

Summary of Independent Counsel Provisions Authorized by Congress

Year	Title	Major Provisions and Changes
1978	Ethics in Government Act of 1978, Titles VI & VII (28 USC. Sec. 595)	Created the office of a "special prosecutor" appointed by a special panel of the US Court of Appeals in DC; dismissal could only be by an attorney general with "good cause" or by special court panel upon completion of an authorized task.
1982	Ethics in Government Act Amendments of 1982	Extended the dates of the act. Reduced the class of people subject to the act. Changed the standards for initiating an investigation. Changed the title from "special prosecutor" to "independent counsel." Added a provision for attorney's fees.
1987	Independent Counsel Reauthorization Act of 1987	Required an attorney general to conduct a preliminary investigation when information is received sufficient to constitute grounds to investigate whether persons subject to the act may have violated a criminal law "other than a petty offense." Prohibited the courts from ordering the attorney general to conduct an investigation.
	No independent counsel law in effect—December 15, 1992, through June 30, 1994	
1994	Independent Counsel Reauthorization Act of 1994	Requires the Justice Department to launch a preliminary inquiry upon receipt of "specific and credible info of criminal wrongdoing" by certain officials; if further investigation is warranted, requires the attorney general to notify a special three-judge panel. Makes dismissal of an independent counsel by the attorney general subject to review by the three-judge panel. An independent counsel is required to submit reports to Congress if investigation uncovers information that might constitute grounds for dismissal or impeachment of the official.
	Independent counsel law expired June 30, 1999	

a prosecutor or independent counsel. The attorney general's decision *not* to appoint a special prosecutor carries with it heightened media attention and the increased scrutiny of Congress. Every cabinet-level official has seen his or her power increase along with the expansion of the federal government as a whole; yet in the process, far more critical functions—many of which require a degree of political independence not expected of other cabinet officials—have fallen on the shoulders of the modern attorney general, backed by a Department of Justice that now employs more than 112,000 people.

Unfortunately, the process of recruiting, selecting, and confirming attorneys general has not undergone a transformation commensurate with this shift in the size and scope of their responsibilities. Since the beginning of the republic, the Senate has formally rejected just nine cabinet nominees (albeit with twelve additional nominees withdrawing their names before a formal Senate vote could even take place). Of those twenty-one ill-fated nominations, only four were slated to become attorneys general: (1) Henry Stanberry (rejected by the Senate by a vote of 29–11 in 1868), (2) Charles Warren (rejected by the Senate 41–39 in 1925), (3) Benjamin Bristow (declined the appointment in 1874), and (4) Zoe Baird (withdrew her nomination in 1993). Notably, of those four only Stanberry was rejected because he was deemed too close to the president (Stanberry had actually resigned from an earlier stint as US attorney general to defend Andrew Johnson at his impeachment trial).[28] Baird withdrew after revealing that she had failed to pay Social Security taxes on illegal immigrants in her employ. Warren was rejected because of his close connection to a sugar conglomerate that was then under investigation by Congress.

In truth, the Senate confirmation process for the nation's chief law enforcement officer continues to offer a virtual rubber stamp for the president's choice. One obvious exception was Warren, who suffered intense scrutiny from senators about his business dealings on the heels of the Teapot Dome scandal. Elliot Richardson's prolonged examination by the Senate Judiciary Committee in 1973 was understandable, given that his predecessor (Richard Kleindienst) had resigned from the post amid allegations that he had lied at his confirmation hearings. Richardson promised to appoint an independent prosecutor in the Watergate matter and was quickly confirmed; Kleindienst was convicted of perjury and given a suspended sentence.

In fact, the confirmation process has run smoothly in the vast majority of cases even when the relationship between the attorney general and the White House is an unusually close one. Consider that the Senate of the past century confirmed to the post of attorney general each of the following: (1) John Kennedy's sibling and campaign manager, Robert F. Kennedy; (2) two presidents' former campaign managers, J. Howard McGrath (in the case of Truman) and

John Mitchell (in the case of Nixon); (3) Franklin Delano Roosevelt's poker-playing pal and companion, Robert Jackson; (4) President Carter's childhood neighbor and close friend, Griffin Bell; and (5) Pres. George W. Bush's disciple and mentee, Alberto Gonzales, who owed nearly all of his most significant professional advancements, including a brief stint as Texas Supreme Court justice, to the president. Edwin Meese, another successful nominee, had been Ronald Reagan's personal friend and colleague for nearly fifteen years. Proposals that occasionally bubble up in Congress to reverse this trend—for example, Senator Lloyd Bentsen's bill to disqualify a president's former campaign manager from becoming his administration's attorney general[29]—address only one symptom of a much larger problem. A clear consensus has emerged among the vast majority of senators that a president should enjoy considerable latitude in choosing members of the executive branch.[30] Not surprisingly, proposals to counter that presumption have met with little success to date. Such deference to the president undermines the need for a serious confirmation check at the very moment when Senate challenges to presidential prerogatives are likely to succeed.

With presidents enjoying nearly unfettered discretion in their selections to head the Justice Department, the legal regimes that rely on the attorney general to offer independent and objective judgment may be essentially compromised from the outset. Certainly every attorney general understands that he or she owes his position to the president, who is constitutionally empowered to terminate the officer without cause. Notwithstanding those legal powers, political conditions and the strength of the opposition may combine to hamper the president's actual discretion. Janet Reno's willingness to expand the jurisdiction of Independent Counsel Kenneth Starr rendered her an occasional thorn in the side of Pres. Bill Clinton and others in his White House, and eventually left her on the outside looking in on most crucial decisions, legal or otherwise, during Clinton's two terms in office. Yet it also rendered her politically untouchable in the eyes of the Republican congressional opposition that came to power after the 1994 midterm elections. President Clinton was hardly the first chief executive to find himself saddled with an attorney general he would just as soon dismiss: upon assuming the presidency under tragic circumstances, Lyndon Johnson was essentially stuck with Robert F. Kennedy as attorney general, at least until the latter resigned from the post to run for the US Senate in 1964.

Many scholars of the presidency have written about the "conflicting loyalties" inherent within the attorney general position. Political Scientist Nancy Baker has identified two attorney general types: the "advocate type," who offers the president "loyalty, support and compatibility," and the "neutral type," whose tenure is characterized by "professional eminence, nonpartisanship and widely recognized integrity."[31] While it is an important breakthrough, the difficulty with Baker's methodology from the perspective of appointment politics is that such judgments must normally wait until after the fact, when the attorney general has served for a relatively significant period of time in the post. That renders it less helpful for purposes of assessing a nominee attorney general's prospects for success. For example, was it clear which of those two types William French Smith and Janet Reno would become before they had been in office for several months, if not years? The search for a "neutral type" who can effectively investigate and prosecute executive branch corruption—as well as assess the need for special prosecutors in a particular case—must rely on evidence and information gathered just *before* the individual's ascension to office.[32]

A more logical avenue for assessing prospective US attorneys general in terms of their capacity to neutrally investigate and prosecute executive branch corruption focuses on their own past connections to the president and other White House officials at the time of appointment. Will this person be an "inner circle" attorney general or an "outer circle" attorney general? Scholar Mary Anne Borelli has argued that the ease of Senate confirmation for any secretary designate in the cabinet varies according to media and public perceptions of his or her "insider" or "outsider" status and whether the nominee is a "policy specialist," "policy generalist," or "issue network liaison."[33] Borelli's notion of an insider encompasses connections within the Washington, DC beltway. Thus an attorney general like former Senator John Ashcroft, barely an acquaintance of George W. Bush's before 2001, would be characterized as an insider under Borelli's formula, due to the time he spent in DC during the 1990s as a US senator. This distinction may prove helpful to analyzing the way certain cabinet members are perceived by the public, but it fails to capture factors that may be more relevant to investigating and prosecuting executive branch corruption, without prejudice.

In assessing what presidents and the political system know about attorneys general at the time of their nominations, at least three relevant categories arise. An "outer circle attorney general" has never been part of the president's personal crowd or close set of acquaintances. Working within the state government under a governor who later becomes president would not disqualify an attorney general for outsider status, absent some other evidence of a day-to-day working relationship between the two. More important, an outer circle attorney general offers perhaps the best hope for maintaining fairness when allegations of executive branch corruption present an occasion for investigation and prosecution.

An "inner circle attorney general," by contrast, presents some tensions and strains in his or her ability to function effectively, as he or she may be closely connected to the White House in general and to the president in particular. Neutrality is difficult, but not impossible, under such a regime. To challenge public perceptions of cronyism or worse, the attorney general must essentially build a wall between the Justice Department and the White House that can be maintained under the most difficult of circumstances, and then rely on political checks to help establish legitimacy with the public. Naturally, there is no way to know in advance whether the attorney general is (1) committed to the ideal of separation in the first place, and (2) willing to sacrifice his or her access to the White House as a close advisor and confidante of the president to maintain that separation. And even if those two obstacles are overcome, a third danger remains: that in an effort to appear neutral, the inner circle attorney general will bend too far in the opposite direction, actually rendering decisions that unfairly disadvantage the executive branch. Political checks and the transparency that comes with them may go a long way toward overcoming those objections.

The third category of attorneys general takes this insider status to its more problematic extreme. The so-called "Oval Office attorney general" is compromised from the outset, as he or she has already served the president in some high-level advisory capacity during the same administration to which he or she is now owes a duty of neutrality and objectivity. Due process is not simply strained under these circumstances; the attorney general who must assess how to investigate (and potentially prosecute) conduct that he or she participated in, condoned, or at least acknowledged, cannot offer neutrality to any satisfying degree in the modern political world. At a minimum, the Oval Office attorney general renders judgments that affect the fate of many former and current officials he or she knows personally and may have worked with closely. Former chiefs of staff, counselors to the president, and formal White House counsel make especially poor candidates for the position of attorney general under any circumstances. A former department head can avoid such status if he or she was never really an integral part of the White House decision-making structure. In an age in which the cabinet no longer serves as the president's sounding board and main source of advice, department heads are more likely to suffer from isolation than from intimacy with the commander in chief.

1. Outer Circle Attorneys General: Judgment from a Distance

An outer circle attorney general can offer a neutral and disinterested perspective on executive branch wrongdoing. Since Watergate, six Department of Justice heads (William Saxbe, Edward Levi, Janet Reno, John Ashcroft, and Michael Mukasey) have fit this ideal type, with Richard Thornburgh's initial

Table 2.2 Attorneys General from 1972–2009
Listed by Their Status within the Executive Branch

Outer Circle	Inner Circle	Oval Office
William Saxbe	John Mitchell	Edwin Meese
Edward Levi	Richard Kleindienst	Alberto Gonzales
Richard Thornburgh (1988–89)	Elliot Richardson	
Janet Reno	Griffin Bell	
John Ashcroft	Benjamin Civiletti	
Michael Mukasey	William French Smith	
	William Barr	
	Richard Thornburgh (1989–91)	
	Eric Holder	

stint as attorney general during the latter part of the Reagan administration also falling into the category.

William Bart Saxbe, the first permanent appointment to head the Justice Department after Elliot Richardson's resignation in October 1973, arrived at the Justice Department after serving fewer than four years as a US senator from Ohio. Representative William J. Keating, a Republican House member from Cincinnati, was primarily responsible for Saxbe's nomination as attorney general; Keating pressed White House Counselor Bryce Harlow to nominate Saxbe in the face of what must have seemed like especially long odds.[34]

Nixon was never comfortable with Saxbe's nomination, and with good reason. As a freshman senator in 1969, Saxby had defied traditional Washington insiders' protocol by challenging Nixon's Vietnam policy during a social gathering at the White House. In response, the president's staff banished Saxbe from the Oval Office for almost two years during Nixon's first term in office. As the Watergate scandal unraveled a few years later, the always-quotable Saxbe continued to show little regard for Nixon, telling one close friend in the press that the president was like "the piano player in a whore house who claims not to know what's going on upstairs."[35] Yet in the wake of Richardson's resignation and the controversial firing of Archibald Cox as Watergate special prosecutor, Nixon needed an attorney general who was perceived as a true outsider to ensure a quick and painless confirmation. Saxbe thus assumed his place in the executive branch as the consummate outer circle attorney general, serving in that capacity during Nixon's final months in office, and then up until Pres. Gerald Ford was able to secure the confirmation of his own attorney general in early 1975. Saxbe may have been a lifelong Republican, but in the conflict between the interests of the White House and those of the country, his allegiances were never in doubt.[36]

As Gerald Ford's selection to head the Justice Department, Edward Hirsch Levi represented a breed of public official entirely different from his recent predecessors, including Saxbe. Not even a registered Republican, Levi had a background that consisted mostly of positions as a scholar and an administrator in academia, save a short stint in the 1940s when he served Franklin Roosevelt's administration as special assistant to the attorney general. Nor was Levi just a symbol of neutrality; unlike some of the other candidates briefly considered for the post, he was a true outsider, having never met Ford before being interviewed by the nation's thirty-eighth president on December 5, 1974. Once confirmed six weeks later, Levi would join Ford in instituting reforms that both men hoped would restore more permanent public trust in the Justice Department. Of most immediate significance, Levi established the Office of Professional Responsibility, which he hoped would serve as the eyes and ears of the attorney general at the Department of Justice.

The tenure of Richard Thornburgh as attorney general straddled two presidencies: he served during the last six months of the Reagan administration and then continued in his position for the first two-and-a-half years of Pres. George H. W. Bush's four-year term. Perceptions of Thornburgh changed as his role and status shifted across the two Republican administrations. After a career spent almost entirely in the state of Pennsylvania climbing up the ladder of state politics (Thornburgh lost a bid for Congress in 1966, but rose to become governor of Pennsylvania for two consecutive four-year terms beginning in 1979), he offered the perfect outside-the-beltway fix after Edwin Meese's trials and tribulations forced his resignation in July 1988. Just as critical, Thornburgh's tenure as US attorney was marked by an aggressive approach to fighting political corruption and organized crime in Pennsylvania. And while Thornburgh had a cordial relationship with President Reagan, it was never close, and was thus a far cry from the chief executive's relationship with his two previous attorneys general, Meese and Smith. Clearly, Thornburgh offered an outer circle antidote to the Meese problem in particular, and the Senate's unanimous confirmation of his appointment clearly demonstrated that reality.

Attorney General Janet Wood Reno was nobody's first choice for a significant position in the Clinton administration. As noted already, Bill Clinton's first choice was Zoë Baird, the general counsel of Aetna. Nor was Reno even Clinton's backup choice. When Baird's nomination collapsed amid charges that she had never paid taxes on an illegal immigrant she employed as a nanny, Clinton turned instead to Federal District Judge Kimba Wood, at least, until Wood confessed to having a "nanny problem" of her own (unlike Baird, Wood actually paid taxes on the illegal immigrant in her employ, a distinction that mattered little to the increasingly testy members of the Senate Judiciary

Committee). Reno got the nod only after those first two choices faltered. Yet as it turned out, the first (and so far only) female attorney general in United States history would eventually become the longest-serving person to hold that position since William Wirt's twelve-year stint in the James Monroe and John Quincy Adams administrations during the early part of the nineteenth century. More important, Reno's tenure was eventually defined by her status as a Clinton administration outsider. She frustrated Democrats and Republicans alike with decisions that did not fall neatly along the pro-Clinton or anti-Clinton storylines those groups tended to adopt.

Reno certainly had the credentials to serve as an effective outer circle attorney general. After working for the Florida House of Representatives' Judiciary Committee for a brief period in the early 1970s, she returned to private practice and almost immediately thereafter (in 1973) landed a position in the Dade County State Attorney's Office. In 1978 she became the head state attorney for the office and was reelected to that position four more times before Clinton appointed her attorney general in 1993.

From the outset Reno found herself isolated from nearly all major policy-making decisions in the Clinton administration. Yet her outer circle status would offer her an essential lifeline during the most difficult moments of Clinton's presidency, and in the end, it would prove a boon to Clinton himself. Despite a series of decisions that seemed to go against his interests in the first term, Clinton made Reno one of only a handful of original cabinet appointments to hang on throughout his second term in office. (Bruce Babbitt, Donna Shalala, and Richard Riley—all administration insiders—were the only others to do so).

In 2000, President-elect George W. Bush rejected calls to name a prominent private attorney or judge to the Justice Department's top slot, turning instead to a seasoned, ideologically conservative politician for the post: the recently defeated US Senator John Ashcroft (R-Mo.). Ashcroft had cut his teeth as a prosecutor in state government. As Missouri's attorney general for eight years (he won two four-year terms in 1976 and 1980), he never shied away from lawsuits that would link him to conservative causes.[37] Most notably, his office steadfastly embraced the pro-life movement's agenda. In 1983, in the US Supreme Court case of *Planned Parenthood of Kansas City v. Ashcroft*, Ashcroft's office defended Missouri's requirement for hospitalization for all second-trimester abortions.[38] (Ashcroft lost that battle by a 4–3 vote). According to Nancy Baker, Ashcroft's "high-profile record" of fighting court-ordered desegregation in Missouri's big cities also earned him steadfast conservative support.[39] Later, as Missouri's governor from 1985 until 1993, and then as US senator from 1995 to 2001, Ashcroft continued to embrace conservative causes. In fact, it would have been hard to imagine a more conservative nominee for the post. Columnist George Will went so far as to call Ashcroft a "pin-up candidate for social conservatives" when the Senator ran unsuccessfully for president.[40]

Ashcroft may have proved too conservative for Missouri voters when he lost his Senate reelection bid in 2000, but he was not too conservative for President Bush to tap him for a high-level cabinet position. The public viewed the December 2000 announcement of Ashcroft's nomination as attorney general as a reward to the Christian conservatives who had helped Bush secure critical primary victories in South Carolina and elsewhere. Defying predictions that Ashcroft's nomination would elicit bipartisan support, Senate Judiciary Committee Democrats fiercely attacked their soon-to-be former colleague. Senator Edward M. Kennedy (D-Mass.) accused Ashcroft of ignoring "the rights and the interests of black students who were trying to get a decent education" when he was still serving as governor of Missouri.[41] Senators Charles Schumer (D-N.Y.) and Dianne Feinstein (D-Calif.) complained about Ashcroft's expansive definitions of gun rights.[42] And Republican senator Arlen Specter (R-Pa.) went after Ashcroft about a speech Ashcroft had given at Bob Jones University in which he had said that "we have no king but Jesus."[43] Ashcroft's personal views were clearly on trial before the Senate. But no senators asked Ashcroft about his views on special prosecutors, in part because the statute had only recently lapsed. Lost to them was the possibility that the need for Ashcroft to maintain independence from his appointing president would grow exponentially in the years to come. Ashcroft was eventually confirmed by a relatively narrow vote of 58–42, with nearly all the Senate Democrats voting against him.

Ashcroft and Bush were never close, and as attorney general, he never did break into Bush's inner circle. Justice Department officials confirmed that throughout Bush's first term, Ashcroft clashed frequently with White House Counsel Gonzales, who was intensely loyal to Bush. Specifically, Ashcroft distrusted Gonzales because his close personal relationship often allowed the White House counsel to exercise unusual control over legal policy decisions that normally belong to the attorney general.[44]

That didn't mean Ashcroft lost *every* battle with Gonzales. For example, when Jay Bybee left his position as assistant attorney general in the Office of Legal Counsel to take a seat on the federal bench, Gonzales desperately wanted John Yoo, a Department of Justice official responsible for defending the administration's program of torturing terrorism suspects, to take Bybee's place. Ashcroft, who did not want someone so loyal to Gonzales to take the position, eventually won the day.[45] But Gonzales won far more of these battles than he lost, overriding Ashcroft's opinion on affirmative action (Ashcroft wanted to take a harder line), on the creation of military commissions (which

Ashcroft opposed), and on gun rights (where Ashcroft again sought a harder-line position).

Of course, Ashcroft's outer circle attorney general status would prove a useful asset when the administration ran into some controversy toward the end of George W. Bush's first term. As the head of domestic law enforcement in the administration's declared "war on terrorism," Ashcroft had tirelessly pressed the administration's position in favor of expanding the powers of the US government to fight terrorism, while curtailing judicial review of defendants' claims in incidents involving domestic terrorism. Yet in the National Security Agency surveillance controversy, a hospitalized Ashcroft stood by his guns (and his own department's policy decision) when he refused to reauthorize the controversial program despite pressure from Gonzales to reconsider his decision. In fact, Gonzales's lobbying probably hurt his own cause, given Ashcroft's dislike of him.

When Gonzales's controversial stint as attorney general ended prematurely in 2007, President Bush did what would have been unthinkable immediately after his successful reelection bid: he chose an attorney general who had been all but pre-approved by key members of the political opposition. Federal District Judge Michael Mukasey, sixty-six, possessed unambiguous credentials as a Republican: he was a veteran of private practice who had served as assistant US attorney under Rudolph Giuliani, and Ronald Reagan had appointed him to the federal district court in Manhattan twenty years earlier. Among the political officials he had impressed most as a jurist was Senator Charles Schumer, who had submitted Mukasey's name to the Bush administration as a possible Supreme Court candidate back in 2003. Nine months after Mukasey announced his intention to retire from the district court in June 2006, Schumer went on *Meet the Press* and urged Mukasey's name as the next attorney general. When Mukasey accepted President Bush's offer to head the Justice Department on September 16, 2007, the nominee drew support as the outsider the administration had so sorely lacked in Gonzales; at the same time, Mukasey provoked concerns at his confirmation hearings when he refused to denounce unequivocally the practice of "water boarding" by the administration.[46] Eventually he was confirmed by a 53–40 count, with Senators Schumer and Dianne Feinstein casting key votes in his favor.

2. Inner Circle Attorneys General—Neutrality Through Politics
Until the 1870s, when the Department of Justice was first created, there were important reasons for choosing an attorney general who was on close personal terms with the president. For much of the nineteenth century, the president's implicit support for the attorney general offered him the only real source of

power he had to exercise as a limited, one-person institution. Yet as the Justice Department bureaucracy grew, so too did the institutional authority of the attorney general. By the end of that century, the attorney general's responsibility extended far beyond simply offering legal counsel to the president and other officials in the federal government. In the modern era, the attorney general has become the nation's chief law enforcement officer, responsible for investigating and prosecuting violations of federal law by anyone, including fellow officials in the executive branch of government. Thus the attorney general's close relationship with the president—once a key ingredient in the attorney's power—now serves as a liability, zapping the credibility he or she needs on Capitol Hill and elsewhere to perform critical functions.

An inner circle attorney general may have maintained a close relationship with the chief executive over the years, whether as the president's childhood friend, as a partner or advisor in some earlier form of government service, as a partner in the private sector, or even as a former campaign manager. Burdened from the outset with the specter of cronyism, the inner circle attorney general must work to overcome the perception that in investigating and prosecuting executive branch corruption, he or she will not place the interests of the president above those of the nation or above more general considerations of due process. Certainly the attorney general can take steps to help accomplish this result, through strategically appointing and empowering subordinate officials such as deputy and assistant attorneys general, and through crafting formal and transparent procedures for communicating with the president and others.

Since President Nixon's election in 1968, at least eight different people have been chosen to head the Justice Department at least in part on the basis of their own successful past relationships with the appointing president. Six of those attorneys general (John Mitchell, Richard Kleindienst, Elliot Richardson, Griffin Bell, William French Smith, and, from 1989–91, Richard Thornburgh) could have fulfilled their investigative and prosecutorial functions successfully, despite their status as inner circle attorneys general. (The other two—Edwin Meese and Alberto Gonzales—are addressed in the next section).

Richard Nixon had consistently emphasized law and order as the centerpiece of his successful 1968 campaign for the White House, and the appointment of a new attorney general offered his administration its first real opportunity to live up to the campaign promise. Given the stakes, Nixon's choice of John N. Mitchell as his administration's top law enforcement official must be considered a strange one on a number of fronts. As a former bond counsel to New York Governor Nelson Rockefeller, Mitchell had become close friends with Nixon after their respective law firms merged to become one in 1966. Though credited with running Nixon's effective 1968 campaign for the presidency, Mitchell openly disdained political work, reportedly much preferring technical legal practice.[47] As Thomas Dewey often quipped, Mitchell may have been "the best bond lawyer in New York, but he's no politician."[48] In choosing Mitchell, Nixon signaled his desire to render law enforcement a political function within his administration. Instead of tapping a career prosecutor or law enforcement official, he turned to someone he liked and trusted.

Predictably, Mitchell had far more access to Nixon than any other cabinet member during Nixon's first term.[49] At least one top official called Mitchell "the second most powerful man in the country."[50] How then did Mitchell take advantage of this extraordinary access and power? When it came to prosecuting outsiders, he brought to bear all the law enforcement powers at his disposal, whether controversial or otherwise. He is famously credited with prosecuting the Chicago Seven for rioting; he also prosecuted US military analyst Daniel Ellsberg for leaking the Pentagon Papers, a controversial US Department of Defense history of the country's political and military involvement in Vietnam from 1945 to 1967. Mitchell backed anticrime legislation to increase police investigative powers and the length of criminal sentences. Even more significantly, he went to great lengths to depoliticize the Justice Department in some important respects. Specifically, he steered free of politicizing the Solicitor General's office, deferring often to Solicitor General Erwin Griswold, a former Harvard Law School dean and a lawyer of stature who had held over from the Johnson administration.[51] According to Thomas E. Kauper, a deputy assistant attorney general in the office of legal counsel, all White House requests for legal opinions from the Office of Legal Counsel were specifically routed to avoid Mitchell, so there would be no question of the Justice Department's providing a neutral opinion on such matters.[52]

Unfortunately, when it came to internal crime matters, including executive branch corruption, Mitchell's focus on Nixon's reelection and his overall political status blinded him to more fundamental issues of fairness and justice. Domestic intelligence-gathering was a priority for the paranoid Nixon, and rather than resisting it, Mitchell pursued it with abandon. Mitchell thus backed J. Edgar Hoover's use of wiretaps and other technology at every turn.

Mitchell had been reluctant to accept the position at the Justice Department, but Nixon eventually persuaded him to do so. The price Mitchell exacted was a deputy attorney general appointment for Richard Kleindienst, the "hard-nosed Goldwater operative" who had worked with Mitchell on Nixon's 1968 campaign.[53] Nixon was nearly as comfortable with Kleindienst as he was with Mitchell, personally appealing to him to come to Washington to help Mitchell in 1969. When Mitchell resigned as attorney general in 1972 to head the Committee to Reelect the President, the president wanted Kleindienst to head the

Justice Department, ensuring that the attorney general would continue to play the trusted inner-circle role in advising Nixon on legal matters. Kleindienst's close relationship with the Nixon White House sowed the seeds of his own political destruction. When G. Gordon Liddy, of the Committee to Reelect the President, personally informed the attorney general of his own involvement in the Watergate break-in and asked for help, Kleindienst failed to report the news or to act at all on the confession.

Elliot Lee Richardson served dutifully in Richard Nixon's cabinet, both as his secretary of Health, Education, and Welfare for two-and-a-half years and then, for five months, as his secretary of Defense. Nixon liked and trusted the former attorney general of Massachusetts, and Richardson enjoyed a strong reputation around Washington as perhaps the best administrator and manager in the Nixon cabinet. Thus it was only natural for Nixon to turn to Richardson as his attorney general after Kleindienst was forced to resign less than a year into his tenure.

Unlike that of his two predecessors, however, Richardson's confirmation came with conditions. The Senate Judiciary Committee that grilled Richardson in May of 1973 extracted on-the-record assurances from the nominee that he would appoint a special Watergate prosecutor and that the prosecutor would have some latitude and independence.[54] Though refusing to abandon his supervisory role, Richardson agreed to stay out of the office's day-to-day decision-making apparatus.[55] With the issue of special prosecutors dominating the confirmation process of an attorney general for the first time in history, Richardson's status as an inner circle attorney general became a front-and-center consideration for senators as well. Later that fall Richardson's principled defense of Watergate special prosecutor Archibald Cox in the face of Nixon's threats to fire him offered proof positive that not all members of the inner circle imperil the Justice Department's independence and effectiveness.

Watergate was still fresh in the American psyche when Jimmy Carter took office as president in January of 1977. Given this recent history, Carter's choice of former judge Griffin B. Bell to serve as his administration's first attorney general was especially curious. Suspicions were immediately raised because, although Carter was six years younger than Bell, they had been childhood friends back in Plains, Georgia.[56] The two men established a professional association in the early 1960s: Carter was the local businessman and civic leader who successfully ran for election to the Georgia state Senate in 1962, while Bell rose from his own modest beginnings to become the managing partner at one of the most prestigious law firms in Atlanta.[57]

In 1961 President Kennedy tapped the forty-two-year-old Bell for a seat on the United States Court of Appeals for the Fifth Circuit. In fifteen years on the bench, Bell did little to establish himself as a prominent jurist, and after returning to private practice in 1976, he would suffer accusations of racism. Specifically, in the late 1950s he had served as a legal aide to Governor Ernest Vandiver, and had often searched for loopholes in the Supreme Court's desegregation decisions that Vandiver might exploit under the right conditions.[58] He also had been a member of two all-white private social clubs in Atlanta: the Capital City Club and the Piedmont Driving Club.

Carter settled on Bell to head the Justice Department even before the 1976 election had concluded.[59] Yet Bell's nomination cast immediate doubt on the credibility of Carter's campaign promise that he would put only the "best and most qualified people" in his cabinet. James Reston of the *New York Times* called Bell's selection "insensitive, willful, stubborn and even selfish."[60] Given the new attorney general's relatively undistinguished judicial record and the questions raised about his racial sensitivity, his appointment as attorney general seemed to be just another example of a president's rewarding an old friend with the keys to the Justice Department.[61]

Unlike his former boss, Bell's successor as attorney general—the former Deputy Attorney General Benjamin Civiletti—was not the president's close personal friend at the time of his elevation in July of 1979. Groomed as Bell's successor from the outset, Civiletti would endeavor to keep politics out of the Justice Department with far more credibility than his predecessor could muster. Civiletti was part of the inner circle in at least one key sense—as the Carter administration's deputy attorney general for two-and-a-half years, he was well known to the president and to White House aides.

An inner circle attorney general of a different sort presided over the Justice Department during Ronald Reagan's first term in office. During the decade of the 1970s, William French Smith had been a senior partner at the law firm of Gibson, Dunn & Crutcher in Los Angeles and a member of various commissions, including the US Advisory Commission on International Education and Cultural Affairs and the World Affairs Council. Like Mitchell and Bell, Smith brought with him to the position little or no experience in criminal law enforcement matters. Yet despite that handicap, the process that led to Smith's nomination as attorney general would become the stuff of legend within the administration. According to Michael Deaver, "In the first [transition] session we had to discuss the cabinet, [and] Reagan came into the room . . . and he said: 'Now listen, before we get started, Bill Smith is going to be my attorney general.' Somebody said: 'Have you thought about the fact that he has no experience?' And the governor said, 'Let me just tell you something, fellows. I have made a decision: he is going to be my attorney general.'"[62]

Reagan's final attorney general, former Pennsylvania governor Dick Thornburgh, rode in from the outside to pick up the pieces of a second term marked by revelations, investigations, and numerous outside prosecutions. Yet in George H. W. Bush's second term, Thornburgh represented the voice of institutional experience as an inner circle attorney general. Accordingly, when he began to promote a culture of secrecy at the Department of Justice, his moves were seen as attempts to circle the wagons around the administration. In what he defended as a move to cut costs, Thornburgh fired eleven of fifteen career officers in the Office of Public Information and cut a third of the employees in the Office of Legislative Liaison. Whether such moves were justified on economic grounds or not, they had the effect of reducing access to his department by both Congress and the public.[63]

Later, Thornburgh prepared a controversial memorandum which declared that state ethics rules would no longer be binding on federal prosecutors. Other Justice Department officials at the time argued that the ethics issue was a false one because as a practical matter, the Department of Justice disciplines its own errant prosecutors anyway. Thus the real contribution of the memo was symbolic as much as anything else: Thornburgh launched a shot across the bow of the law enforcement world by announcing that his own lawyers were above the laws that applied to every other lawyer in the country. It was an inauspicious beginning, to be sure, for President Bush's chief law enforcement officer and the successor to the embattled Edwin Meese. And it foreshadowed significant struggles ahead that would test President Bush's commitment to produce an ethical administration.

When Thornburgh left the first Bush administration in 1991 to launch an unsuccessful race for the US Senate, his replacement was the understated William Pelham Barr. Thornburgh's successor came to the position sporting significant experience as an administration insider. He had served as assistant attorney general for the Bush administration's Office of Legal Counsel from 1989 to 1990 and then had become deputy attorney general during the summer of 1990. Barr's primary contribution to the position of attorney general came through diplomacy. Whereas Thornburgh's heavy-handed quest for secrecy had invited distrust of his motives from congressional Democrats, Barr offered a lighter touch. When Representative Henry Gonzales (D-Tex.) threatened to hold hearings about the Banco Nazionale de Lavoro's securing of $4 billion in unauthorized loans to Iraq, Thornburgh's hard-nosed attempts to persuade him against the move proved futile, and even led to the subpoena of documents from the FBI and other investigating entities. Barr, by contrast, instead of appealing to Gonzales on grounds of executive privilege, argued that public disclosure of the classified information would harm national security.[64]

Barr's argument failed in that case, but his credibility helped him in other matters, such as the INSLAW affair. While Thornburgh had repeatedly reneged on agreements with Congress to provide full access to Justice Department witnesses in that scandal, Barr's middle ground of appointing a retired judge as "special counsel" to advise him on INSLAW was greeted as a step in the right direction. Barr thus offered a blueprint for inner circle attorneys general to be successful: a dash of modesty, a hint of diplomacy, and a willingness to seek outside counsel to diffuse charges of a Justice Department cover-up.

3. Oval Office Attorneys General: Project Impossible

In 1985, President Reagan appointed Edwin Meese to succeed William French Smith as head of the Justice Department. A longtime friend and associate of Reagan's dating back to the 1960s, Meese served as counselor to the president throughout his first term in office. In that position Meese became one of Reagan's most important advisors on policy; he was a member of the "troika" that ran the White House during Reagan's first term, along with Chief of Staff James Baker and Deputy Chief of Staff Michael Deaver.[65] Within that troika Meese was "responsible for relationships with the departments and agencies, for development of policy, for the administration of the cabinet, and for daily operations of the Executive Branch."[66] In truth, little occurred during the period that was not in his bailiwick. Thus when President Reagan nominated Meese to serve as his administration's new attorney general after the 1984 election, he was placing in power one of only a handful of people who could not possibly separate themselves in theory or practice from allegations that might arise of executive branch misconduct or corruption during that first term. Meese was an "Oval Office attorney general" in the tradition of Robert H. Jackson, although in the post-Watergate era he had responsibilities that Jackson never had.

The Senate Judiciary Committee offered fierce opposition to Meese's candidacy, but *not* on the ground that his earlier tenure as counselor to Reagan created an irresolvable conflict of interest. Rather, Senate Democrats questioned Meese principally on his politics on civil rights, as well as his so-called "personal ethics."[67] Meese confessed to having paid no interest at all on an unsecured twenty-month loan from John McKean, his tax counselor. During his confirmation hearings, several senators raised questions about the matter; McKean had twice been appointed to the Postal Board of Governors and was serving as its chairman at the time Meese's confirmation hearings were reaching their climax.[68] In addition, there were allegations that Meese had arranged federal jobs for several other people who had also done him financial favors, and that he had accepted preferential treatment in getting an Army Reserve promotion.[69] The committee was going over well-trodden ground: in 1984

William French Smith had referred all of these inquiries to an independent counsel (the special panel eventually appointed Jacob Stein to the matter), who subsequently cleared Meese of any criminal wrongdoing.

In fact, one of the few senators who questioned Meese about his close relationship with Reagan was a Republican, Senator Charles Mathias (R-Md). Specifically, Mathias raised the argument that an attorney general who had been in a "close, personal or political relationship" with the president would "lack the objectivity to stand back and look at the President's situation, and to advise him and to advise the nation in an independent way."[70] Meese's response was telling, as he focused on expanding communications with the chief executive rather than on the issue of loyalty: "Going back now almost 20 years . . . I have taken a more independent stand, brought the President, and earlier the government, more bad news, and told him more things that he couldn't do or shouldn't do in giving him legal advice, than almost any other person, and I would continue that independence."[71]

Meese's comments, of course did not reflect the potential need to keep the president out of the loop, such as when he might compromise an investigation. The attorney general's decision making, about hiring a special prosecutor, for example, generally precludes the possibility of consulting with the president. In fact, Meese's example provides evidence of his lack of independence, if anything.

Senate Democrats sustained a filibuster of Meese's nomination for five days in early February of 1985. Finally, on February 23, the Senate approved Meese by a 65–31 vote. Those thirty-one votes were the largest number cast against an attorney general nominee since the Senate rejected Calvin Coolidge's nomination of Charles Warren in 1925 by a 41–39 vote.

According to John Ehrman, "the common thread linking the scandals of Reagan's second term is that they originated in [Meese's] lack of attention to the details of his administration."[72] Narrowly confirmed as attorney general, Meese was already licking his wounds from one series of investigations before talk began of his involvement in the so-called Wedtech scandal. Whether or not Meese weathered this new set of charges, his reign as head of the Justice Department soon became a joke around Washington. Even within the administration itself, Meese's leadership was viewed as an embarrassment.[73] By some accounts, "morale among career law enforcement officials dropped to its lowest point in many years. . . . Inside the Justice Department, Meese became an object of scorn and derision."[74] As to helping put out other fires, his earlier role as an advisor made fulfilling that function close to impossible. According to Haynes Johnson, "Meese had to excuse himself from so many major federal inquiries because of association with Reagan officials or friends being questioned."[75] What may have been possible in an earlier age was no longer possible in the post-Watergate era. And the Oval Office attorney general was never able to break out of his role as Reagan's companion, advisor, and friend during an era when the attorney general's functions demanded he do exactly that.

Twenty years after Meese's ill-fated move to the Justice Department, Pres. George W. Bush made a similar appointment. Bush's selection of White House Counsel Alberto Gonzales to serve as John Ashcroft's successor had many of the same markings as the Meese appointment. As White House counselor, Gonzales became one of President Bush's most trusted advisors during his first term in office. Indeed, he was considered loyal to a fault in some quarters.

Perhaps more than any other official in federal government, Gonzales owed his political career to one man. After little more than a decade in private practice, he was chosen by then-Governor George W. Bush to become his general counsel in 1994. In that post Gonzales helped his mentor in matters ranging from avoiding jury duty to processing clemency requests from Texas prisoners on death row. Bush made Gonzales Texas' secretary of state in 1997 and two years later named him to the Texas Supreme Court, a post he would hold for less than two years before receiving his appointment as Pres. George W. Bush's White House counsel in early 2001. Through President Bush's first term, his affection for Gonzales kept him on nearly every short list floated for potential Supreme Court vacancies. Yet that same affection also neutralized Gonzales's effectiveness once he moved out of the White House counsel's office.

When Gonzales was first appointed attorney general in 2005, conservatives feared that a true conservative (Ashcroft) was being replaced with a moderate. They based that judgment on Gonzales's less strident positions on abortion and affirmative action. Yet such fears were quickly allayed as it became clear that Gonzales's own views on the law were not a factor at all in the decisions he made. The attorney general would remain a steadfast enthusiast for White House policy and preferences even in his new position at the Justice Department. As Commerce Secretary Don Evans observed, "He is totally loyal to the President."[76]

At his hearings, Gonzales promised senators that "if confirmed as attorney general, I will no longer represent the White House; I will represent the United States of America and its people."[77] Yet that distinction was not always so easy to articulate. When Senator Russell Feingold (D-Wisc.) asked the nominee whether the president could violate the law as commander in chief, Gonzales's response was revealing. Laws were "assumed to be constitutional," he said, and "to the extent that there is a decision made to ignore a statute, I consider that a very significant decision and one that I would be personally involved with, I commit to you on that, and one I will take with a great deal of care and seriousness."[78]

Feingold was left unsatisfied by these answers, perhaps because they sounded more like responses from the president's attorney than from the next attorney general of the United States. Gonzales's striking lack of independence in theory and in practice only served to strain relations between the administration and Congress, and left the attorney general ill-suited to weather Bush administration scandals once Congress shifted into Democratic hands after the 2006 midterm elections.

• • •

The demise of the independent counsel provisions of the Ethics in Government Act of 1978 marked a return to reliance on a system in which the primary check on prosecutorial abuse would be politics itself. The same could be said for checks on the misuse of power by routine prosecutorial authorities who report to the attorney general, and indirectly to the president himself. If the attorney general is not capable of neutrality, the system becomes strained; and even if the attorney general is capable of neutrality, he or she may require other types of political checks to be able to fulfill the duties of office without undue interference.

chapter 3

When All Bets Are Off

Presidents, Vice Presidents, and Their Family

Members on Trial

The 1870 statute that formally established the Department of Justice granted the new agency "control over all criminal prosecutions" in which the United States maintained an interest, and it vested its head officer with control over all "federal law enforcement."[1] In the case of misconduct by public officials, the operating presumption of the Justice Department appeared straightforward: its staff of US attorneys and other prosecutors would actively investigate and prosecute any and all cases against federal officials, supervised by an attorney general who could make impartial decisions in those cases or, alternatively, defer to deputies and assistant attorneys general who could.

In this age of the revolving door between government and industry, proper management of conflicts of interest has become the price of conducting government business. And the sheer size of government has increased the number of conflicts that arise even within government itself. This is especially true in the case of government lawyers, whose duty of loyalty to their client (in this case, the US government) expressly prohibits them from taking on assignments that create the appearance of impropriety or conflict of interest. Given these strictures, allegations lodged against the president of the United States are especially problematic. Is there any Justice Department prosecutor who would not find himself or herself caught in a web of conflicts while investigating such matters?

Given the vice president's position in the hierarchy, and the political symbolism attached to it, allegations against the vice president pose problems and conflicts similar to those posed by allegations against the president. And allegations leveled against the president's family members are likely to create issues equally treacherous for a federal prosecutor who must defer to the attorney general and, ultimately, to the president of the United States as well.

The presumption against deviating from routine Justice Department investigative procedures does not simply disappear under these circumstances. While a Justice Department prosecutor has to wonder about the political implications of his or her investigation and prosecution of a sitting president or vice president, appointing a special prosecutor may tip the balance too far to the other side, as the new prosecutor seeks to justify the decision to deviate from routine procedures in the first place. Recognizing this problem, some special prosecutors and independent counsels—including Whitewater Independent Counsel Kenneth Starr—have introduced incentive structures into their offices designed to "reflect, in essence, the Justice Department at its very best," including an elaborate pre-indictment review process and a staff of investigators whose backgrounds "reflect the experience and concerns of the prosecutors within the department."[2] Of course, as one writer aptly notes, such a strategy of "replication" is flawed from the outset: the decision-making processes in the Department of Justice are in fact "multilayered" and "infused with the institutional memory of long-serving career officials."[3] Additionally, the staff recruitment process itself, no matter how fairly conducted, disproportionately attracts those from the opposition party, and those who dislike the president most are "apt to stick around the longest."[4]

No mathematical formula can pinpoint some magical "mean of aggressiveness" in a prosecutorial office, and attempting to pinpoint one by adhering to strict rules for hiring independent counsel staffs is an ineffective strategy at best. Nor is it wise to hamper independent or special prosecutors at the outset with artificially imposed restrictions. Attorneys general and other political officials must accept the premise that while special or independent prosecutors offer significant benefits, such as circumventing the problem of conflicting loyalties, they also carry with them significant disadvantages, such as reduced accountability in expending resources. These factors tend to be even more exaggerated when the president or vice president is the target of an investigation, but they are also relevant when a president's family members become targets of their own federal investigations.

In the final analysis, no statutorily authorized special prosecutor or independent counsel provisions can significantly reduce the element of discretion that an attorney general must exercise when considering the need for a special counsel. Inquiries into that need should include these questions:

- Do the allegations of criminal activity clearly and directly implicate the president or vice president, or do they do so only indirectly?
- For how long have Justice Department prosecutors already been involved in the investigation, and to what degree are they involved?
- Are Justice Department officials, past or present, implicated in the alleged wrongdoing?

- In the case of allegations against the vice president, would his resignation offer political benefits (as well as costs) to the White House?
- In the case of allegations made against a president's immediate family member, does that person maintain a formal or informal role in political decision making, such that investigating and prosecuting him or her might do even greater political damage to the White House?

The attorney general must deliberate on all these questions when considering his or her fitness to investigate the chief executive without the assistance of a special prosecutor. Further complicating the matter, the attorney general must also consider the nature of the allegations themselves: sometimes the charges are not too serious to be addressed fairly without resorting to outside counsel and without inviting waves of criticism. At other times, of course, there is no scenario under which the attorney general will *not* be subject to some form of legitimate criticism.

Agnew Agonistes: A Vice President in the Cross Hairs

Just as Watergate Senate Committee Chairman Sam Ervin (D-N.C.) was gaveling into session that body's first day of hearings on May 17, 1973, Justice Department lawyers were focusing their attention on another scandal involving the vice president of the United States and his role in certain official activities while he was still governor of Maryland in the mid-1960s. Spiro Agnew was hardly the first vice president in American history to face the possibility of criminal charges: 167 years earlier, former vice president Aaron Burr was tried for treason on charges that were ultimately dismissed. In 1872 Vice President Schuyler Colfax was jettisoned from the Republican ticket as a result of his links to the Crédit Mobilier scandal involving the Union Pacific Railroad and the revelation that various congressmen had received bribes in the form of corporate shares. (While he left office in disgrace, Colfax avoided actual indictment.) By contrast, the investigation of Spiro Agnew in the spring and summer of 1973 for tax evasion and money laundering held profound implications for American government. Agnew's eventual resignation at the conclusion of that investigation led to the first appointment of a vice president (Gerald Ford) under the terms of the six-year-old Twenty-fifth Amendment. It would also set the stage for the promotion of Ford to the presidency itself.

To be sure, Agnew's rise to national prominence had been nearly as quick as his downfall. After serving one term as a Republican Baltimore County executive in an overwhelmingly Democratic district, Agnew ran for governor of Maryland in 1966. He immediately found himself blessed with an opponent who was sitting on the wrong side of history; the Democratic nominee, George P. Mahoney, was running on an anti-integrationist platform in a state that was far more progressive than the Deep South. The more moderate Agnew benefited greatly when Mahoney's position on the issue essentially splintered the Maryland Democrats. As members of the Democratic Party who actually supported integration crossed party lines in droves, they helped Agnew become the unlikely Republican governor by a margin of just 82,000 votes.

Agnew's moderate image and nominal connection to the South caught the attention of Nixon's aides at the 1968 Republican National Convention; his meteoric rise was complete when he was tapped as Nixon's running mate that year. Once elected, Vice President Agnew abandoned his image as a moderate compromiser, taking on the role of chief "hatchet man" for an administration that would become known for its vitriol against the press and against Democratic opponents. Four years later, Nixon and Agnew became the first full ticket to be reelected intact since 1956.

Unlike more modern vice presidents like Al Gore, Dick Cheney, and even Joseph Biden, all of whom became highly influential members of their presidents' inner circles, Agnew fit the more traditional role of a vice president relegated to making stump speeches on behalf of the president's policies and representing him at funerals and other chiefly ceremonial events. Indeed, Vice President Agnew was often so divorced from the administration's high-level decision making that he began to complain publicly about his "poor treatment" by the White House and even attacked the administration's overtures to Communist China as bad policy.[5] Later, in a decision that would determine the future course of the presidency, Agnew refused White House entreaties to voluntarily step down from the 1972 ticket in favor of Treasury Secretary John Connally.

During the winter of 1972–73, the US Attorney's Office in Maryland, headed by George Beall, the younger brother of US Senator J. Glenn Beall (R.-Md.), began investigating numerous leads pointing toward "illegal practices on the part of contractors doing business with Baltimore County."[6] Several witnesses and their lawyers agreed to describe testimony they were prepared to give as part of a cooperation agreement with the government, alleging that "payments had been made to or on behalf of the Vice President."[7] The cash payments, some of which occurred while Agnew was still governor of Maryland, and some of which were made after he had assumed the vice presidency, were regarded by the payers as "necessary to obtain county or state business" in Maryland. (In Maryland at the time, the governor chose architects and engineers for state construction jobs from lists generated by the Maryland State Roads Commission.)

On July 3, 1973, barely six weeks into his new position as attorney general, Elliott Richardson was briefed on the Agnew investigation for the first time. During that meeting he assured Beall that the Justice Department's central offices in Washington, DC, would not interfere with or compromise his work in any way.[8] Eight days later, Richardson received a fuller briefing from Beall and his assistants. This time Richardson brought with him a list of four questions that needed answers in the near future:

1. When, if ever, and under what conditions should Agnew be confronted with the allegations against him and given an opportunity to answer questions under oath?
2. Should the attorney general advise the president that the investigation was going on?
3. Which potential witnesses in the investigation should be given complete immunity from prosecution?
4. Did the investigation fall under the jurisdiction of Watergate special prosecutor Archibald Cox?[9]

Convinced by the prosecutors that the evidence against Agnew was strong, Richardson discussed with Beall and his staff the possibility that Agnew might willingly resign if confronted with the facts. Beall's assistants weren't so sure. Richardson was inclined to defer to his US attorneys on most issues, but as attorney general he had especially strong feelings about the second question—he believed that the president had a right to know what was going on before they confronted Agnew.[10] Of greater significance, Richardson told the prosecutors that he did not think Cox should get involved at all—apparently, he was convinced by Beall that at a time when public confidence might be waning, the Agnew case offered an ideal opportunity "to demonstrate the [Justice] department's ability and willingness to vigorously enforce the law, even if it involved the vice president of the United States." [11]

The third meeting between Richardson and the prosecutors occurred on July 27, 1973.[12] One of Beall's assistants, Barnet Skolnik, told the attorney general at that point that he thought press discovery of the investigation was imminent because the scope of the investigation had expanded.[13] At that point none of the anti-Agnew witnesses had received immunity, which raised an important concern for Richardson. Richardson asked: "Do any of you have any moral doubt as to Agnew's guilt?" As none of them did, Richardson informed them that it was now time to brief the president.[14]

Although Agnew had already informed the White House that he was under investigation (and there was good reason to assume Nixon was aware of the investigation even earlier), Richardson formally reported the exact nature of the charges to the president on August 6, 1973. Nixon indicated that he wanted Richardson's office to provide its own "fresh assessment" of the case; he asked Richardson to get Assistant Attorney General Henry Peterson, head of the Justice Department's Criminal Division, to provide his own judgment. Richardson agreed, but indicated that the evidence so far was "cut and dried" in terms of "documentary evidence as well as sworn testimony."[15] President Nixon also told Richardson to immediately confront Agnew with everything he had, and to get his reaction as soon as possible. Thus later on the afternoon of August 6, Richardson met to discuss the case with Agnew and his attorneys. According to Richardson's memo filed a week later, Agnew remarked that "the whole thing was a fabrication," and that at least one of the witnesses was "crazy." The vice president also complained that the Baltimore-based prosecutors were not objective; that Beall had lost control of the investigation to his "zealous young assistants"; and that he wanted to be "sure he received the treatment afforded a normal defendant," since Agnew noted a tone of contempt in the way prosecutors had referred to him in their various statements.[16]

Agnew and his attorneys agreed that Peterson should conduct his own investigation while the case remained confidential. He then met with the president and professed his total innocence of all the charges.[17] At the same time, White House Counselors Fred Buzhardt and Leonard Garment informed Nixon that the case against Agnew was quite strong—over forty counts were being considered in a potential indictment. Thus an important question remained. Would the Nixon administration publicly defend Agnew against the charges, or would it adopt a neutral and deferential stand while the US Attorney's Office in Maryland moved forward with its investigation? The decision was a political rather than a legal one: Could the White House, already engulfed in defending itself against a special prosecutor investigating the Watergate affair, realistically expend itself in Agnew's defense without dragging the presidency down even further in the process? Moreover, if Nixon came to Agnew's defense, calls for Cox or some other special prosecutor to take over the investigation would likely ensue.

According to author J. Anthony Lukas, that same day Nixon sent White House Chief of Staff Alexander Haig to Agnew to suggest that the vice president consider resigning.[18] Only a president sitting high atop the polls, and with few other looming crises, would have the capital to wage effective war on his vice president's behalf to avoid this more limited form of political damage. With the Watergate investigation heating up in the Senate, President Nixon was in no such position.[19] Of course that made the threat to Agnew's due process rights even more substantial.

Initially, Agnew resisted Haig's entreaties. But with Nixon's own impeachment a distant but not altogether unrealistic possibility, pressure on Agnew to resign grew at a fever pitch, for influential Republicans feared the prospect of handing the White House over to a Democratic speaker of the house if both men were removed from office at the same time. The next day, August 7, 1973, the Justice Department's investigation of Agnew made the front pages of the national media. In his news conference on August 8, Agnew called reports of his illegal activities "damned lies, false and scurrilous and malicious," and promised full cooperation with the investigators. The evidence itself began filtering down to the press soon thereafter, and at least one Justice Department official leaked that "the evidence is so strong that the case must be taken to trial." At another news conference on August 21, Agnew complained about leaks from the Justice Department that he called "a clear and outrageous effort to influence the outcome of possible grand jury deliberations."[20]

The only real conflict between the attorney general and the Baltimore prosecutors occurred during the first week of September. On Thursday, September 6, Petersen directed the US Attorney's Office in Baltimore to prepare a written status report on the investigation of Vice President Agnew. George Beall's prosecutors told Peterson that they were unanimous in their opposition to preparing such a memorandum, as the memo itself might fall into the hands of the press, or worse, it might be discoverable by Agnew's attorneys in the course of the prosecution. To the Baltimore prosecutors, all of the information contained within such a memo could just as easily be conveyed orally. Further, disclosing the information to the White House would invite White House leaks for political purposes. But Petersen felt such a memo was necessary "to enable the appropriate officials in the department properly to exercise their heavy responsibilities and to make the important decisions that must be made in the near future."[21] According to Lukas, Petersen craved vindication after earlier accusations that he had mishandled the Watergate investigation by keeping it focused solely on the burglary and "issuing press releases extolling the virtues of the ongoing investigation."[22] Yet as a career Justice Department bureaucrat, Petersen kept counseling in favor of caution—he was prepared to be as deferential to the vice president as necessary.

Throughout the month of September 1973, the attorney general focused on what he determined was the desired outcome for all concerned: Agnew's resignation. On September 15, a working group consisting of Richardson, Deputy Attorney General William Ruckelshaus, Petersen, and the Baltimore prosecutors reached a consensus on a plea offer: in return for his resignation, Agnew would be offered a plea of no contest to income tax evasion. Yet Agnew balked at one additional condition. He was asked to formally admit to accepting the payoffs. If he was hoping he would have the president's support in these negotiations, he was badly mistaken—by late September Nixon had resigned himself to the inevitability of Agnew's resignation and he now wanted it to proceed as quickly as possible. No less significant to Nixon, he did not want to cause a break with the attorney general, whose support he would need as he fended off the Watergate special prosecutor in the months to come. Once President Nixon's sympathy had dissipated, the vice president's hopes for a defense went out the window.

On October 9, 1973, at a conference with Agnew's lawyers, Richardson agreed to recommend against prison time before the judge assigned to the case. With that critical piece in place, Agnew met with the president and agreed to resign.[23] His resignation arrived on Secretary of State Henry Kissinger's desk early in the afternoon on October 10. That same day Agnew appeared in Baltimore District Court, where he pleaded no contest to the charge of income tax evasion. Following the department's recommendation, he received a sentence of three years of unsupervised probation and a $10,000 fine.[24]

The case of Spiro Agnew offers a fitting lesson in how the attorney general, working without special prosecutors, can nevertheless effectively perform prosecutorial functions in the event of wrongdoing by the vice president. In this case, an inner circle attorney general was able to prevail because political circumstances worked in his favor. President Nixon's refusal to fight for Agnew (in part driven by the president's own concerns about Watergate) laid the groundwork for the attorney general's success, as did the absence of conditions such as intervening elections that might have biased the investigation. A Democratic Congress, already on guard against the administration because of Watergate, stood ready to add Agnew to its list of targets if necessary. Certainly it is unlikely that a special prosecutor could have moved so quickly, and failure to do so would have all but ensured that the president's and the vice president's offices would both be under siege at the exact same time.

Watergate: Investigating the President of the United States

The story of the Watergate scandal has been told and retold so many times that its most essential details can be boiled down to a handful for purposes of assessing Justice Department participation in resolving the scandal early on, before a special prosecutor was named in the crisis. It still remains the only scandal in American history to end a presidency midway through its term. That it spelled the end for a president who was riding high politically just eighteen months earlier—Richard Nixon won a forty-nine-state landslide with over 60 percent of the vote in his reelection in November 1972—serves as a stark reminder of just how quickly good fortunes can turn bad. For better or worse,

Watergate became the dominant paradigm driving all the ethics reforms of the late 1970s and beyond.

The roots of the scandal dated back more than a year before the infamous break-in at the Democratic National Committee offices in the Watergate Hotel on June 17, 1972. In 1970 White House aide Tom Charles Huston, liaison to an interagency committee on intelligence, authored a forty-three-page report calling for numerous extreme measures in the name of national security, including strategic domestic burglaries, unauthorized electronic surveillance, the opening of "radicals'" mail, and even detention of antiwar protestors in camps.[25] The plan was initially ratified by Nixon, but it was ultimately defeated by the combined objections of J. Edgar Hoover (reasserting his own agency's near exclusive control over surveillance activities) and Attorney General John Mitchell. However, the immediate fallout from the defeated plan was a sudden new interest on the part of the president in surveillance activities, which he hoped to control within the White House itself. In short, if the White House could not manage surveillance activities taking place in other agencies through an interagency committee on intelligence, it wanted the capacity to conduct some covert activities on its own without having to go through the FBI, the CIA, or anyone else.

President Nixon charged John Ehrlichman, his assistant for Domestic Affairs, with responsibility for solving the problem. Ehrlichman's response was to form a "Special Investigations Unit" under White House control beginning on July 24, 1971. Nicknamed the "plumbers" because it was charged with working on government leaks, the unit was led by thirty-four-year-old David Young, who had just joined the White House from Henry Kissinger's staff on July 1, as well as by one of Ehrlichman's young aides, thirty-one-year-old Egil "Bud" Krogh. In an effort to beef up the operation, top White House aide Charles Colson recommended E. Howard Hunt to Krough and Young. White House Counsel John Dean then recruited a friend of Hunt's, G. Gordon Liddy, to join the operation too. Whether or not Nixon and his aides knew all the specifics of the plumbers' activities, they certainly knew in a general way what the unit was charged with doing.

Working out of a room in the Executive Office Building, Young and Krogh were first charged with addressing the ultimate administration leaker, Daniel Ellsberg. Six weeks earlier, Ellsberg had been the Pentagon aide accused of delivering copies of the controversial Pentagon Papers, detailing government decision-making processes concerning the Vietnam War, to Neil Sheehan, a reporter from the *New York Times*. The plumbers' first task was to break into the office of Ellsberg's Los Angeles psychiatrist, Dr. Lewis J. Fielding, in an effort to uncover information that might discredit Ellsberg. In the words of

Fred Emery, "Nixon wanted to get to the bottom of the Ellsberg affair . . . he wanted Ellsberg, his motives and his message discredited."[26] The plumbers also expanded the scope of their investigative activities to look into Senator Ted Kennedy's Chappaquiddick affair (the Democratic presidential hopeful in 1972, Kennedy had pled guilty to leaving the scene of an accident in which a woman in his car had drowned) and the Kennedy administration's alleged involvement in the assassination of Vietnamese president Ngo Dinh Diem on November 2, 1963.

Once the White House reelection campaign began in earnest, the plumbers shifted their activities to work more directly on behalf of the Committee to Reelect the President (CREEP). The decision to break into the Democratic National Committee offices at the Watergate Hotel and to plant surveillance bugs there grew directly out of this effort. The June 17, 1972, break-in was actually the second in a series; the five burglars caught that night, including former CIA agent James W. McCord, had three weeks earlier broken into the same Watergate Hotel office, but that time had managed to avoid capture.

Aware that the FBI had assumed control over the Watergate investigation from the outset, President Nixon met with his aides throughout the latter part of June 1972 to discuss how they might contain the FBI's investigation into the incident. Unfortunately for Nixon, circumstances had aligned so that the FBI would not be easily influenced by political considerations. For starters, the bureau was experiencing a leadership vacuum at the top for the first time in its history. J. Edgar Hoover had died just six weeks before the Watergate break-in; his temporary replacement, L. Patrick Gray, deferred to long-term FBI regulars to oversee the day-to-day operations of the bureau while he served as acting director, awaiting his Senate confirmation hearings. That left operational command of the bureau to W. Mark Felt, a long-time FBI official now frustrated at having been passed over for the top leadership post by the Nixon administration.[27] It was a situation ripe for division and conflict, but that did not seep down to the actual Watergate investigation. While Gray was busy "trying to be director so bad and ingratiate himself with the White House," the FBI agents who "did the job, day in and day out," apparently did it quite well.[28] While Nixon and his aides plotted their next move, the FBI was already racing ahead with its investigation, tracing money the burglars had, with the help of Mexican banks, indirectly funneled to the Committee to Reelect the President.[29]

Initially, the prosecutor heading up the criminal investigation of the Watergate affair was thirty-six-year old Earl Silbert Jr., the Principal Assistant US attorney in Washington, DC. If White House aides were determined to end the investigation at Liddy, Silbert was the ideal prosecutor for the purpose. In the days after the break-in, Silbert did not so much as ask the court for a search warrant for McCord's house. At first Silbert also did not contest the White House request to have lawyers John Dean and Fred Fielding sit in on FBI interviews of White House personnel that touched in any way on the Watergate affair.[30] Thus if Silbert and his colleagues wanted to interview the witnesses, the meetings would occur in Henry Peterson's office at the Justice Department, outside the hearing of the Grand Jury.[31] Nor did Silbert question White House claims that the national security aspects of the case[32] required discretion from him—along with willingness to keep the White House lawyers informed of his progress. Finally, neither the FBI nor Silbert interviewed Robert Reisner, the assistant to a major target of this early investigation, Jeb Magruder.[33]

Peterson was only a bit more active on the investigative front than Silbert. As head of the Justice Department's Criminal Division, he ordered the FBI's Washington field office to ask the CIA whether the suspects in the burglary were then actively employed by the agency. And he requested that all new information developed by the FBI be forwarded directly to him, so that he could then pass it to the White House.[34] This last request proved a boon to the White House, as it allowed the president and his aides to review details soon after they came in, and plan their responses accordingly. Where was the attorney general during all this commotion? Richard Kleindienst, partial to the interests of Mitchell and Nixon, was unwilling to assert himself in the process. This breakdown at the highest levels of the Justice Department initially went unchecked, aided and abetted by a White House with nothing to gain and everything to lose from the Watergate scandal. Not even the Democratic Congress could offer an effective check on the attorney general under such conditions.

Eventually Silbert tried the burglars in January of 1973 on the theory that they, Hunt, and Liddy were "off on an enterprise of their own"; he continued to assure reporters that there was no criminal conspiracy.[35] From the perspective of Nixon and his aides, Silbert was simply too good to be true. (Eighteen months later, in July of 1974, the Nixon administration would reward Silbert for his discretion by offering him the US attorney's post in Washington, DC.) But Silbert's credibility was already coming under fire from the trial judge, John J. Sirica of the US District Court for DC. Sirica never accepted Silbert's claim that the burglars had acted alone, and his doubts were not lost on the head burglar, McCord, who feared that if Silbert's claim was accepted, the White House would eventually cut off any assistance to the burglars. Thus on March 19, 1973, McCord wrote a letter to Sirica stating that his plea and testimony, some of which he claimed was perjured, had been compelled by pressure from White House Counsel John Dean and former attorney general Mitchell. His letter launched the Watergate investigation in earnest and soon resulted in the resignation of Kleindienst and the formation of a Senate Select Watergate committee that summer.

Though the Senate Watergate Committee did not open public hearings into the matter until May 17, 1973, behind-the-scenes maneuvering was already underway. Prior to resigning, Attorney General Richard Kleindienst pressed Nixon to hire a special prosecutor for the investigation. The president resisted at first, but once McCord's letter went public, Nixon began to see at least one advantage to such an appointment: if the Watergate prosecutor was not hostile to the administration, he might actually validate the work already done by Silbert.[36] When Nixon fired his top two White House aides, Chief of Staff H. R. Haldeman and John Ehrlichman, on April 30, 1973, Kleindienst and Dean elected to leave the administration as well.

During confirmation hearings for Kleindienst's successor, Elliot Richardson, the issue of the special prosecutor arose once again. Silbert's investigation had already lost credibility with the public and the courts. Thus before accepting his nomination as attorney general, Richardson extracted the president's promise that once in office, he would have full charge of the Watergate case and "could name a special prosecutor if he thought it appropriate."[37] Weeks before he was formally confirmed, Richardson was concocting lists of prospective special prosecutors that he might float before the Senate committee that grilled him. High on his list were esteemed senior jurists like Judge J. Edward Lumbard of the US Court of Appeals for the Second Circuit and Chief Justice Joseph Weintraub of the New Jersey Supreme Court.[38] In Richardson's mind, Lumbard ranked first because of his "flawless reputation for honesty, integrity and fairness," his "considerable reputation as a prosecutor," and his "complete familiarity with federal criminal law."[39] Several advisors also suggested the name of Leon Jaworski, the former president of the American College of Trial Lawyers, and Harvard Law professor Archibald Cox.[40]

The Senate hearings into Watergate began even before Richardson's confirmation hearings had formally concluded. With his appointment imminent, the prospective attorney general tentatively named Cox as the Watergate special prosecutor.[41] What was the understanding of Cox's role going forward? The last cases in which a special prosecutor had been named to investigate and prosecute executive branch corruption had occurred several decades earlier. In each instance, the administration had limited the powers of the special prosecutor to crimes directly linked with the scandal for which he had been named. In the 1920s, Atlee Pomerene and Owen Roberts litigated only civil and criminal cases arising directly from the Teapot Dome scandal.[42]

This built-in limitation was what concerned Cox most before he accepted the assignment from Richardson. As originally proposed by Richardson, the

Watergate special prosecutor had jurisdiction over only those crimes "directly linked to the Watergate break-in." It was unclear at that point whether allegations about illegal campaign contributions, or the break-in at the office of Ellsberg's psychiatrist, had any relationship to Watergate. Cox wanted authority to investigate leads wherever they took him, without assuming what would become the difficult burden of proving a link to the Watergate burglary in every instance.[43] Richardson eventually agreed to "insert language giving the special prosecutor wide jurisdiction over allegations of criminal conduct involving White House assistants or presidential aides, past or present."[44] This was an enormous grant of discretion and latitude to Cox, and would create significant problems for the White House that Nixon had not anticipated when he first agreed to a special prosecutor. Even more telling, it established a precedent for future special and independent prosecutors to cite in their own investigations. When Kenneth Starr more than two decades later asked for authority to investigate allegations about a White House intern named Monica Lewinsky, he was drawing on the experience of Cox and others who claimed that such latitude was necessary, if not absolutely inherent within the position itself. Though the Justice Department's broader agenda and responsibilities require such wide-ranging authority to ensure flexibility, the narrower purpose of the special prosecutor usually does not.

Cox's appointment transformed the Watergate investigation and altered the course of American politics in the process. Unlike Silbert, who formally continued working on the investigation up through June, Cox would not accept White House attempts to intimidate him and his investigation. More importantly, the notion of a White House cover-up, which Silbert's office had not pursued, became a central aspect of Cox's investigation. Although Silbert and his aides secured John Dean's testimony and provided a detailed blueprint of the case, Cox asked them on June 29 to formally withdraw from it.[45] For the first time there was a prosecutor working outside the White House and the Justice Department's day-to-day supervision. In fact, the memo of understanding between Richardson and Cox established that Cox alone would "determine whether and to what extent he [would] inform or consult with the attorney general about the conduct of his duties and responsibilities."[46] A greater degree of latitude would be difficult to imagine.

The remainder of the Watergate investigation unfolded in the glare of the public spotlight. When Cox joined the Senate investigators in pursuing White House tapes containing presidential discussions about the Watergate break-in, all other investigations stopped in their tracks. Nixon attempted to fend off the subpoena by claiming executive privilege; he eventually ordered Cox, through Richardson, to drop the subpoena or be fired from his position. The decision to fire Cox spelled the beginning of the end of Nixon's presidency. Two top Justice Department officials, Richardson and Deputy Attorney General William Ruckelshaus, resigned rather than fire Cox and essentially go back on the attorney general's original promise to the Senate Judiciary Committee that he would name and support a special independent counsel. That left Solicitor General Robert Bork to carry out the firing, which he did on October 30, 1973.

The Cox firing thus backfired on Nixon in two fundamental ways. First, it turned public opinion against his presidency for good; second, it accomplished little in the long run, as Nixon was forced to approve the appointment of another special prosecutor, Leon Jaworski, in his place. Nixon continued to fight the subpoena until July 24, 1974, when the US Supreme Court by an 8–0 decision sided with Jaworski and ordered the White House to hand over the tapes.[47] On July 30, 1974, Nixon complied with the order; ten days later he resigned from office.

The lessons of Watergate are many. Rather than empowering career Justice Department attorneys to conduct an impartial investigation, White House officials, acting through Justice Department official Henry Petersen, put the onus on Earl Silbert to conduct an investigation, and then took steps to ensure that he would be straitjacketed by his superiors. Meanwhile, the attorney general's office was in flux and continued to be so throughout the period. No one could think that a special prosecutor would be duplicative under such circumstances.

Silbert was not the only Department of Justice lawyer straitjacketed in the crisis; Richardson was similarly denied the opportunity to conduct his own preliminary inquiry to determine whether he needed to fall back on a special prosecutor appointment. By early 1973, the issue in Watergate was no longer prosecutorial effectiveness; it was a question of public trust. Nixon's actions had married the public with the prosecution, much to his own detriment.

Billygate: It's a Family Thing

Embarrassing relatives have long been political thorns in the sides of US presidents. The embarrassment hits closest to home when the relative is the president's sibling. Sam Houston Johnson, younger brother of Lyndon Johnson, often got drunk and blabbered to the press until Lyndon intervened with the help of the Secret Service. President Nixon could not have been too pleased with his younger brother Donald, who started a fast-food chain that would sell "Nixonburgers" using money borrowed from millionaire Howard Hughes.

These sibling offenses, however, did not compare in political significance with those of William "Billy" Carter, the younger brother of Pres. Jimmy

Carter. At first glance, Billy's antics after his older brother became president seemed harmless enough. In early 1977 he lent his name and credibility to a product called Billy Beer, helping the beer company conjure up the image of a beer-guzzling, overweight southerner who was distinctly fond of a good time. Billy Carter's endorsement of Billy Beer made some White House officials uncomfortable, but it had few implications for US foreign policy.

The same could not be said for Billy's actions as a registered agent of the Libyan government. In late 1978 and early 1979, the president's brother visited Libya at least three times as a guest of that nation, insisting throughout that he was just a "friend" of the Libyans.[48] After one of his trips, in March 1979, Billy met with the press and made derogatory remarks about Jews; he then proceeded to halfheartedly defend Libya against charges that it had sponsored terrorism, noting that "a heap of governments support terrorists and [Libya] at least admitted it."[49] Public outrage swiftly followed. After many protests, in July of 1979 Billy Carter formally registered as a foreign agent. Adding insult to injury, the press reported that he had accepted $220,000 in "loans" from the Libyan government.[50]

Nothing the Justice Department did during the summer and fall of 1979 could calm an increasingly violent storm of public opinion after the discovery of the loans from Libya. The press demanded to know (1) what Billy Carter had done to earn the loans, (2) why he had agreed to register as a foreign agent after insisting that he wasn't one, and (3) what role the White House had played in his Libyan activities.[51] Just as significantly, reporters asked whether the White House had played any role in influencing the Justice Department investigation. The White House responded on July 22, 1979, with the formal statement that President Carter did not condone having any of his close relatives acting as foreign agents, and that at no time had there been any contact between the Justice Department and the White House concerning the investigation into Billy Carter's actions. Yet as author Burton Kaufman notes, the statements only seemed to make matters worse: information about Billy's trips continued to leak out during the years that followed, implying that both the president and the First Lady had known about his visits and had simply not stopped them.[52]

Griffin Bell resigned from the Justice Department in 1979 to become special ambassador to the Helsinki Convention. Billy Carter's case thus offered Attorney General Benjamin Civiletti his first significant challenge.[53] Eventually the new attorney general admitted to the press that he had discussed the case with the president, undercutting previous statements made by his office and the White House.[54] The Billy Carter affair thus fed the perception that family and friends of the president were judged by a different standard than others, notwithstanding the Justice Department's pleadings that the letter of the law had not actually been violated.

With the 1980 presidential and congressional elections coming increasingly into focus, no high-profile Democrat would stand in the way of calls for a Senate investigation into the Billy Carter affair. Yet just as the Justice Department's Office of Professional Responsibility uncovered no actual criminal wrongdoing, the Senate subcommittee investigating the matter reported that Billy Carter had no influence over US foreign policy and that no one in the White House had engaged in any improper or illegal activities.[55]

Eventually, Billygate came to stand for a scandal in which various people acted in highly inappropriate ways, but in which no illegal activity took place. Griffin Bell's close connections to the Carter family would have rendered him powerless to address the matter with legitimacy; Civiletti's presence at least offered the Justice Department some distance from Carter personally. Because there were no allegations of criminal activity to pursue, the Justice Department was never forced to seriously consider appointing a special prosecutor. Civiletti's mistakes in the case did not justify such an intervention, in part because, even after he had made them, he was able to maintain a level of public credibility.

Travelgate: The First Lady and the White House Travel Office

On May 19, 1993, the Clinton White House fired seven longtime employees of the White House Travel Office. No fewer than eight investigations were eventually launched into the matter and its handling by the White House: (1) the White House's own internal investigation, labeled the "White House Travel Office Management Review"; (2) a US Department of Justice investigation, which included an FBI investigation as well; (3) a General Accounting Office investigation; (4) a House Government Reform and Oversight Committee investigation, with hearings chaired by Rep. William Clinger (R-Pa.); (5) a Senate Whitewater Committee investigation administered by the Senate Committee on Banking, Housing, and Urban Affairs, which held hearings chaired by Senator Al D'Amato (R-N.Y.); (6) an investigation by the Department of Justice's Office of Professional Responsibility into FBI contacts with the White House regarding the matter; (7) an investigation by Special Counsel Robert B. Fiske Jr., authorized by his appointment in January 1994 under Department of Justice Regulations (beginning on August 5, 1994, Fiske's team examined the Travel Office firings for any possible connection to the July 20, 1993, death of former Deputy Counsel Vincent Foster), and (8) an investigation by Independent Counsel Kenneth Starr. There were also other investigations begun by Fiske and subsumed into Starr's own portfolio. Starr's investigation began in

August 1994 and, under successive independent counsels, extended until a final report was issued on June 23, 2000, and filed with the court on June 30, 2000.[56]

These multiple inquiries raised important questions concerning the state of the independent counsel regulatory scheme that was at work during the mid-1990s. The high costs of the inquiries contributed in part to the demise of the independent counsel provisions in June of 1999. Regardless, critical questions must be raised concerning whether the participation of a special prosecutor was even necessary in the Travelgate matter. The role of First Lady Hillary Clinton also warrants consideration, as her involvement offered perhaps the strongest argument for appointing a special prosecutor.

When President Clinton first took office in January of 1993, the White House Travel Office was responsible for administering White House travel and accompanying press flights. The controversy arose after the seven Travel Office employees were fired within a matter of weeks. By some this would be seen as "an effort to slime and sack long-serving officials in order to replace them with presidential cronies—and to claim credit along the way for cleaning up corruption."[57] Hillary Clinton at first denied any role in the firings, but eventually she conceded that while she had no *decision-making* role in the removal of personnel, she had in fact expressed her concern (to several persons) that "if there were fiscal mismanagement in the Travel office or in any part of the White House it should be addressed promptly" so that the administration would "not be blamed for condoning any existing fiscal mismanagement problems."[58]

One critical issue remained. If the First Lady had somehow encouraged the firings, weren't such actions within the discretion of the White House? Even if they were, the Clinton White House was at risk of embarrassment, given that close friends of the Clintons, including Harry Thomason (who owned an air charter company), were vying to take over the White House travel business at that time. Still, vacating offices to staff them with friends, while not praiseworthy, falls well short of criminal misconduct that might justify a special prosecutor's involvement. Later Hillary Clinton was accused of giving testimony that was "factually inaccurate" to the Office of the Independent Counsel, though the independent counsel's final report found the evidence "insufficient to prove a cover-up."

Upon leaving office in early 2001, Janet Reno—a steadfast supporter of the independent counsel statute at the time of her confirmation as attorney general[59]—declared that she had reversed her position on it. The reasons she offered were clear enough: once she was forced to grapple with the statute for the first time, Reno realized that she had to play a critical role in making decisions, and that her decisions would be "second-guessed and criticized no matter what decision [was] made."[60] If the purpose of the statute was to restore public confidence in the process, Reno erred when she named special prosecutors to relatively minor matters. The Travelgate matter would figure prominently in the attorney general's change of heart on this subject.

The FBI weighed in first with its report of May 28, 1993; not surprisingly, it exonerated itself of any wrongdoing. (In a March 1994 report, the Office of Professional Responsibility concurred in the FBI's finding.) On July 3, 1993, the White House issued its own self-report, which, somewhat more surprisingly, was highly critical of several White House officials, including Chief of Staff Mac McLarty. Still, it found no criminal wrongdoing. The Government Accounting Office weighed in a year later, concluding that Hillary Clinton had indeed played a role in urging the firings, but that no criminal wrongdoing had taken place. Whitewater special prosecutor Robert Fiske had already been looking into Travelgate as part of his investigation into the Vince Foster suicide. Thus when Fiske gave way to Independent Counsel Kenneth Starr on the Whitewater and Vince Foster matters in 1994, Starr assumed control of the Travelgate investigation as well. Starr's involvement, which was supposed to instill public confidence in the process, did not satisfy a Republican Congress emboldened by its newly captured control of both houses after the midterm elections of 1994. Thus both the House Government Reform and Oversight Committee and the Senate Whitewater Committee launched their own investigations into Travelgate in 1995. Four years later, Kenneth Starr exonerated Pres. Bill Clinton of any involvement; seven-and-a-half years later, Starr's successor as Independent Counsel, Robert Ray, found insufficient evidence to prosecute Hillary Clinton for any wrongdoing as well.[61]

The Whitewater Land Deal: Old Friends, New Problems

Travelgate proved to be an ancillary matter, producing headlines embarrassing to the Clinton administration, but little else. By contrast, the Clintons' involvement in the Whitewater land deal was a more significant matter, potentially capable of undermining an entire presidency—that is, if the public could ever truly understand it. Of all the allegations leveled against Bill Clinton during his two terms in office, few were as complicated as the real estate deal that eventually came to be known simply as "Whitewater."

On March 8, 1992, months before Bill Clinton had even secured the Democratic presidential nomination, the *New York Times* first reported that as early as 1978, the Clintons had passively invested and lost between $37,000 and $69,000 in the Whitewater land project situated along the south bank of the White River near the Ozark Mountains.[62] The floundering partnership known as the Whitewater Development Corporation had planned to sell lots for the construction of vacation homes. Years later a US Securities and Exchange Commission investigation found that the partnership's two principals—Jim and Susan McDougal—had committed crimes when they arranged for a fraudulent $300,000 loan to shore up the struggling company. Meanwhile, Jim McDougal's bank, the Madison Guaranty Savings & Loan, failed in 1989, costing taxpayers over $60 million. The Whitewater corporation was then permanently dissolved in 1992, though the Resolution Trust Corporation (RTC) continued to act in the role of receiver for any savings and loan that closed after January 1, 1989. Two months before Clinton's election as president, the RTC forwarded a criminal referral to the FBI and the US attorney in Little Rock regarding Jim McDougal's fraudulent use of different bank accounts at Madison Guaranty, including that of the Whitewater development.[63]

Federal investigators examining these issues in late 1993 raise two principal questions concerning President Clinton's involvement in the Whitewater matter: (1) Did Clinton, as governor of Arkansas, pressure a former municipal judge (David Hale) to make the fraudulent $300,000 loan to the McDougals? and (2) Did President Clinton or his wife knowingly participate in any criminal conduct related to Madison Guaranty, CMS, or the Whitewater Development, or did they have knowledge of such conduct by the McDougals or others? President Clinton's immediate response to the accusation regarding Judge Hale was that no conversation between himself and the judge ever took place. And indeed, Hale never mentioned Clinton when the FBI originally investigated Madison Guaranty's failure in 1989—it was only when he was indicted for fraud in September 1993 that Judge Hale first made public his allegations against Bill Clinton.

The second allegation raised a thornier set of issues, in the tradition of the Watergate scandal: "What did they know, and when did they know it?" Both the president and the First Lady understood the seriousness of the matter and the conflicts of interest that were sure to arise. Just consider the chronology of events that occurred late in 1993:[64]

1. September 29, 1993—Treasury Department officials alert White House Counsel Bernard Nussbaum that the RTC plans to issue criminal referrals on Madison Guaranty.
2. October 14, 1993—White House officials meet with Treasury Department officials concerning RTC criminal referrals.
3. October 27, 1993—US attorney for the Eastern District of Arkansas, Paula Casey, declines to investigate the first RTC criminal referral.
4. November 5, 1993—The Clintons' private attorneys meet with White House attorneys regarding Whitewater.

5. November 9, 1993—The Fraud Section of the Justice Department's Criminal Division takes charge of matters involving Madison Guaranty.

It became increasingly clear that the Clintons' personal involvement in the Whitewater land deal, whatever the nature of that involvement, was making life very difficult for those charged with investigating the RTC's criminal referrals.

On January 12, 1994, President Clinton requested that Attorney General Reno appoint a special prosecutor. With the independent counsel provisions of the Ethics in Government Act of 1978 having temporarily lapsed, Reno had available to her an alternative mechanism to address the issue: the regulatory independent counsel authorized under 28 C.F.R. Section 600.1 et seq. (1993). On January 20, 1994, she turned to respected New York Attorney Robert Fiske to assume the role of independent counsel. Fiske was a moderate Republican who had rankled conservatives by opposing some of the Reagan administration's more extreme conservative nominees from his position on the American Bar Association's judicial screening committee.[65] Reno's charge to Fiske was to investigate the Whitewater controversy and the controversy surrounding White House Counsel Vince Foster, whose death by suicide the previous summer had raised a cloud of questions as well.

Whitewater at the outset offered a textbook case for turning to a special prosecutor. The president and the attorney general—both public supporters for renewing the defunct independent counsel law—immediately saw the need for an outsider with extensive prosecutorial experience, but who maintained no ties whatsoever to the current administration. The president apparently supported the decision to go outside the Justice Department hierarchy, paving the way for at least some degree of cooperation between the special prosecutor and the White House. And in fact Fiske deposed both the president and the First Lady on June 12, 1994.

On June 30, 1994, Fiske issued a report indicating that he would not bring charges against the White House alleging improper contacts between the Clintons and the RTC. He also concluded that Vincent Foster had committed suicide. However, that same day President Clinton signed into law the Independent Counsel Reauthorization Act of 1994. Approximately a month later, Fiske was replaced as Whitewater Special Prosecutor by former Judge Kenneth Starr, over the protests of Reno, who had pleaded with the Court that Fiske continue in his position. The entire Justice Department was confident that Fiske would be retained because of his "reputation for integrity and competence."[66] White House Counsel Lloyd Cutler had told Clinton that "no court would ever get rid of an independent Republican like Fiske," but that is exactly what happened.[67]

What ensued was an investigation that extended for over six years at a cost of nearly $60 million. When it was over, Starr publicly acknowledged certain errors, including having taken on "so many different subjects" as part of the investigation.[68] The Whitewater land deal, however, was not one of the subjects he ever publicly regretted pursuing.

Reno Agonistes: Vice President Al Gore's 1996 Campaign Fundraising Mishaps

The most highly publicized political scandal that did *not* lead to appointment of an independent counsel during the Clinton years concerned allegedly illegal campaign contributions and fundraising practices during Bill Clinton's 1996 reelection campaign. In addition to President Clinton, Vice President Al Gore was specifically implicated in numerous questionable activities. If any of the charges had stuck, they might well have torpedoed the future political hopes of Gore, who was already the presumptive frontrunner for the 2000 Democratic nomination. Moreover, if substantiated by a neutral authority, complaints about the 1996 elections would have added a measure of credibility to many of the other investigations already under way at that time.

The controversy over the 1996 election focused on several questionable sources of donations and on illegal fundraising activities. One source was the People's Republic of China, which had allegedly attempted to influence the 1996 election through campaign contributions to both Republicans and Democrats. Born in Taiwan, California businessman Johnny Chung allegedly made forty-nine visits to the White House over a two-year period, donating to the Democratic National Committee money that he had acquired from China's military intelligence establishment.[69] Other allegations concerned Yah Lin "Charlie" Trie, who had allegedly donated $460,000 to Bill Clinton's legal defense fund, after which he lobbied the president against intervening in China's disputes with Taiwan. Additionally, one Wang Jun, despite his association with a front company for the Communist Chinese army, had attended a White House function.

Another questionable source of donations originated in California with a sect of Buddhist nuns, which had made contributions to the Clinton-Gore campaign despite having sworn a vow of poverty. Taiwan-born Maria Hsia allegedly facilitated $100,000 in illegal contributions to the 1996 campaign through her efforts at the Buddhist temple.[70] Yet another set of allegations arose during the summer of 1997; this time the charge was that Vice President Al Gore had solicited contributions to the Democratic National Committee from his White House office in ten separate sessions between November 1995 and May 1996.[71]

Investigation of these and other allegations related to the 1996 campaign proceeded on several fronts. The House Committee on Government Reform and Oversight, led by Chairman Dan Burton (R-Ind.), began meeting in March 1997 to discuss 1996 Democratic campaign practices. Unlike its House counterpart, the Senate Committee on Governmental Affairs, chaired by Fred Thompson (R-Tenn.), focused on both Democratic and Republican activities. Yet Thompson and his fellow senators faced a frustrating investigative process hampered by witnesses' fleeing the country or taking the Fifth Amendment.[72] It soon became evident that Congress's role in the political maelstrom would be a limited one indeed.

Was the Department of Justice up to the task? Attorney General Janet Reno certainly thought so, despite the political minefield that comes with investigating a sitting vice president. On December 19, 1996, Reno expanded her department's ongoing investigation of party fund-raising practices to include the activities of President Clinton's legal defense fund, and she further declared that the Department of Justice's Public Integrity Section task force would issue subpoenas in the matter. Reno did not indicate that she was refusing to appoint an independent counsel, but she withheld judgment for the time being. More than nine months later, on September 21, 1997, Reno initiated a more specific probe into whether illegal fundraising telephone calls were made by Vice President Al Gore and others from inside the White House, in violation of federal law.

The Department of Justice secured a series of indictments in these matters beginning in 1998. First came Yah Lin "Charlie" Trie, sentenced to four months of in-home detention for funneling illegal foreign money into Democratic coffers. Then came Maria Hsia, sentenced to ninety days of home detention and forced to pay a $5,300 fine for laundering illegal contributions through the Buddhist temple. Later came Johnny Chung, sentenced to 500 hours of community service and forced to pay a $10,000 fine for funneling donations from Chinese businessmen and military officers to the Clinton campaign. Other indictments focused on similar charges of funneling foreign contributions to the Democratic National Committee and other political committees. Accusations swirled around the use of the Lincoln Bedroom in the White House to entertain some of these donors. Despite indications from Chung and others that top Democratic National Committee officials had continued to solicit donations they knew to be illegal, no indictments were ever handed down in the matter against top Democratic committee officials, or against the president or vice president.

Behind the scenes, debates over whether Reno should have appointed an independent counsel in the first place were fierce indeed. FBI Director Louis Freeh in November 1997 wrote to Reno in a twenty-two-page memo that it would be difficult to imagine a situation "more compelling" for the appointment of an independent counsel.[73] The Justice Department's task force head, Charles LaBella, echoed Freeh's sentiment because he believed a clear conflict of interest was present.[74] Yet despite continued calls from within her own department, and despite public opinion polls favoring the appointment of an independent counsel by nearly a 2–1 margin, Reno held firm to her conviction that an appointment was not warranted.

Perhaps Reno feared a continuous cycle of partisan retribution, with members of the losing party calling for independent counsels to investigate campaign abuses after each presidential election. (The use of career prosecutors would have mitigated that fear, but only to a degree.) Perhaps she was also influenced by the conduct of the Starr investigation, which by late 1997 had expanded well beyond its original scope, thanks in part to statutes that encouraged the attorney general to authorize such expansions whenever they were requested. By the end of her tenure in office, Reno could point to convictions secured against twenty-two people by the task force. She also fell back on her own record of having called for special or independent counsels in many prior instances. The claim that she was a party hack or a rabid Clinton supporter flew in the face of the reality that she had become an alienated outsider in her own administration. That she survived the episode bruised but intact is a testament to her status as an "outer circle attorney general," one with credentials as a neutral decision-maker that were well established with both parties. It is perhaps ironic that only an outsider could have resisted the pull to appoint an outsider.

"So Many Different Subjects": The Paula Jones and Monica Lewinsky Affairs

Future assessments of Bill Clinton's presidency will focus less on his questionable 1996 campaign practices than on the scandal that led to his impeachment and nearly ended his presidency. When Paula Jones filed a sexual harassment suit for $700,000 against Clinton in US District Court in Little Rock, Arkansas, on May 6, 1994, she set into motion the chain of events that led to the scandal. The suit charged Clinton with having engaged in "willful, outrageous and malicious conduct" by propositioning and then exposing himself to Jones, then an Arkansas state employee, at a hotel in Little Rock on May 8, 1991. The Supreme Court in 1997 ruled that the lawsuit could move ahead while Clinton was president.[75] In an attempt to establish a pattern, Jones's lawyers then subpoenaed numerous individuals, including a White House intern named Monica Lewinsky, whose affair with Clinton had been inadvertently discovered by Whitewater Independent Counsel Kenneth Starr.

With the Jones trial already scheduled for May 27, 1998, Starr applied for and was granted approval from Reno and the special three-judge appeals court on January 16, 1998, to investigate the possibility that Clinton had suborned perjury or obstructed justice in the Jones case in order to hide his relationship with Lewinsky. This was an ideal moment for attorney general review, which is a crucial element in the independent counsel provisions. In the text of her petition seeking expansion of the investigation, Reno wrote this:

> The Department of Justice has received information from Independent Counsel Kenneth Starr that Monica Lewinsky, a former White House employee and a witness in the civil case *Jones v. Clinton*, may have submitted a false affidavit and suborned perjury from another witness in the case. In a taped conversation with a cooperating witness, Ms. Lewinsky states that she intends to lie when deposed. In the same conversation, she urges the cooperating witness to lie in her own upcoming deposition. I have determined that it would be a conflict of interest for the Department of Justice to investigate Ms. Lewinsky for perjury and suborning perjury as a witness in this civil suit involving the president, in light of the allegations involved in the lawsuit. I have also determined that the taped conversation establishes that further investigation of this matter is warranted. It would be appropriate for Independent Counsel Kenneth Starr to handle this matter because he is currently investigating similar allegations involving possible efforts to influence witnesses in his own investigation. Some potential subjects and witnesses in this matter overlap with those in his ongoing investigation.[76]

It is hard to establish from Reno's statement just what her "preliminary investigation" included. Certainly there was little assessment of the "cooperating evidence's credibility" (Linda Tripp, the witness, had been relocated out of the White House in 1994); nor was there in the application direct consideration of what wrongdoing the president himself might have committed, making the conflict-of-interest claim seem even more tenuous.

To be sure, the independent counsel provisions then in place were stacked heavily in favor of the independent counsel's petition. Section $592(c)(2)(A)$ required that the attorney general "give great weight to any recommendations of the Independent Counsel." The statute thus removed from the Department of Justice the power to use traditional investigative tools such as the grand jury to further develop the facts as part of its preliminary investigation.[77] And a 1996 court ruling further held that the three-judge panel could expand the jurisdiction of the independent counsel *despite* the objections of the attorney general.[78] Of course, many other routes were available to Reno. Under 28 US

Section 593(c) (1994), she could have taken up to thirty days to investigate the matter, and under the statute she was also authorized to interview witnesses. Moreover, she could have sought authorization to apply for an extension if necessary.[79] Finally, the she could have requested appointment of a *new* independent counsel if she felt the matter was not related to Starr's original charge to investigate the Whitewater matter.

On April 1, 1998, President Clinton successfully won a motion to dismiss the Jones lawsuit for its failure to prove any substantive harm or distress. Meanwhile, Starr's investigation continued without pause. Even the settlement of the Jones lawsuit in November for $850,000 had no effect on Starr's investigation, which culminated in a full report to Congress, a House vote on impeachment in December 1998, and contempt of court citations for perjury and false affidavits that were filed against Clinton the following April in US District Court.

More than a decade of hindsight suggests that the logic of using a different outside counsel to investigate the Lewinsky matter was at least arguable. The more contentious issues concerned (1) whether the case should have been handled by Whitewater counsel Kenneth Starr, or by a new independent counsel altogether; and (2) whether the investigation should have continued even after the Jones lawsuit was dismissed. Starr's admission years later that he should not have led the investigation that resulted in Clinton's impeachment was based on his argument (perhaps disingenuous) that "there was a sense on the part of the country that my Lewinsky efforts [were] an effort somehow to expand the [Whitewater] investigation, when it was separate."[80] In that sense, the Independent Counsel's extra responsibilities had rendered him less than independent; he was certainly not the type of "outsider" needed to ensure objective and disinterested judgment. Attorney General Reno herself was thus the only true outsider left.

chapter 4

A Bit *Too* Familiar

When the Justice Department Investigates

the Justice Department

Perhaps the most obvious conflict of interest that arises in the investigation and prosecution of executive branch corruption occurs when the hunter becomes the hunted. Officials within the Department of Justice and its many law enforcement agencies sometimes find themselves in the cross hairs of one of their department's investigations, whether as the primary targets of an inquiry or as individuals whose activities are swept up in a larger investigation that originated elsewhere. In 1975, when Attorney General Edward Levi established the Office of Professional Responsibility within the Justice Department to investigate misconduct by its attorneys, the Office of Inspector General—also within the Justice Department—retained its primary responsibility for investigating misconduct by nonlawyers in the department. Ultimately, both those offices must answer directly to the attorney general and his deputies. Given how quickly public suspicions may arise when Justice Department lawyers are essentially investigating their own colleagues, the use of a special prosecutor can never be ruled out.

When the attorney general falls under scrutiny, any preliminary inquiry that turns up evidence of criminal wrongdoing offers a highly persuasive argument for letting an outside attorney or special prosecutor lead the investigation. Yet most cases are not so cut and dried, notwithstanding the presence of a legitimate conflict of interest. Indeed, if a special prosecutor had to be named every time a member of the Justice Department or one of its divisions played even a modest role in the factual circumstances of a crime (perhaps in the course of doing routine agency business), special prosecutors would soon outnumber career prosecutors by more than a handful.

From the public's perspective, it is doubtful whether federal police and prosecutors can investigate their own ranks with the same energy and enthusiasm they bring to other investigations. The propensity of some presidents to select attorneys general from their own inner circle—John Kennedy's selection of Robert Kennedy and Ronald Reagan's selection of Edwin Meese quickly come to mind—only exacerbates this problem, for then misconduct within the Justice Department may reflect very directly on the president, creating additional incentives for the attorney general to be less than vigilant in conducting investigations.

The Unauthorized Surveillance of Martin Luther King Jr.

Soon after Watergate, the Ford administration was forced to address allegations of misconduct on the part of officials in the Department of Justice. The activity in question—surveilling private citizens without legal authority—had allegedly begun at least two decades earlier, authorized by J. Edgar Hoover, who had died in 1972. Even so, key officials responsible for implementing Hoover's controversial surveillance policies remained very much in power.

This time it was the legislative branch controlled by the Democrats in opposition that fired the first warning shots across the agency. In late 1975 and early 1976, the US Senate's Select Committee to Study Governmental Activities with Respect to Intelligence Activities—aka the (Frank) Church Committee—considered numerous questionable FBI undertakings from the 1950s and the 1960s. These included the surveillance of civil rights hero Dr. Martin Luther King Jr., beginning in 1963, when William Sullivan was the FBI's assistant director in charge of the Domestic Intelligence Division. At a hearing in April of 1976, senators listened to testimony that Sullivan had initiated the surveillance of King and others in the civil rights movement and that he had done so based on his hatred of King personally. They also heard testimony about Sullivan's having argued internally that communists had influenced King's actions. Sullivan evidently hoped to provoke the communist-obsessed Hoover to support his surveillance proposals.[1] If that was his plan, it was for the most part successful.

On April 26, 1976, Attorney General Levi directed the Justice Department's recently formed Office of Professional Responsibility to investigate the matter fully. Sparked by the Church Committee's inquiry, the Justice Department's Civil Rights Division had already begun a preliminary review under the personal direction of Assistant Attorney General J. Stanley Pottinger. The attorney general's referral to the Office of Professional Responsibility now required this newly established office to conduct an additional examination of records at FBI headquarters and field offices before formally completing its review.

Jesse Jackson, head of Operation PUSH (People United to Save Humanity), and other civil rights leaders remained unsatisfied with the department's announced plan of action. On May 10, 1976, Jackson requested that President Ford appoint a special prosecutor to more fully investigate the affair. Jackson, who had been a presence in King's Southern Christian Leadership Conference, based his argument on the discovery that "the person primarily responsible for outlining the campaign against King" was still at the FBI."[2] Less convincingly, Jackson expressed his suspicion that there were "undoubtedly, other skeletons yet in the closet" that only a special prosecutor could get to the bottom of.[3]

Yet Levi (bolstered by President Ford's strong show of support) was undaunted in his effort to maintain the Office of Professional Responsibility's jurisdiction over the matter. In a letter responding to Jackson, White House Counsel Philip Buchen detailed the office's specific duties, which included—in addition to examining the harassment campaign against King—making these determinations:

1. whether the FBI investigation of Dr. King's assassination was thorough and honest
2. whether there was any evidence that the FBI had been involved in the assassination of Dr. King
3. whether, in light of the first two matters, any new evidence had come to the attention of the department concerning the assassination of Dr. King
4. whether the nature of the relationship between the FBI and Dr. King called for criminal prosecutions, disciplinary proceedings, or other action.[4]

In truth, these types of allegations seemed made to order for the newly created Office of Professional Responsibility (OPR). In his short time as attorney general, Levi had somewhat curtailed the independence of the FBI, leaving it with only a small fraction of the autonomy from its parent body (the Department of Justice) that it had maintained throughout Hoover's stormy tenure.[5] Given the tenuous status of the OPR, to strip it of its authority so early in the King investigation, and in the absence of any conflict with the attorney general or his deputies, would have marginalized its critical role as a centerpiece of post-Watergate reforms. The department attorneys assigned to the case had previously worked in the Civil Rights, Criminal, and Tax Divisions; but none had any connection with the FBI. Moreover, even if the investigation implicated officials still in the Justice Department, the incidents had occurred long before Ford assumed the presidency. Thus under the circumstances, Attorney General Levi and President Ford had no incentive to countenance efforts that might have slowed down or quashed the inquiry.

The Office of Professional Responsibility's investigation of FBI abuses under Hoover and Sullivan continued well into the Carter administration. In the end, its findings confirmed much of what Congress had learned from the Church Committee and elsewhere about the campaign of harassment conducted against King. Yet the passage of time and Hoover's utter dominance of all FBI activities during that period rendered actual indictments of other individuals in the matter unfeasible. Sullivan's death in November of 1977 at the age of sixty-five put to rest Jackson's complaints as well, though the suspicious circumstances (a hunter in the woods near Sullivan's home shot the ex-FBI official with a telescopic site on a .30 caliber rifle) would raise new questions that may never be answered.[6] Did Sullivan have even more files and transcripts on King that he was prepared to reveal, even if they might further embarrass the FBI and its current leadership? Disappointed that President Nixon had passed him over as Hoover's successor, Sullivan may have harbored and intended to satisfy a grudge against his old agency.

The Misappropriation of Funds by FBI Director Clarence Kelley

The Justice Department's ability to police itself was put to an even more stringent test during the summer of 1976, when government prosecutors began investigating allegations that current high-level FBI officials had mishandled government funds and property. According to a memo written by Edward Levi to the president at the end of the summer, the investigation focused on three separate sets of allegations: (1) that kickbacks had been taken by FBI officials in the course of purchasing electronic equipment for the agency, (2) that funds established for confidential expenditures and for the FBI Recreation Association had been misappropriated, and (3) that government goods and services had been systematically stolen by FBI officials.[7]

The media's interest in the affair focused in particular on the role played by the highly controversial new FBI chief, Clarence Kelley, who was specifically targeted with the last two allegations. Kelley, who had taken over as the second permanent director of the agency on July 9, 1973, now would be forced to fend off allegations that he had misappropriated government funds, goods, and services for his own personal use.

To be sure, Kelley had invited some of this attention by maintaining an especially high profile in the years following J. Edgar Hoover's exit from the bureau. Under his leadership, the Department of Justice was conducting a nationwide investigation of burglaries allegedly conducted by the FBI dating back to 1971. Kelley informed the Senate Select Committee on Intelligence Activities that the FBI had no record of using burglary in domestic cases after 1966, when Hoover ordered the practice halted. Soon thereafter, it was discovered that additional break-ins did in fact occur during the 1970s. Although none of the revelations concerned burglaries conducted during Kelley's tenure, many believed that Kelley had intentionally failed to disclose evidence of such acts, or, even worse, that people within the bureau had failed to disclose evidence of them to their superiors.[8] Either way, the FBI found it hard to shake the perception that just over a year after Hoover's death, the agency was veering out of control. In this increasingly hostile public environment, new allegations of misappropriation and waste were sure to fuel public skepticism and distrust even further.

As he had done with the charges concerning the harassment of King, Attorney General Levi now turned to the Office of Professional Responsibility to conduct the inquiry into misappropriations and theft on the part of FBI officials. A copy of that office's report was eventually provided to Deputy Attorney General Harold Tyler Jr. for his recommendation. Tyler in turn asked two assistant attorneys general and the head of a different bureau in the department to examine the report and the recommendations it included and to provide him with their individual conclusions as to the action they thought appropriate.[9] Thus three consultants and the deputy attorney general were all accountable for the report that would eventually come before Attorney General Levi. These multiple layers of checks were compelled by the need to combat unwarranted perceptions of a whitewash, especially with a tough general election fast approaching.

On September 2, 1976, Levi issued his final report on the various allegations of stealing and misappropriation against Kelley. In it, he concluded that (1) while the FBI director had received numerous gifts for his newly acquired apartment, he could have reasonably believed these were housewarming gifts from friends in the bureau, and (2) although bureau resources of time, personnel, and property were used for Kelley's personal benefit, he had not intended that to be the case, and in each instance had offered to reimburse the bureau.[10] Meanwhile, Levi also identified no substantial evidence to support allegations that other FBI officials had received kickbacks.

The recommendations offered to Levi by his aides were conflicting. The Justice Department attorney assigned to conduct the investigation recommended that the director be removed from office. That attorney's supervisor had recommended a lesser penalty for Kelley, such as a letter of reprimand or admonishment. He had also recommended that Kelley reimburse the bureau for the value of the goods and services that had been of personal benefit to him, and that he publicly admit to having received them. The consultants and the deputy attorney general, and ultimately Levi, all agreed that the record warranted an instruction to the director to reimburse the bureau for any goods and services he had received.

Yet on the matter of possible criminal charges against Kelly, Levi backed off. He concluded that because the director had not willfully used his office for personal benefit, there was no impropriety that warranted further criminal inquiry, or even dismissal. To support his conclusion, Levi cited Justice Department regulation 28 C.F.R. Part 45.735–14(e)(1967), which stated specifically that officials may accept "a voluntary gift of nominal amount made on a special occasion." He argued that Kelley's arrival in Washington could be interpreted as just such a "special occasion."[11] He found no impropriety in the director's benefiting from the use of bureau resources in these cases, since Kelley had attempted in each instance to reimburse the bureau and avoid repetition of the incidents. And the attorney general found the director's refusal to accept other items additional "evidence of his effort to be honest and careful." Thus Levi recommended against further criminal inquiry and against asking Kelley to resign. His recommendations were approved by the president immediately thereafter.

The Kelley affair presented Levi with the closest and most controversial decision of his two-year tenure as head of the Justice Department. On one hand, Kelley was a high-level official within the Justice Department whose ties to the FBI dated back to World War II—he had joined the bureau in 1940 and had held one or another administrative position in it during the quarter century before being named director in 1973. Barely a handful of the current Justice Department officials or prosecutors had failed to cross Kelley's path or interact with his office at one time or another, making conflicts inevitable. Finally, with the general election season approaching, Levi was surely wary of being perceived as playing politics with an investigation so soon after the Watergate scandal.

On the other hand, President Ford and Levi were both eager to see the Office of Professional Responsibility, still in its infancy, survive yet another early test of its independence and integrity. Ultimately the two factors that weighed most heavily against going to the more extreme measure of naming a special prosecutor were Kelley's status and the nature of his offense. Kelley was an appointee of Ford's predecessor, Richard Nixon, and thus neither Levi nor Ford had any personal or partisan stake in seeing him survive; and the nature of the charges ensured that Ford and Levi had more than enough incentive to investigate Kelley's wrongdoing, as the FBI chief was essentially accused of theft from Levi's own agency. In short, there were significant and effective political checks at work in this case. These were not simply abuses of the public trust; they were a squandering of resources within the very department Levi was trying to lead. As an outer circle attorney general, Levi had more than enough credibility to sell this argument to Congress—if such a sales job was even required. Finally, a special prosecutor inquiry that began at scratch might well have extended past Election Day, inviting charges of delay and whitewashing from the media and the political opposition.

The Kelley investigation did claim some victims. The FBI's associate director was removed from office on the ground that he had misappropriated funds belonging to the Recreation Association. The Justice Department's investigation also revealed that John Dunphy, the head of the Exhibits Section, which constructed items for the bureau, had converted to his own use several thousands of dollars' worth of government property, was a partner in fraud with respect to a bureau fund, and had encouraged his own subordinates to obstruct the Office of Professional Responsibility's investigation. (Dunphy later pleaded to a misdemeanor for the conversion of government property and resigned from his post.) In the absence of a special prosecutor, the Department of Justice was held accountable in the court of public opinion for the way it had conducted the affair. Speaking to a reporter on September 7, 1976, presidential candidate Jimmy Carter said, "Knowing what I know now, I would have fired FBI Director Clarence Kelley. . . . when you see the head of the FBI break a little law and stay there, it gives everybody the sense that crime must be OK."[12] Was Carter's victory in November influenced by the public's perception of continued corruption in Washington? At least in this one case, the Ford administration's actions—as determined primarily by the outer circle attorney general Edward Levi—render that a difficult claim to support.

The Superfund Scandal Ensnares the Justice Department

The Superfund scandal described at the outset of chapter 1 did not go away with the dismissal of administrator Rita Lavelle. In fact, the Environmental Protection Agency's head at the time, Ann Burford Gorsuch, was busy getting into some hot water of her own. The Superfund scandal eventually ensnared several members of the Department of Justice as well.

Gorsuch was following administration protocol when she took action to dismantle her own agency, as environmental cleanup had never been that high on the new administration's list of priorities. President Reagan's first secretary of the interior, James G. Watt, was openly hostile to environmentalism and supportive of the development of natural resources by commercial interests. In September of 1983 Watt indiscreetly mocked affirmative action policies by referring to his own staff as "*a black, a woman, two Jews and a cripple*," and as a result was forced to resign from office. As for Gorsuch, the former corporate attorney from Mountain Bell in Denver made it clear from the outset that she would not oppose any of Watt's controversial proposals for reform. In fact, Gorsuch immediately embraced budgetary cuts for her own agency. Under her leadership, the EPA's budget (excluding Superfund) dropped by $200 million, while its staff was slashed by 23 percent. All of this only contributed further to accusations that the agency had expressed favoritism toward the very industries that it was supposed to regulate.[13]

In late 1982, just a few weeks before Lavelle was scheduled to testify before Congress, the House Energy and Commerce Committee, chaired by John Dingell (D-Mich.), requested that both Lavelle and Gorsuch produce all relevant Superfund enforcement documents. Both were cited for congressional contempt in December 1982 when they refused to do so. Then, in early 1983, congressional leaders including Dingell and Rep. Elliott Levitas (D-Ga.), chairman of a separate House subcommittee, heard unconfirmed reports of automated shredders being moved into the Superfund Offices. Accordingly, on February 10, 1983, the general counsel to the clerk of the House of Representatives wrote to Environmental Protection Agency lawyers inquiring specifically about the moved shredders and the agency's failure to date to produce documents.

To head off perceptions of stonewalling, Gorsuch formally requested on February 14 that the Justice Department investigate these matters for possible criminal prosecution.[14] Yet she also continued to deny Congress the documents they requested, claiming executive privilege in accordance with a memorandum sent by President Reagan to Environmental Protection Agency officials on November 30, 1982. That memorandum set forth "the historic position of the Executive Branch, with which I concur, that sensitive documents found in open law enforcement files should not be made available to Congress or to the public except in extraordinary circumstances."[15] Though the Justice Department chose not to bring Gorsuch's case before a grand jury, the die was cast against her continuing in her post, and she resigned on March 9, 1983, amid accusations that she too had politically manipulated Superfund money.

As Congress geared up for a protracted battle over the documents, the central player within the Justice Department was Assistant Attorney General Theodore Olson. Two decades later, Olson would go on to argue on behalf of Governor George W. Bush in the US Supreme Court case of *Bush v. Gore* that effectively secured the presidency for his client; he subsequently served as the Bush administration's first solicitor general. But back in the mid-1980s, Olson had been dutifully laboring as a lawyer in the Office of Legal Counsel in Ronald Reagan's Justice Department under the leadership of Attorney General William French Smith. Charged by his bosses with defending Gorsuch's assertion of executive privilege, the Justice Department was essentially at war with itself, as department lawyers were investigating wrongdoing in the Environmental

Protection Agency at the same exact time as Olson and some of his colleagues at the Department of Justice were busy arguing that certain of the environmental agency's documents should never be disclosed.

Not satisfied with this state of affairs, the House Judiciary Committee launched an investigation of its own after both Lavelle and Gorsuch had departed the scene. Called to testify before the House Judiciary Committee's subcommittee, Monopolies and Commercial Law, on March 10, 1983, Olson was asked whether the Environmental Protection Agency had at any time indicated a willingness to turn over documents. Olson's answer proved quite controversial: "I don't recall having been told that by anybody associated with EPA. I did read the newspapers, and it seemed to be that . . . that sentiment seemed to be being expressed, especially in the last week or two. But that's all I know."[16]

Olson also indicated that everyone involved had agreed that this was a proper occasion for the invocation of executive privilege. As for documents regarding the advice given to President Reagan about executive privilege, Olson indicated that the only documents not yet turned over to the committee were "scraps of paper." Many of the answers he gave that day were at a minimum evasive, as Olson was construing each question in the narrowest possible way. At worst, they were misleading. Either way, the Justice Department was slowly getting wrapped up in the matter in ways that would come back to haunt it later.

More than two years later, during the late spring and summer of 1985, members of the House Judiciary Committee alleged that the Justice Department officials responsible for defending the Environmental Protection Agency's executive privilege claim (Edward C. Schmults, Carol Dinkins, and Olson) had obstructed congressional investigations into the agency's scandals by withholding documents and hiding the existence of certain work product.[17] Recognizing the obvious conflict, the department's Office of Public Integrity began its own investigation into the matter. Thus began an intramural squabble between the three officials in question and those now charged with investigating the matter, including John C. Keeney (deputy assistant attorney general for the Criminal Division) and William F. Weld, the attorney general's special assistant during the preliminary investigation.[18]

The preliminary investigation resulted in the appointment of an independent counsel at the request of Attorney General Meese. That result was inevitable, given the proximity of the investigators to the investigated. Weld specifically recommended that an independent prosecutor investigate both Schmults and Olson, but Meese overruled him and referred only the allegations against Olson to the three-judge panel. After one independent counsel was forced to resign due to conflicts, Alexia Morrison was eventually appointed on May 28, 1986.

As scandals go, "Sewergate" could have been dealt with more effectively by the Justice Department if the White House had elected to waive all claims to executive privilege. But by standing on that privilege to shield documents from Congress, and using Justice Department officials to do so, the White House set in motion a chain of events that made appointing an independent counsel necessary. Nor did it help that the new attorney general, Edwin Meese, who knew most of these players from dealing with them as presidential counselor during the first term, was not in a position to resolve in-house squabbles to anyone's satisfaction.

The Wedtech Scandal Brings Down an Attorney General

President Reagan's decision to promote his long-time advisor Edwin Meese to the position of attorney general came back to haunt him and his presidency in many ways. As an "oval office attorney general," Meese was never able to achieve enough distance from the White House to become an effective chief law enforcement officer in the eyes of Congress or the public. The principal test of his tenure at the Justice Department came in late 1986 with the revelation that administration officials had first sold arms to Iran and then illegally diverted the proceeds of the sales to fund the resistance movement in Nicaragua. During his preliminary investigation of the Iran-Contra affair, Meese bungled the process so badly that he made both an investigation by Congress and the appointment of an independent counsel inevitable. He was desperate to downplay the extent of the misconduct committed, and his lack of aggressive law enforcement virtually paralyzed the Reagan administration throughout late 1987.

In the final analysis, Meese's reputation as a politically motivated attorney general who was fiercely loyal to the president made him less rather than more useful to the administration, and left him with little capital on the Hill. Still, after he had survived one independent counsel investigation intact before his appointment in 1985, there was little reason to suspect he would land in hot water yet again. But that is exactly what happened during the summer of 1987.

A defense contractor named Wedtech provided the first cracks in the attorney general's already weakened armor. Originally a manufacturer of baby carriages, Wedtech shifted its focus in the 1980s to fill numerous contracts for the Department of Defense. According to reporter Haynes Johnson, Wedtech, after losing several Federal bids, succeeded "by winning no-bid federal contracts established to assist minority-owned companies that it had lost previously."[19] In 1981, when Meese first joined the administration as a top counselor to the president, Wedtech placed Meese's personal lawyer, E. Bob Wallach, on its payroll as an attorney.[20] A year later, Wedtech hired Lyn Nofziger, a former Reagan administration political affairs officer who had just recently left the White House. As part of his compensation package, Nofziger received Wedtech stock and approximately $1 million in fees.

In April 1982, Nofziger met with Meese in hopes of persuading him to help secure an army contract for Wedtech. James Jenkins, a high-level aide to Meese, convened a controversial meeting at the White House the next month, against the advice of White House Counsel. [21] Attending the meeting were representatives of Wedtech and the US Army, and officials of the Small Business Administration. Jenkins later testified that Meese had ordered him to arrange the unusual session despite warnings that it might conflict with ethics laws.[22] Wedtech eventually received $27.7 million from the army, as well as a loan of $2 million and a grant of $3 million from the Small Business Administration. Together, these last two sums represented a full third of all grants awarded in 1982 by the agency. Like Nofziger, Jenkins eventually left the Justice Department to accept a position as a consultant to Wedtech.

During the four-year period between 1983 and 1986, Wedtech paid former White House insiders and consultants "nearly $11.6 million in salaries, fees, bonuses and other incentives" as part of its extensive lobbying operation, and "seven of Wedtech's officers and advisers [including Nofziger] later sold their Wedtech shares for $10 million."[23] A prime beneficiary of all this largesse was Wallach, who continued to persuade Wedtech officers that it was in the company's best interest to pay him substantial sums of money to subsidize his services to Meese.[24] For his part, Wallach served in several official capacities for Meese: first as his confirmation counsel when he was nominated to be attorney general, then as his assistant in helping him reorganize the Justice Department, and finally as his official counselor.[25] All these connections between Wedtech and former Reagan administration officials were eventually referred to the Securities and Exchange Commission and other state and federal regulatory agencies.

Once the truth of Wedtech's peddling was revealed, convictions started rolling in. The former director of the navy's Office of Small and Disadvantaged Business Utilization, Richard D. Ramirez, and Lyn Nofziger were guilty of misconduct in violation of the 1978 Ethics in Government Act, which, in addition to creating the independent counsel provisions, imposed heavy restrictions on former government employees working in the private sector. For two years after leaving government service, all former employees of executive branch agencies were expressly restricted from representing anyone before an agency on matters that came within the former employees' sphere of responsibility. And the law prohibited the former government employee from representing anyone before his or her own former agency for at least a year, even if the former employee had no connection with the matter while in the government.[26]

As for Meese himself, there was no way for him to justify *not* naming a special prosecutor, given the charges then before the Justice Department. Meese even admitted to interceding on behalf of Wedtech back in 1982, when he was still a White House counselor. In this instance, a special prosecutor was necessary if there was to be any sense of accountability whatsoever. Thus on February 2, 1987, Deputy Attorney General Arnold Burns, one of Meese's own subordinates, formally asked that the special court name James McKay as independent counsel. Department spokesman Terry Eastland noted that McKay's involvement would allay all concerns about Meese's conduct.

The naming of a Wedtech special prosecutor spelled the beginning of the end of Meese's tenure as attorney general. In early 1988 the independent counsel found that Meese had filed a false income tax return while serving as attorney general, and that he had likely also violated federal conflict of interest laws; yet he declined to recommend that Meese be indicted, because he had not found reason to think that the attorney general was motivated by a desire for personal gain.[27] As for the most significant complaint under investigation—that Meese had taken bribes or illegal gratuities—the prosecutor stated only that there was "insufficient evidence" to indict.[28] Still, with a Democratic Congress in place and the Reagan administration's window for policymaking beginning to close, the president could no longer countenance Meese as a continued distraction at the Justice Department. On July 5, 1988, Reagan accepted Meese's resignation as attorney general.

The William Gray Leak Investigation

In its first years after being established in 1976, the Office of Professional Responsibility survived some especially hard tests of its authority to investigate wrongdoing by Justice Department lawyers. It weathered those tests in part because it enjoyed the strong support of Attorneys General Edward Levi and Benjamin Civiletti, among others. The need for high-level support, however, would also prove to be the office's Achilles heel: if an attorney general ever lost faith in the office, or refused to use it in appropriate cases, it would be undermined, and the Justice Department would find itself facing an unpleasant set of choices. Without a working Office of Professional Responsibility, the Attorney General would be forced to either (1) turn prematurely to special prosecutors or (2) suffer far greater and more intrusive forms of public scrutiny, as wrongdoing by government attorneys went unchecked. Already under some suspicion for his secretive department policies, Thornburgh undermined the

OPR at a critical juncture and eventually found himself in so much trouble that his support from the White House would soon diminish as well.

Thornburgh's problems began with a leak—the kind of leak that Justice Department officials routinely confront in the course of their criminal investigations. The subject of the leak was Philadelphia Congressman William H. Gray III (D-Pa.), one of the most influential members of the House of Representatives during the late 1980s. Gray was first elected to his congressional seat in 1978. His service in the House was marked by several notable milestones: he became the first African American congressman to chair the prestigious House Budget Committee and eventually the first to serve as a major party's majority whip. It was a series of unlikely events, however, that would tie the fate of the powerful House Democrat to Attorney General Thornburgh. Those events may have also expedited the latter's eventual exit as head of the Justice Department.

The real trouble started with Justice Department allegations of wrongdoing leveled against an accountant who had worked in Gray's congressional office. This type of personnel investigation normally remains confidential, but a CBS News story on May 31, 1989, reported that the FBI had been investigating "financial irregularities" in Gray's office.[29] Department of Justice attorneys informed Gray that the investigation into his accountant had actually begun several months earlier—they even issued a statement confirming that the congressman was a target of the investigation. Nonetheless, Gray's reputation clearly suffered from the leak. The timing of the leak was suspicious as well: the news report noted that Gray was in the process of seeking the majority whip position recently vacated by Rep. Tony Coelho (D-Calif.). Gray immediately requested that the Justice Department initiate a full-blown investigation into the source of the press leak.[30] For his part, Thornburgh assured Gray that he had indeed ordered an appropriate investigation into the leak. In a CBS News follow-up report two days later, Thornburgh even declared that he would fire employees responsible for the leak, though in a clear swipe at the media, he told the reporters gathered that they too were responsible for their part in reporting leaks.[31]

Not surprisingly, Thornburgh, who was on the public record as an opponent of frequent independent counsel investigations, rejected calls from the Congressional Black Caucus that he name an independent counsel to investigate the leak in question. Instead, he fell back on routine Justice Department channels, ordering the Criminal Division to open its own investigation. Still, the attorney general diverged from the ordinary course in one important respect: he directed Edward S. G. Dennis Jr., the assistant attorney general in charge of the Criminal Division, to supervise the investigation personally.[32] Rejecting the advice of Deputy Attorney General Donald B. Ayer, Thornburgh chose not to rely on the Office of Professional Responsibility as the primary investigative authority.

In an effort to determine the source of the CBS report, Dennis's investigation solicited sworn statements from 109 people and subjected another ten to lie detector tests, including the attorney general himself. [33] Two of Thornburgh's top aides—Press Secretary David Runkel and Thornburgh's own executive assistant, Robert S. Ross Jr.—actually failed their polygraph tests outright, leading them to be reassigned immediately.[34] When confronted, Runkel admitted that he had indeed played a role in confirming the information broadcast by CBS. Ross told investigators that he had never had any contact or dealings with the network's reporter.

Meanwhile, Ayer never wavered from his contention that the Office of Professional Responsibility (and not Dennis) should have handled the matter in the first place. On January 30, 1990, Ayer pressed the attorney general to remove himself entirely from the leak investigation, as his close ties to Ross and others presented an irreconcilable conflict. Finally, in May of 1990, Ayer resigned in protest.[35] The public resignation put Thornburgh in an uncomfortable position, but he would not budge. Addressing the perception that there had been unethical conduct in his department, he argued that there was in fact a critical distinction between employees who volunteer information to the media (which amounts to clear-cut wrongdoing) and those who simply confirm or deny reports when asked (which was essentially Runkel's offense). He added that the information provided by other secondary sources was so uncertain as to render a prosecution based on it futile.

What should have been the next step in this quickly evolving process? On the face of it, the Office of Professional Responsibility remained the logical venue for the investigation. Staffed by career lawyers who maintained no clear ties to Thornburgh, that office offered a hope of objective review, without resorting to the extreme measure of appointing an independent counsel. Ayer's protest actually went a step further, arguing that Michael Shaheen (and not the department's Criminal Division) should have conducted the investigation from the start. Now the investigation was closed without Shaheen's review of the evidence.

Instead of bringing Shaheen into the process, or appointing an independent counsel, Thornburgh looked for a middle way out. His solution: invite an attorney from an altogether different unit in the department, Solicitor General Kenneth Starr, to investigate Runkel and Ross further. The move sent up a red flag: On what basis could the attorney general justify the involvement of Starr, who at the time was not even serving as a full-time prosecutor? A full year later, Starr cleared the attorney general and his aides of any legal wrongdoing in the Gray leak investigation. Few could have been satisfied with this outcome. For his part, Thornburgh permanently reassigned Runkel and Ross, a tacit admission that the two had at least engaged in actions with the appearance of impropriety, notwithstanding Starr's legal conclusions.

In the final analysis, the real casualty of the affair was Thornburgh, whose reputation even within White House circles suffered greatly as a result of this and other incidents. Thornburgh did little to reassure congressional Democrats that he took the matter seriously. In May of 1990, the *New York Times* reported that White House officials were privately starting to express their misgivings about Thornburgh's stewardship.[36] Over a year later, Thornburgh received the White House's blessing to run for senator of Pennsylvania in a special election, which he eventually lost to Harrison Wofford, a former civil rights attorney—and with it any long-term hopes of seeking national office in his own right. In this way the Gray leak had contributed to Thornburgh's eventual undoing.

The INSLAW Software Piracy Scandal

In March of 1982, the Justice Department awarded the small nonprofit Institute for Law and Social Research (INSLAW) a $10 million, three-year contract to implement a public domain version of the automated Prosecutors' Management Information System (PROMIS) for use in US attorneys' offices across the country. What should have been a simple matter of executing a government contract eventually evolved into a widespread corruption scandal that would extend across three continents and last for the better part of two decades. Ultimately it would fall to the Justice Department more than a decade later (during the presidencies of George H. W. Bush and Bill Clinton) to sort out the mess and determine how to hold the responsible officials accountable, if at all, for their wrongdoing.

The Justice Department's interest in PROMIS arose out of the longstanding desire of its leaders to establish a standardized case management system for its own prosecutors. William Anthony Hamilton, a brilliant young computer programmer and principal owner of INSLAW, originally developed the prosecutor management software. It worked so well that, starting in 1982, the Justice Department became his primary customer. Problems began when INSLAW revealed to all of its customers that it had actually improved the public domain version of the software to create an enhanced version of PROMIS. In November 1982, the Justice Department requested copies of the enhanced PROMIS. INSLAW then sought additional compensation in return for the enhanced program. Following an April 1983 modification of the original contract, the updated software was finally installed in a handful of offices at the Department of Justice. As a condition of this modification, the government was required to make additional payments to INSLAW, while INSLAW was required to verify that it had created the enhanced software strictly through the use of private, rather than government funds.[37]

Once the Department of Justice assumed control of the enhanced software, an unusually bitter conflict with INSLAW ensued. For its part, the Department of Justice refused to verify INSLAW's ownership of the enhanced software and withheld payments under the modified contract. In response, INSLAW initiated a number of lawsuits against the department for allegedly "stealing" the enhanced PROMIS software through "trickery, fraud, and deceit." According to INSLAW, the 1983 modification did authorize the enhanced software to be installed without payment first being rendered. INSLAW further charged that the department's actions—with the full encouragement of Ed Meese and Deputy Attorney General Lowell Jensen—were a "sham contract dispute" over the terms and conditions of the contract, calculated to run INSLAW out of business so that it would be unable to seek restitution against the government through the judicial process.[38] INSLAW was especially suspicious of the role played by a former employee, C. Madison Brewer, who was now a Department of Justice official. Hamilton had dismissed Brewer from INSLAW on bad terms several years earlier.

INSLAW declared Chapter 11 bankruptcy in February 1985, but that did not prevent the company's securing favorable rulings against the government from two federal courts during the late 1980s. The first of these came in 1987, after INSLAW filed a claim against the Department of Justice in bankruptcy court, alleging that Justice officials had conspired to steal the computer program. A bankruptcy judge found in favor of INSLAW, ruling that the Department of Justice had stolen PROMIS through "trickery, fraud, and deceit."[39] In 1988, a federal district court upheld the ruling. (A court of appeals reversed the case on a technicality three years later, finding that the bankruptcy court had no jurisdiction to hear the damages claim.)

The wrongdoing in the INSLAW case clearly implicated Department of Justice officials who held their positions during the Reagan administration. According to the House Judiciary Committee report, a handful of those officials had apparently executed a premeditated plan to destroy INSLAW and co-opt its rights to the PROMIS software.[40] What was their motive? There were already allegations that Justice officials were trying to push INSLAW into bankruptcy in order to avoid paying restitution. The allegations about Brewer's vindictiveness against INSLAW were also revived. Additional accusations maintained that high-level friends of the Reagan administration sought to secretly market the PROMIS software to foreign countries. Specifically, Earl W. Brian, the former California health secretary under Gov. Ronald Reagan and a close personal friend of Ed Meese, was allegedly responsible for reselling the software to Israel and several other countries.

The most dramatic charges of all could have been lifted right out of a best-selling spy novel. Alleging an elaborate plot that combined elements of international intrigue with the vagaries of American electoral politics, INSLAW's lawyers claimed that the Department of Justice had stolen the PROMIS software as part of a payoff to Brian for his assistance in getting Iranian leaders to collude in a plot to hold up release of the Iranian hostages during the fall of 1980.[41] Reagan campaign officials at the time feared that release of the hostages right before the general election would amount to a so-called "October surprise," helping President Carter to defeat Reagan. Although few of the witnesses willing to back such allegations could boast unstained reputations, the stories told were consistent enough that, when considered in light of the two favorable court rulings, they warranted at least some investigation. Whatever one believed or didn't believe about the scandal, the owners of INSLAW had, as Jack Brooks (D-Tex.) put it, been "ravaged by the Justice Department . . . treated like dogs."[42]

One journalist later remarked that "among the more baffling elements of the case for students of INSLAW [was] the role of Dick Thornburgh."[43] In theory, the attorney general who succeeded Ed Meese maintained no ties at all to the Department of Justice attorneys who had allegedly committed questionable activities in the case; in fact, at the time the software was purportedly stolen in the early 1980s, Thornburgh was still serving as governor of Pennsylvania. Later, when the allegations first started flying, Thornburgh was entrenched as director of the Institute of Politics at Harvard University's John F. Kennedy School of Government. Thus when Thornburgh was first appointed to head the Justice Department in 1988, many expected him to address the case more expeditiously than any insider reasonably could. Former Attorney General Elliot Richardson, serving as one of INSLAW's attorneys, wrote an encouraging letter to Thornburgh soon after his appointment, noting that the INSLAW matter would be on his desk when he arrived, and praising Thornburgh's reputation for fairness.

In May of 1989, with a new administration in place and yet another favorable court decision for INSLAW on the books, Richardson wrote again to Thornburgh, this time calling for him to appoint an independent counsel to investigate the INSLAW matter.[44] Congress's interest was also heating up. Yet Thornburgh withheld some key documents from the House Judiciary Committee looking into the case, and he refused to acknowledge even the possibility of a conspiracy that might justify either appointing an independent counsel or using Justice Department resources for an investigation. Thornburgh's resistance in the INSLAW case is hard to fathom, except possibly as an indication of his reflexive, circle-the-wagons mentality. According to Ronald LeGrand, chief investigator for the Senate Judiciary Committee in 1988, at least one trusted Department of Justice source told him that the INSLAW case "was a lot dirtier for the Department of Justice than Watergate had been, both in its breadth and in its depth."[45] Still, any wrongdoing would have reflected badly on Meese and his predecessors, rather than on Thornburgh. When the court of appeals reversed the bankruptcy court ruling on a technicality in May of 1991, it noted that INSLAW could file a new suit. Meanwhile, a Senate subcommittee conducting its own staff inquiry into the case was terminated without reporting any conclusions.

Thornburgh's departure from the Justice Department in August 1991 spurred a slight shift in its approach to the case. His successor, attorney general designate William Barr, also refused to appoint a special prosecutor, but in a nod to political reality, in November 1991 he announced the appointment of Nicholas Bua, a retired US district judge in Chicago, as "special counsel" to assist the Justice Department in reviewing INSLAW. Bua eventually cleared the Justice Department of any wrongdoing, though he was clearly hampered in his efforts by coming to the case so many years after the alleged corruption had occurred. Regardless, the 1992 House report noted that "as long as the investigation of wrongdoing by former and current high level Justice officials remains under the control of the Department itself, there will always be serious doubt about the objectivity and thoroughness of the inquiry."[46] In a sense, that may be INSLAW's most lasting legacy: it undermined the premise that structures within the Justice Department can address allegations of internal wrongdoing. In the George H. W. Bush administration's handling of the IN-SLAW matter, the Office of Professional Responsibility never had the chance to do that either.

It was not until September 27, 1994—almost two years into the Clinton administration—that Justice Department officials finally offered some form of closure to the INSLAW case. In a 187-page report, the department (now headed by Janet Reno, a Democrat) announced that "it could find no credible evidence that department officials conspired to steal computer software from the private firm of INSLAW, Inc." Yet the INSLAW case never disappeared. The 1990 death of Danny Casolaro, a journalist investigating the case, kept it alive well into the 1990s even though his death (West Virginia law enforcement authorities called it a suicide) was never considered an integral part of the core

INSLAW matter. Casolaro reportedly saw the INSLAW case as part of a broad and far-reaching conspiracy, which he labeled an "octopus," and at the time of his death he was seeking to confirm the link between the sale of INSLAW and the release of the Iranian hostages.[47]

Additionally, in May 1995 *Wired* magazine published a report charging senior Justice Department officials with appropriating PROMIS as part of a covert intelligence operation that allowed the US government to browse through the computers of foreign banks and intelligence services. This much was evident: as long as the matter was left unresolved, it would never disappear entirely. Nearly two decades later, the INSLAW case still remains a blot on the Department of Justice, if only because the whole truth is still not known.

The Dexter Lehtinen Travails

Dexter Lehtinen had the right connections and pedigree to rise quickly in Florida politics. After graduating first in his class at Stanford Law School, he logged time initially as a federal prosecutor and later as a Florida state senator. Once his unsuccessful first marriage was behind him, Lehtinen went on to marry Ileana Ros-Lehtinen, who would eventually become the first Cuban-American and the first Hispanic woman to serve in the US Congress. (She accomplished both those feats in 1989, winning out over a highly favored Democrat in a traditional Democratic district along the way.) Dexter Lehtinen also enjoyed the good graces of Vice President George H. W. Bush's son Jeb, a rising political player in the sunshine state. With Jeb Bush's encouragement, Attorney General Meese named the forty-three-year-old Lehtinen as interim US Attorney in Miami in 1988. Lehtinen would eventually become a thorn in the side of the Justice Department in Washington, DC, even as his office was successfully prosecuting high-profile criminals and receiving national attention for doing so.

Lehtinen's three-and-a-half-year tenure as interim US attorney was marked by several high points and just as many low points. On the plus side, his office was responsible for the successful prosecution of Panamanian General Manuel Noriega on charges of drug and other racketeering in 1990. He also gained positive publicity when, early in his tenure, he successfully sued the state of Florida for violating its own water standards and permitting the deterioration of the Everglades. The state eventually agreed to clean up the polluted water, and the lawsuit garnered Lehtinen significant support from environmental groups. In fact, the Florida Wildlife Federation became one of Lehtinen's biggest supporters when he sought Senate confirmation for his appointment as permanent US attorney beginning in 1990.

On the minus side, Lehtinen failed in his attempt to indict Cuban art collector Ramon Cernuda on charges of illegally trading with the Castro regime. According to outside prosecutors who followed the case closely, Lehtinen's motives in going after Cernuda were more political than legal, as he sought the indictment at a time calculated to help his wife in her race for the US House.[48] US district Judge Kenneth Dyskamp eventually ruled that the seizures of Cernudo's art were unconstitutional and threw the case out.

Lehtinen was also plagued by controversies that not only raised questions about his judgment, but also implicated him in some criminal activity. His troubles began with multiple accusations dating from before his tenure as interim US attorney: that he had (1) violated the Bar's ethics rules by concealing assets during his divorce from ex-wife Donna Stevenson, (2) committed domestic violence and abuse against her, and (3) improperly accepted a $676,960 referral fee when he was a private attorney.

A Florida bar report in May 1990 eventually exonerated Lehtinen of all these charges; for her part, Stevenson publicly denounced the charge that Lehtinen had ever "mistreated or abused" her "in any way."[49] Still, questions lingered about the thoroughness of the bar's inquiry.[50] And the bar's favorable review of Lehtinen's case occurred at the exact same time that consumer groups and others were busy finding fault with attorney discipline systems around the country. In one high-profile case, a professional court in California had taken over discipline of the state's 122,000-plus lawyers in the wake of widespread dissatisfaction over a system that relied on volunteer lawyers to settle charges against fellow attorneys. Even the Bush White House had gotten into the act of piling on the law profession at that time: after a speech by President Bush promising to restore "common sense and fairness" to the medical malpractice system, Press Secretary Marlin Fitzwater badmouthed lawyers as deserving "all the criticism that they can get."[51] The administration's decision to look past some of the allegations leveled at Lehtinen smacked of a degree of hypocrisy. That perception duly haunted Lehtinen when the White House formally nominated him to serve as the permanent US attorney later in 1990.

As head of the second biggest federal prosecutor's office outside of Washington, DC, Lehtinen also clashed directly with the Justice Department on a number of fronts. He offended some in Washington when he demanded more prosecutors for the drug war right after receiving the interim appointment. Even Associate Attorney General Frank Keating, who praised Lehtinen's appointment initially, complained that he had not really been acting as a "team player." Before a successful outcome was certain, Lehtinen and his bosses in Washington fought over the details of the Panamanian dictator's prosecution. Lehtinen had wanted to participate personally in the trial of Noriega despite his ten-year absence from the courtroom. The Justice Department pulled Lehtinen off the trial team, both because it favored seasoned trial lawyers and because of concerns that the allegations about Lehtinen's personal life, which by then had been aired publicly, might undermine confidence in the integrity of the proceedings. Lehtinen even had to push to overcome the Justice Department's initial reluctance to keep him abreast of the negotiations over the seizure of Noriega's assets.[52]

Lehtinen also committed a number of missteps while investigating allegations of corruption in the Broward County Sheriff's Office, which was under the direction of Sheriff Nick Navarro. In July 1991 Lehtinen met twice privately with Navarro, and then announced in front of him and the press that Navarro was "not the target of a Federal grand jury investigation."[53] Lehtinen apparently took these actions without providing any notice to either his assistants or the FBI agents who were investigating the case. He also quashed two subpoenas that would have required Navarro to hand over his office records. Two of his own assistants officially protested Lehtinen's unorthodox handling of the matter to Washington. Lehtinen removed both from his office and then handed them unofficial demotions. Attorney General Barr referred the matter in its entirety to the Office of Professional Responsibility.

Lehtinen's appointment as permanent US attorney was clearly in danger; it is unusual enough for a nominee under Senate scrutiny to be defending himself from an internal investigation run by the same Justice Department he was hoping to serve. In fact, the Office of Professional Responsibility opened up a second investigation into Lehtinen's actions as interim US attorney. This time the complaint stemmed from his handling of personnel. Specifically, in a letter to the *Miami Herald* his executive assistant had publicly criticized former assistant US Attorney David DeMaio for "egregious conduct," even though that same assistant had been rated as outstanding and had been awarded a merit raise right before his departure. Lehtinen's prospects for a permanent appointment clearly suffered from his office's unwarranted criticism of DeMaio.

The last straw for Lehtinen's few remaining supporters in the Senate was a controversy involving Alberto San Pedro, a convicted state felon who was awaiting trial on charges of federal drug smuggling, money laundering, and perjury. San Pedro complained to a federal judge that Lehtinen had improperly asked him questions about suspended Hialeah Mayor Raul Martinez, even though Lehtinen had personally recused himself from the Martinez prosecution. Regardless, this last complaint occupied the attention of Justice Department investigators at a time when Lehtinen would have benefited most from staying out of the spotlight entirely.

All these incidents together created sizeable political and legal headaches for the Bush administration. Consider the intricate politics of Lehtinen's nomination for the permanent position of US attorney. Despite his nomination's remaining in Senate limbo, Lehtinen was legally allowed to continue serving, thanks to his formal appointment by fifteen of south Florida's federal judges. Meanwhile, the Senate refused to act on his nomination in 1990, declaring in October of that year that there were "concerns" about his background. The Senate again refused to take up the nomination in August 1991. Given the impending presidential election and the political importance of Florida, did President Bush risk backlash from the nomination of the federal prosecutor who had convicted Noriega and cleaned up the Everglades? Or did Lehtinen's troubles, if left unaddressed, create an even greater risk of embarrassment? As late as September 1991, the White House still had not committed on whether to resubmit Lehtinen's nomination in hopes of forcing the Senate's hand during an election year. That issue eventually resolved itself in January 1992, when a frustrated Lehtinen permanently resigned from his position as interim US attorney.

A second set of issues was even more vexing. The Office of Professional Responsibility—an agency that Attorney General Thornburgh had sidestepped earlier—was now handling two of Lehtinen's matters. Did multiple allegations put too much stress on that office and necessitate an expanded investigation, possibly including the introduction of an independent counsel?

Lehtinen's case proved once again how political accountability sometimes works more effectively than legal accountability. It wasn't until a full year into his presidency—in January of 1990—that Pres. George H. W. Bush was finally ready to seek Senate confirmation for Lehtinen. Still, a majority of senators was never able to look past all these issues. Though Senator Connie Mack (R-Fla.) persistently pushed Lehtinen's cause, reports continued to crop up raising questions about his tenure and cautioning a slowing of the process.

The NSA Surveillance Controversy

The US National Security Agency (NSA) is located within the executive branch and remains fully accountable to the president. By Pres. George W. Bush's secret executive order issued in 2002, the NSA, as part of its terrorist surveillance program, was authorized to monitor (without warrants) phone calls and other communication involving any party ,even if the other person involved in the communication was actually within the United States. Before August 2007, the Federal Intelligence Surveillance Act (FISA) established a secret court to meet and approve all requests for search warrants, including those sought in pursuit of the war on terrorism.[54] Yet during Pres. George W. Bush's first term as president, a fundamental controversy arose with respect to the NSA's surveillance activities: Did the administration's program of warrantless surveillance violate the Fourth Amendment? If not, did it violate FISA, and thus was its continued existence essentially circumventing congressional authority?

The warrantless surveillance program was not even revealed to the public until December 2005, when the *New York Times* first reported that it had been proceeding under a presidential order signed in 2002.[55] At that time, the Bush administration defended the program, arguing that FISA had been implicitly amended by the "authorization for the use of military force" against terrorists, which Congress passed in the weeks following the September 11 terrorist attacks. Opponents of the administration countered that the amendment authorized action only against those "who planned, authorized, committed or aided" the attacks.

At first the debate over the legality of NSA surveillance appeared to be a political controversy more than one addressing criminal misconduct on the part of public officials. That began to change once Attorney General Alberto Gonzales testified before Congress about the program in February 2006. After a series of evasive answers, including his blanket statement that he would not let the courts decide the constitutionality of the administration's position, Gonzales provided controversial testimony arguing that all of the Justice Department officials in 2002 were "essentially in agreement" about the validity of the administration's position.[56] Congressional leaders knew that the Office of Professional Responsibility had launched its own investigation into the matter at the time the program was first revealed. According to Gonzales's own written responses to the committee, H. Marshall Jarrett, counsel for the Office of Professional Responsibility, had repeatedly requested the clearances necessary to investigate the Department of Justice's alleged approval of the NSA surveillance program.[57] When all such requests were denied, the office was then forced to close its own investigation. Was the OPR investigation shut down for national security reasons, or to protect Gonzales from such a probe?

If questions about Gonzales's role in the controversy boiled down to an issue of trust, the attorney general did not help his case any with his evasive and conflicting answers to the senators' questions. The Senate committee eventually discovered new evidence that pointed to a "revolt" from within the Justice Department over the program's legality and to a White House attempt to quell the revolt by allowing it to continue solely on the basis of Justice Department approval. The most damaging testimony came from the former deputy attorney general, James Comey. Testifying before the Senate on May 15, 2007, about an entirely different scandal involving the dismissal of US attorneys, Comey indicated that during March 2004 he had personally refused to sign a presidential order reauthorizing the warrantless surveillance program, on the ground that it needed more safeguards.[58] At the time, Comey was acting attorney general because Ashcroft had been temporarily hospitalized for gall bladder surgery. Unwilling to accept no for an answer, then–White House Counsel Alberto Gonzales, joined by White House Chief of Staff Andrew Card, attempted to bypass Comey by visiting Ashcroft in the hospital to get the signature. Ill and barely conscious at the time, Ashcroft refused to authorize the program.[59] He offered lucid enough reasons for his refusal: first, he remained concerned about the legality of the surveillance program, and second, he was not then the attorney general, as Comey was acting attorney general while he remained hospitalized. It was a telling moment for Gonzales, who feared Bush might be in violation of the procedures Gonzales had helped to establish for the NSA operation without the Justice Department's sign off.[60] Later, Gonzales would testify before Congress that there had never been any legal disagreement over the NSA's eavesdropping program.

Gonzales attempted to contradict Comey's testimony about the hospital visit when he reappeared before the Senate in late July 2007. Specifically, he argued that the visit to Ashcroft's hospital room was for a discussion of "other intelligence activities." But with trust in the head of Justice already at a low point, many senators responded in disbelief to the attorney general's denials. According to Arlen Specter (R-Pa.), the ranking Republican member of the committee, Gonzales's "credibility has been breached to the point of being actionable."

In subsequent days, Gonzales's fate was sealed as Director of National Intelligence John Negroponte and FBI Director Robert Mueller both challenged his version of the events of early 2004. A memo from Negroponte dated May 17, 2006, was released to the Associated Press; in it Negroponte contradicted Gonzales's testimony regarding the subject of a March 10, 2004, emergency congressional briefing that preceded his hospital-room meeting with Ashcroft. Meanwhile, Mueller seemed to dispute Gonzales's testimony with his own sworn testimony on that subject before the House Judiciary Committee.

Gonzales's announcement of his resignation on August 27, 2007, did not end the congressional inquiries into his actions, though it did temporarily squelch calls for appointing a special prosecutor and for initiating an impeachment inquiry in the House of Representatives. Once again, an attorney general was not able to square his previous work as counselor to the president with his new role as the nation's chief law enforcement officer. To be sure, Gonzales's road to resignation was perhaps inevitable once congressional Democrats were in a position to put him on the hot seat.

Alberto Gonzales's Controversial Dismissal of US Attorneys

Each of the ninety-three US attorneys representing federal judicial districts across the country holds office at the discretion of the president of the United States. After every election of a new president, a brand new coterie of chief prosecutors—normally with ties to the victorious president's political party—assumes its place in these posts with little fanfare or controversy. A successfully reelected president normally enjoys the same opportunity to clean house for his second term. Yet such removals have in fact been exceedingly rare, absent some serious cause for dismissal that extends beyond simple partisan considerations. For example, Presidents Richard Nixon and Bill Clinton fired just one US attorney each after their successful reelection bids in 1972 and 1996, respectively.[61] US attorney dismissals are also exceedingly rare midway through the president's four-year term, as such firings may be perceived—whether accurately or not—as partisan in nature. According to a congressional Research Service report issued in February of 2007, between 1981 and 2006 just two out of 486 US attorneys were forced from office by presidents midway through their terms.[62]

Given this modern tradition of deference, Pres. George W. Bush's midterm dismissal of seven US attorneys on December 7, 2006, without any formal explanation, was certain to cause an uproar among the administration's critics in Congress. When the Democrats took control of Congress exactly one month later, their anger was expressed in formal legislative demands. The first shot across the bow came in the form of an official letter from Senate Judiciary Committee member Dianne Feinstein (D-Calif.) and Committee Chairman Patrick Leahy (D-Vt.) to Attorney General Gonzales. It was dated January 9, 2007.[63] The immediate concern of the two senators was that the president might appoint interim US attorneys to the newly vacated spots under a controversial provision of the USA PATRIOT Improvement and Reauthorization Act of 2005,[64] thus bypassing the traditional Senate confirmation process. (The act eliminated the traditional 120-day maximum term for such appointments, giving the president a chance to appoint U.S attorneys for an indefinite period without Senate approval). Two days later those two senators, joined by Senator Mark Pryor (D-Ark.), introduced legislation to prevent circumvention of Senate consent for new US attorneys under the act.[65]

On January 18, 2007, Attorney General Gonzales testified before the newly constituted Senate Judiciary Committee run by Chairman Leahy.[66] The Democratic senators' inquiries focused on whether the firings in question had been politically motivated. Gonzales denied the allegations, referring to the firings as the outcome of a "routine" evaluation of the performance of individuals in the Bush administration. Still, the media suggested that something else was afoot, with unnamed GOP sources indicating that the Bush administration had in fact been attempting to rid the Justice Department of disloyal prosecutors.[67] Some senators' ire was raised further by the curiously changing testimony of Deputy Attorney General Paul McNulty. On February 6, 2007, McNulty told Senators that the seven US attorneys fired in December had all had job performance issues.[68] Then, within a matter of days, McNulty recanted his testimony and apologized to the committee for statements that he labeled "inaccurate," as six of the seven US attorneys in question had in fact received outstanding job performance ratings. Senators learned that in one of the more egregious cases, US Attorney Bud Cummins of Arkansas, the head of the office and a man with positive job ratings, had been dismissed in favor of Timothy Griffin, a former aide to White House strategist Karl Rove. Meanwhile, Justice Department officials who had told Senate Democrats they did not know that Rove was lobbying for Griffin's appointment, were forced to backtrack from their statements as well.[69]

After two months of continuously negative revelations about the firings—which in turn invited public calls for Gonzales's dismissal by senators hailing from both sides of the political aisle[70]—the attorney general appeared once again before the Senate on April 19, 2007.[71] This time Gonzales accepted formal responsibility for the firing of the seven US attorneys, although he continued to disavow knowledge of the specific process by which they had been fired, much to the dismay of perplexed senators. Even more troubling, Gonzales stated that the fired US attorneys had lost his confidence, an argument that drew looks of incredulity from senators in light of his own recent acknowledgement that he had never investigated why they had been fired in the first place. Gonzales's evasive testimony led Senate Judiciary Committee members Tom Coburn (R-Okla.), Lindsay Graham (R-S.C.) and Jefferson Sessions (R-Ala.)—normally stalwart supporters of the Bush administration—to join calls for the attorney general's resignation. President Bush's April 23, 2007, expression of confidence in the attorney general proved to be too little, too late. Gonzales's tenure in office was already nearing its conclusion; later that summer the president accepted his formal resignation. To those who feared setting a precedent for making federal prosecutors look over their shoulders for approval from the White House, Gonzales's dismissal served as tacit vindication of their position.

Gonzales's resignation was not the only event that occurred in the aftermath of the scandal. Another was the rescinding of the 2005 USA PATRIOT Act reauthorization clause that had permitted unlimited terms for unconfirmed-by-the-Senate interim attorneys in the first place. At the time the clause was rescinded, twenty-three of ninety-six US attorneys' offices were headed by interim or acting US attorneys, and twenty-one of those offices had no presidential nominee pending for the vacancy.

Meanwhile, many questions remained about the activities of Gonzales and others. If the White House had indeed pressured US attorneys to remain loyal and partisan on behalf of the administration, that would have run afoul of the US Hatch Act, which flatly prohibited most federal employees from engaging in political activities while on duty.[72] Monica Goodling, who had served as the Justice Department's liaison to the White House at the time of the firings, testified before the House Committee of the Judiciary on May 23, 2007, under a grant of immunity.[73] Goodling admitted that she had broken civil service laws on hiring and improperly weighed "political factors" in her decision making.

When Gonzales announced his resignation on August 28, 2007, other investigations were freed up to go forward. The Justice Department's inspector general, Glenn Fine, had been hampered to that point in his own research on the matter; however, two days after Gonzales's announcement, Fine disclosed in a letter to the Senate Judiciary Committee that his office was now looking into whether Gonzales had made "intentionally false, misleading, or inappropriate" statements to Congress about firing the federal prosecutors and about the terrorist surveillance program. [74] Yet Fine was still hamstrung in one important respect: the Office of the Inspector General was not empowered to review the misconduct of lawyers, which included Gonzales and Goodling, among others. Thus Fine's office agreed to a joint investigation with the Office of Professional Responsibility into the dismissal of the US attorneys

Almost a year later, on July 29, 2008, the Justice Department office, headed by Fine, and the Office of Professional Responsibility issued a joint 146-page report concluding that actions of Attorney General Gonzales and his aides constituted "official misconduct" in violation of federal civil service laws and Department of Justice policies.[75] The report accused Gonzales of having "abdicated his responsibility to safeguard the integrity and independence of the department."[76] But Fine's report was qualified by his investigation's failure to secure the cooperation of numerous officials, including Karl Rove and Harriet Miers, among others. Thus the larger issues of White House involvement remained unanswered.

By August of 2008, Congress had been looking into the matter for more than eighteen months, and internal investigations had proceeded as far as possible. With many issues still left unresolved, Gonzales's successor as attorney general, Michael Mukasey, had to make yet another decision in this long-running controversy: whether or not to appoint a special prosecutor to pursue the investigation a step further. As an outer circle attorney general, Mukasey showed little hesitation on this front: on September 29, 2008, he appointed Nora Dennehy, acting US attorney for the District of Connecticut and eighteen-year veteran of the Justice Department, as special prosecutor. As in the CIA tapes scandal, Mukasey was not willing to go completely outside the Justice Department with his appointment power. But unlike his predecessor, Mukasey did not view appointing a special prosecutor as a sign of defeat, either. He was simply using the power of his office to offer a creative solution to one of the most vexing questions every attorney general must face: How can the Justice Department investigate itself? In this case, the absence of a formal independent counsel statute and overwhelming cries for one to be invoked gave Mukasey the opportunity to find a quintessential third way.

chapter 5

More Political Considerations

Departed Officials, Looming Elections,

and the Influence of Partisan Opposition

An attorney general who is considering whether or not to appoint a special counsel or independent prosecutor is swimming in dangerous waters. The issues that he or she must sort out are many and complex, and the consequences of even one misstep along the way can be profoundly damaging. Three concerns are conspicuous among those that must be taken into account in this decision-making process. First is the political status of the official to be investigated; second, the timing of the investigation; and third, the extent to which united or divided government may affect the proceedings.

1. The political status of the official in question. When assessing the political context of a prosecution, the attorney general must of course consider the positions held by the targeted individuals, which are addressed extensively in chapters 3 and 4. Additionally, he or she must weigh (1) whether the targeted official owed his or her original appointment to the current president rather than to a past president who has left the scene, (2) whether the targeted official maintains strong partisan connections to the current president, as opposed to those who hail from the opposition party, and (3) whether the targeted official still holds the position or works in the office in which the misconduct is alleged to have taken place. Sometimes officials remain in the executive branch working in a different capacity; in other cases they may have left the administration altogether. Special prosecutor and independent counsel provisions tend to assume that misconduct has emanated from someone who still remains in a position to pose conflicts of interest.[1] Clearly those who continue to hold the same public office in which they were accused of misconduct may be treated differently from those who no longer maintain their position of trust.

2. The timing of the investigation. As a president's reelection campaign approaches, his administration begins to focus on expressly political concerns, such as serious primary challengers to the president, and perhaps on undecided voters who may prove crucial to the looming contest. Of course scandals and allegations of wrongdoing can derail even the most carefully crafted political plans, especially when the wrongdoing implicates either of the two people at the top of the ticket. As much as the attorney general may prefer adhering to normal Justice Department protocols under such circumstances, the temptation to refer an issue to a special prosecutor can be overwhelming.

With respect to timing, it should also be noted that special prosecutors are not hampered by other cases demanding their attention and forcing compromises and shortcuts to balance limited resources. As a result, these specially appointed outsiders tend to take longer than other attorneys in building their cases. Thus if the appointment of a special prosecutor goes forward, critics may accuse the attorney general of jettisoning executive accountability to a distant point in the future when the election is safely behind the president he or she serves. On the other hand, if no appointment goes forward, accusations of a cover-up will fly, and the report the attorney general issues to justify the decision not to appoint may be dismissed as politically motivated. In sum, the attorney general's exercise of discretion will receive scrutiny, no matter what he or she decides to do.

3. The influence of partisan opposition in Congress. Finally, an attorney general deciding whether to name a special counsel must consider whether the government is divided or united. During the course of a preliminary investigation, the legislative branch may become the attorney general's best friend—or worst enemy. When the opposition party controls one or both houses of Congress, calls for a special prosecutor may become heated, especially during politically charged hearings. In the hands of the president's own party, of course, that same Congress will offer little such rhetoric, save for the occasional barkings of a frustrated minority. The position of attorney general is at its core a political one, appointed by the president and confirmed by the Senate; even a neutral, outer circle attorney general cannot ignore the political context that surrounds his or her office. United party government means that a special prosecutor may offer the only real opportunity to investigate administration wrongdoing, while divided government may threaten to politicize the prosecution, even when it is the hands of an independent counsel.

The attorney general must take all these (and other) factors into account when conducting a preliminary investigation into the nature and source of official wrongdoing.

Most (but not all) of the case studies that follow concern lower-level or mid-level officials. Upon the very first whiff of wrongdoing, cases that directly implicate presidents or vice presidents tend to invite public calls for the appointment of a special or independent prosecutor. As a result, attorneys general or others entrusted with decision-making authority must be on guard against the pressures imposed on them to appease congressional leaders and the public at large with special prosecutor appointments that undermine, rather than preserve, due process principles.

Cases of misconduct alleged against any of the hundreds of other "covered individuals"[2] under the now-defunct Independent Counsel Act, or against any of the thousands of people who could be targeted by a garden-variety special prosecutor, tend to fly below the public's radar screen, and so pressures to appoint special prosecutors for them are fewer. But this does not mitigate what may be at stake for these people; nor does it lessen the problems associated with either naming a special prosecutor prematurely in their cases or failing to name one at all once other avenues of investigation have been severely compromised.

Former Political Officials under Fire: The Curious Case of EEOC Chairman John Powell

As the president who inherited the federal government in the wake of the Watergate scandal, Gerald Ford had to set a solid public example of ethical conduct and integrity in order to secure credibility with the American public. By the summer of 1976 the Justice Department's Criminal Division had identified at least twelve ongoing corruption cases involving officials of the executive branch. The cases included "allegations of obstruction of justice, receipt of illegal campaign contributions, fraud, misuse of public funds and civil rights violations."[3] An especially high-priority target on this list was John H. Powell Jr., the embattled fifth chairman of the Equal Employment Opportunity Commission (EEOC).

A former general counsel to the US Commission on Civil Rights, Powell began his five-year term as EEOC chairman on December 28, 1973. At the time of his appointment by President Nixon, there seemed little reason to suspect that Powell would not enjoy a successful tenure. He had already served successfully in both the private and public sectors; most recently he had been general counsel of the US Commission on Civil Rights. Yet charges of unethical conduct by Powell arose during his first eleven months in office as head of the EEOC. These included allegations that (1) he had met with an officer of a corporate defendant in a Title VII case without the knowledge of the other commission members and (2) he had attempted to issue contracts without the approval of the commission members. White House Counsel Philip Buchen authorized Assistant White House Counsel Jay French to conduct a preliminary review of both those matters, and French's initial examination turned up evidence of criminal activity. Specifically, French learned that Powell had (1) wasted appropriated funds by issuing unnecessary contracts or contracting to pay more than the value of the service to be performed, (2) made fraudulent claims for reimbursement of travel expenses, (3) issued directives to his personal staff to ignore Commission decisions he disagreed with, and (4) been intimidating and harassing employees.[4] Subsequently, French drafted a formal request to the FBI that it conduct its own investigation to determine whether the EEOC chairman had violated bribery and graft laws. Meanwhile, the Office of Management and Budget (OMB) conducted a separate investigation into budget irregularities at the EEOC. Finally, the General Accounting Office began investigating the charge that Powell had unilaterally and improperly issued numerous contacts.[5]

On January 22, 1975, Deputy White House Counsel Philip Areeda forwarded relevant materials gathered by French to the Justice Department.[6] A response came quickly: Justice officials Jack Keeney and Lawrence Silberman suggested that there were more than enough materials to warrant further inquiry, although probably not enough to warrant an all-out FBI investigation at that early stage.[7] Keeney and Silberman also suggested that the OMB be asked to broaden its investigation of Powell into matters of waste and irregularities in personal accounts.[8] Finally, they suggested that the Civil Service General Counsel's Office had the capacity to examine Powell's ethical violations, which were the original subject of French's inquiry.[9] Before any of these inquiries reached their conclusions, however, on March 19, 1975, President Ford requested and received Powell's formal resignation from the EEOC. The Justice Department eventually determined that Powell had not violated any criminal laws, but his violation of commission rules and procedure were by then a matter of public record, making it impossible for him to continue in his position.

A dissection of the investigation of Powell after the fact suggests that all the conditions were in place for a fair and balanced inquiry by White House and Justice Department officials. Powell had little direct contact with Justice Department officials before the investigation. More important, none of the allegations called into question the judgments of the current administration, as President Ford had not appointed Powell to his position in the first place. Nor was any election immediately pending, and so the opportunity to politicize Powell's case was minimal at best. Finally, if the Justice Department had not given appropriate attention to the matter, a Democratic-led Congress with bolstered majorities following the 1974 midterm elections was in a strong position to conduct its own aggressive inquiry or to exert pressure on the administration as necessary. In short, the investigation of EEOC Chairman John Powell Jr. offered little reason to circumvent routine protocols for addressing executive branch corruption.

Death and Intrigue: The Final Years of the Civil Aeronautics Board

The US government has always struggled with the issue of how to best organize and oversee the nonmilitary aviation industry. Established by Congress in 1938, the Civil Aeronautics Board (CAB) was responsible for air traffic control safety programs and airway development in the United States. It was also initially responsible for accident investigations, as well as other airline issues, like market entry, supply, and price, that tended to affect the airline companies' own economic health.

The CAB found itself at the center of a continuing controversy throughout the early 1970s. In one instance, a dispute over the scope of CAB's investigation into illegal campaign contributions made by American Airlines and Braniff surfaced after the death of the board's enforcement bureau chief, William M. Gingery, who committed suicide on February 17, 1975. The chain of events set off by Gingery's death once again tested the young Ford administration and its new attorney general, Edward Levi, just a short time after the Watergate scandal had soured the public on the likelihood that the executive branch could fairly investigate its own wrongdoing. The CAB case confirmed that the executive branch is in fact eminently capable of professionally investigating and prosecuting official misconduct, especially when the officials in questions have already left their original positions of influence.

Gingery left a suicide note behind that charged his immediate predecessor, as head of CAB's enforcement bureau (acting CAB chairman Richard J. O'Melia) with having prematurely terminated several investigations into illegal political contributions and having improperly ordered the files from those investigations impounded. Before his death, Gingery was scheduled to give testimony to the Senate Judiciary Committee's Subcommittee on Administrative Practice and Procedure, headed by Senator Edward Kennedy (D-Mass.). The committee had been investigating CAB practices and policies. Gingery requested that the suicide note be sent to the subcommittee directly. More than a month later, on March 21, 1975, O'Melia told the subcommittee that in November 1973, when he had headed the enforcement bureau, then-CAB Chairman Robert D. Timm had ordered an abrupt end to the investigation of political gift-giving by airlines. O'Melia also accused Timm of having prohibited investigators from pursuing leads in the case. Those accusations set off a wave of events that would take down Timm and the entire CAB. Adding to the problem was O'Melia, who testified that while he had received the order in a memo from Timm, he could not produce a copy of it because he had refused to accept it.

For President Ford and his administration, Timm's case presented a continuing problem. The former CAB chairman was already suspected of maintaining improper ties to the airline industry while he was in office. Those suspicions led President Ford to refuse to reappoint Timm as chairman of CAB, although he stayed on as a member of the board. Testifying after O'Melia, Timm admitted to having limited the scope of questioning that the enforcement board could pursue when investigations were initiated in July 1973, giving some credence to the second of O'Melia's two charges. But Timm adamantly denied ever sending a memo of the kind O'Melia described. Critical questions thus remained: Was Timm guilty of criminal misconduct? And who would be charged with the responsibility of rendering that determination?

Further complicating the matter were revelations in May 1975 that O'Melia had failed to accurately define a conflict of interest in his own background check when he had originally come up for confirmation as head of CAB. From the White House's perspective, it seemed possible that O'Melia had lied in his allegations against Timm, perhaps to deflect attention from his own problems.[10]

With the blessing of the White House, Senator Kennedy referred the entire matter to the Department of Justice, which then launched a preliminary investigation into the affair. Ultimately, the Justice Department concluded that while Timm's undisputed actions had caused a failure to adequately investigate political contribution violations, his actions were not technically in violation of any provision of the criminal code and thus did not warrant any further investigation.

Nevertheless, the president was empowered by 49 USC. Section 1321(a)(2) to remove members of CAB for "inefficiency, neglect of duty, or malfeasance in office." Buoyed by the Justice Department's report, the White House began taking steps to remove Timm from office. Although he resisted at first, Timm finally resigned in a letter dated December 10, 1975. Although the Justice Department investigation turned up no evidence of criminal conduct, it did provide the White House with the means to invoke CAB statutory provisions that allowed the president to remove CAB members for "malfeasance."

Is there reason to question the thoroughness and fairness of the Justice Department's investigation of Timm? Based on the factors outlined above, the risk of bias in this case appears minimal. Like John Powell at the EEOC, Timm was a Nixon administration appointee whose ties to Ford were limited. Indeed, Ford had already refused to reappoint Timm to his CAB post. The recent controversy stemming from the attempt of former attorney general Kleindienst to improperly influence the Antitrust Division's investigation of ITT, a large manufacturing conglomerate, rendered President Ford wary of any official actions that could be perceived as improperly protecting corporate interests. Timm's actions certainly fit that description. Finally, Timm's alleged improper conduct occurred entirely within the scope of the Nixon administration; thus prosecution by the Ford administration's Justice Department was unlikely to produce skeletons that could be linked to the current White House administration.

Investigating Officials in the Eye of an Electoral Storm: The Campaign Irregularities of Congressman Gerald R. Ford

On July 16, Attorney General Edward Levi faced one of the most difficult decisions of his short tenure as head of the Justice Department. Three days earlier, a public relations bombshell had been dropped on FBI Director Clarence Kelley: an informant revealed serious allegations of wrongdoing against President Ford for actions he had taken in congressional campaigns dating back a dozen years or more. Levi now had to decide whether to refer those allegations to the Office of the Watergate Special Prosecutor, now led by Charles Ruff. Complicating Levi's decision was his assumption that, whether or not the charges were eventually substantiated, they could be used against Ford in his current campaign for reelection. And yet they were not charges that had anything to do with Ford's presidency or even his work as congressman.

More than two years after Nixon's resignation and nearly two years after his controversial pardon, Ruff's office was still investigating various Watergate-related allegations of wrongdoing concerning the 1972 presidential campaign. By the summer of 1976, Ruff's hefty to-do list still included pursuing (1) appellate arguments to uphold the convictions of Watergate criminals H. R. Haldeman, John Ehrlichman, and John Mitchell on appeal, (2) claims that President Ford had lied to Congress when he denied at his vice presidential confirmation hearings that the Nixon White House had ordered him as House minority leader in late 1972 to block the first congressional investigation into Watergate, and (3) allegations that illegal contributions had been made to Nixon's 1972 campaign by members of industry, including Armand Hammer, chairman of Occidental Petroleum.

The new allegations being raised against Ford over past congressional campaigns specifically concerned funds from two large maritime unions (the National Marine Engineers Beneficial Association and the Seafarers International Union) that might have been laundered through Republican committees in Michigan and then covertly paid to Gerald Ford beginning in 1964 and continuing through 1974. During that decade Ford's reelection was all but guaranteed in his overwhelmingly Republican district, and he had collected far more money than he needed for his electoral campaigns. Because his position as minority leader meant that he also received money from sources outside his district, it had been his practice to divert some of it to other Republicans around the country.[11] Under Michigan state and federal law, both Ford's own campaign committees and the Kent County Republican Committee were required to report all such contributions. If the money received by the county committee had been secretly diverted to President Ford, that might constitute an illegal contribution under federal election laws in place at the time. And if Ford had converted any of these funds to his own personal use, as the informant suggested, that would constitute a criminal offense as well. Finally, Congress's Code of Official Conduct specifically stated that each member "shall keep his campaign funds separate from his personal funds."

With the November election bearing down on the administration, Levi had to make his decision in a hurry. The informant's report indicated that in at least one instance Ford had technically dipped into campaign funds for personal use. That occurred in late November 1972, when he wrote a check for $1,167 on his official campaign account to buy personal air tickets for his family. He apparently tried to reimburse the account with a personal check two weeks later, but his own account was overdrawn at the time, and so he did not actually repay the campaign account for six weeks. Levi was also aware of allegations that the maritime unions had paid stipends to Ford and others of about $2,000 per month, but he believed that the charges had never been substantiated.[12] Eventually Levi bowed to the reality that even if the charges were either frivolous or immaterial, only a special prosecutor could end the speculation with any credibility. Thus after engaging in numerous discussions with FBI Director Clarence M. Kelley, Associate FBI Director James B. Adams, and Deputy Attorney General Harold Tyler, Levi decided on July16, 1976, to refer these allegations to the Watergate special prosecutor already in place.[13]

Working quickly, the special prosecutor's office attempted to trace the disposition of contributions made to Ford's campaigns by the two committees. FBI agents working on Ruff's behalf interrogated Ford's former campaign aides in Michigan and subpoenaed the records of three Republican campaign committees in Ford's old district. Several of the aides reported that they knew of no improper payments or instances in which campaign contributions were mishandled.[14] Accordingly, on October 14, 1976, just three months after the referral, Ruff announced that his office had found "no evidence to support an allegation that President Ford had misused political contributions . . . or [committed] any other violations of law."[15]

Was the referral to the special prosecutor necessary in this case? Perhaps few investigations meet the criteria for referral so well. The allegations implicated President Ford directly, thus inviting the public to look for bias in the very attorney general he had appointed less than a year earlier. (See chapter 3.) Far more important, the timing of the investigation (during the summer and early fall of the general election contest) placed Levi in a no-win situation if he tried to oversee the investigation himself. A quick report on the allegations would have spurred Democratic charges of a political whitewash, while a late announcement after the election would have fueled speculation that the Department of Justice had stalled the investigation to limit political fallout. Thus in this instance, the only means of non-partisan investigation and prosecution lay in invoking the special prosecutor mechanism.

Leaving No Stone Unturned: Elizabeth Tamposi and the Passport Search Scandal

The so-called "passport search" scandal that arose during the fall of 1992, just as Pres. George H. W. Bush's reelection campaign was drawing to a close, could not have been timed much worse from the perspective of the forty-first president. Notably, it was not just an unrelated scandal that broke during a campaign; the alleged wrongdoing—if the claims proved true—had actually been conducted on behalf of the president in order to provide him with an advantage over his Democratic opponent, Arkansas Governor Bill Clinton. The scandal began with the oft-repeated election rumor that Clinton, while studying in England during the Vietnam War, had written a letter renouncing his US citizenship or seeking dual citizenship for purposes of evading the draft.[16] Following up on the rumor, several news organizations used the Freedom of Information Act (FOIA) to file requests with the State Department and the Justice Department seeking information about Clinton's citizenship and military draft status during the period in question.[17] Congressman Gerald Solomon (R-N.Y.) made a similar request through the State Department's legislative affairs office. On September 16, 1992, Bush's White House Chief of Staff, James A. Baker, discussed the requests for the first time with the White House assistant for political affairs, Janet G. Mullins.[18]

Elizabeth M. Tamposi was the Bush administration's assistant secretary of state for consular affairs. On September 30, 1992, Tamposi directed three consular affairs officials to conduct a search for passport records related to Clinton.[19] At this time, Tamposi spoke with Assistant Secretary of State for Legislative Affairs Steven K. Berry to let him know the search was underway.[20] She also spoke to Margaret Tutwiler, the assistant to the president for communications, and asked her to notify Baker about what was happening.[21] According to Tamposi, Berry represented himself as working on behalf of Mullins.

The searchers apparently located the file but were unable to find the letter in which Bill Clinton had allegedly renounced his citizenship (or at least had sought information about renouncing it). The next day the searchers resumed their search from 10:15 A.M. to 4:30 P.M. Meanwhile Tamposi informed Berry that while no letter had been found, she had discovered evidence of possible tampering with the file, including a suspicious tear in the upper left corner of one of the documents.[22] Tamposi then contacted the State Department's inspector general, Sherman Funk, to report the possible tampering to him as well. Funk in turn reported the incident to the FBI for further investigation.

In addition to the charges of possible tampering, two other red flags were raised. First, as department officials later acknowledged, such an accelerated response to FOIA requests from media outlets was highly unusual, to say the least.[23] Second, while Berry specifically denied that the White House itself had ever specifically asked him to search for the files, he did admit that he might have told Tamposi about the White House's interest in Clinton's passport files. Any search for such files in an attempt to influence a presidential election campaign would clearly violate State Department protocol about access to individuals' passport files. Passing such records to news organizations might violate federal privacy laws as well.

On October 9, 1992, the FBI announced that it had found no evidence of tampering. Still, stories about the purported tampering were now being reported widely in the media, and some reporters were asking why the passport files search had even been conducted in the first place.[24] In the weeks following these revelations, two primary questions arose about the search: (1) Who approved of it in the first place? and (2) Why exactly did political appointees at the State Department make an exception to the first-come, first-serve queue for FOIA requests? The first question was a political hot potato that might cause serious problems for an administration in a close election campaign; the second opened up the possibility of criminal wrongdoing by high-level administration officials.

Despite the FBI's announcement, Funk continued his own investigation on behalf of the State Department's Office of the Inspector General. Given the approaching presidential election, the familiarity of the Office of the Inspector General with State Department procedures offered perhaps the only means of reaching any conclusions on the matter before Election Day. On the other hand, as political appointees, inspectors general may be somewhat suspect—they are often selected, if only in part, because of their political relationships and party affiliation.[25] Moreover, because inspectors general lack direct prosecutorial authority, their capacity to investigate criminal activity is limited; they must essentially refer issues on to other authorities, who then conduct their own investigations. Nor would uncooperative witnesses have much incentive to talk to most inspectors general.

Funk did not issue his final report until November 18, 1992, two weeks after

Election Day. Based on 107 interviews of seventy people, he concluded that Mullins might have made false statements to investigators and thus referred the case to the Justice Department for further action.[26] Still, the limits of Funk's report were obvious from a careful reading of the final product. The report depicted Secretary of State Baker—then on leave from the State Department to run the president's reelection campaign—as having indirect knowledge of the search either while it was in progress or within a few hours of its completion.[27] The report also suggested that Republicans inside and outside the administration had been encouraging reporters to request information on Clinton. Funk noted that it was "perfectly legal" to conduct the search in response to the news organizations' FOIA requests. Additionally, Funk's report indicated that White House officials would not cooperate with him, which rendered him unable to piece together a complete account of activity at the White House on the night of September 30, when the search began. Not one of the seventy people interviewed was associated directly with either the Bush-Quayle 1992 campaign or the Republican National Committee, although Funk's report acknowledged that the search might well have involved political appointees trying to influence the election.

On December 10, 1992, the Justice Department's Criminal Division recommended to outgoing Attorney General William Barr that he seek the appointment of an independent counsel in the matter; the following day Barr asked the special panel of the DC Court of Appeals to do exactly that. The court then appointed Joseph DiGenova as independent counsel just one day before the statute was scheduled to expire.

Up to that point, the only review for evidence tampering had been the FBI's brief one. Why didn't the Justice Department conduct its own full-fledged investigation? Certainly the Justice Department was not implicated in the events. Meanwhile, the heavily qualified findings of the inspector general satisfied few beyond the confines of the outgoing administration itself. Still, Election Day had cast enough of a shadow on the proceedings to discourage any more comprehensive inquiry.

Three years later, DiGenova's $2.2 million investigation into the matter concluded that while "there were some stupid, dumb and indeed partisan things done by Bush Administration people"—among them that James Baker may have indirectly encouraged the review of the files—none of them rose to the level of criminal activity.[28] Far from defending his own investigation, DiGenova used his report as an opportunity to decry the use of independent counsels in all but the most significant matters, such as Watergate and the Iran-Contra affair.

Yet history suggests that it is not so easy to categorize a scandal as "significant" or "insignificant" without some form of comprehensive investigation by a neutral party at the outset. Once Election Day of 1992 came and went, the passport tampering scandal seemed far less significant. Hindsight offers that assessment, and even the independent counsel assigned to the case would eventually question the basis for his own appointment. Still, no one could have known how the matter would conclude back during the fall of 1992, when an undermanned inspector general toiling without the tools of a full-fledged prosecutor's office was conducting his investigation. At that earlier juncture, the political stakes seemed enormous, and even the lowliest members of the Department of Justice would have been absolutely immune from political pressures.

When Congress Defers to the Executive: The Illegal Loans of OMB Head Bert Lance

In 1977, accusations of improprieties leveled against Bert Lance, the first director of the Office of Management and Budget, ended Pres. Jimmy Carter's brief honeymoon with the public.[29] Certainly some credit for stoking public opinion goes to *New York Times* columnist William Safire, who on July 21, 1977, kick-started the public's obsession over the Lance affair with a column entitled "Carter's Broken Lance.[30] Still, it was Lance's own actions that contributed most directly to the administration's growing public relations problems. To many it appeared as if Lance's presidential appointment was a product of personal ties, rather than of his merits as public servant. Like Bell, Lance was an old acquaintance of Carter's from Georgia. The future president first met Lance in 1966, and as governor of Georgia in the early 1970s, Carter had appointed Lance to serve as his director of the Georgia Department of Transportation.[31] Though Lance's appointment as OMB director kept him far from law enforcement duties, it did not relieve him of the need to help set a strong ethical tone for the new administration. During the 1976 presidential campaign Carter had promised over and over that if elected, he and his aides would take the high road by avoiding even the appearance of impropriety. Of course this promise was never limited to federal law enforcement positions. Even if Lance had proven to be a squeaky clean public servant, his appointment on primarily personal grounds would have been problematic. And since he was not squeaky clean, the ethical problems that pursued him caused further scrutiny of the circumstances surrounding his original appointment. Many quickly reached the conclusion that "Lance, whether guilty or innocent, [had] violated Carter's high ethical standards for public servants."[32] President

Carter's willingness to publicly defend his embattled OMB chief only served to validate the widespread suspicion that the new president had helped friends at the expense of the public interest.

The allegations that arose just six months into Lance's tenure at OMB concerned his participation in illegal banking practices while serving as president of the Calhoun First National Bank at Calhoun, Georgia, and at the National Bank of Georgia (NBG) in Atlanta. In the early 1970s Lance was allegedly involved in a series of fraudulent and fictitious loans from the bank. The proceeds of the loans had been used to purchase and improve land near Calhoun.

Why had these allegations not come to light during the administration's elaborate vetting process? Although President Carter's Georgia friends may have received some benefit of the doubt on any number of issues, the problems Lance faced were glaring. As a result of routine bank examinations, the Calhoun Bank's operations had been scrutinized as far back as 1974. After securing agreements to correct unsound banking practices, the bank examiners eventually referred possible violations of campaign laws to the Department of Justice in early 1976. The US Attorney's Office in Atlanta, after looking into allegations that Lance had violated federal banking laws during his race for governor, closed the case against him on December 2, 1976, after Carter's election but before Carter formally took office.[33] Had the US Attorney's Office been pressured to make a decision that would satisfy their new boss? Although the comptroller of the currency, John G. Heimann, did brief the chairman of the Senate Governmental Affairs Committee, Senator Abraham Ribicoff (D-Conn.), concerning the investigations, he predicted to Ribicoff that the investigation of Lance would probably go nowhere. Unfortunately, Heimann briefed Ribicoff even before the IRS had completed its own full report.

The Senate Budget Committee—still in friendly Democratic hands—had also been derelict in its duties. At his Senate confirmation hearings, Lance agreed to divest himself of $3.3 million in National Bank of Georgia stock holdings in accordance with President-elect Carter's insistence that his nominees meet heightened standards for avoiding conflicts of interest. Yet some negative publicity about the NBG eventually ensued, leading Lance to seek an extension from the Senate committee to wait beyond the December 31, 1977, deadline to sell the stock. The committee dutifully deferred. Then, in an ironic twist, President Carter himself intervened on Lance's behalf with Ribicoff,[34] undermining his own publicly articulated commitment to the new standards.

Lance then violated another promise he had made to the Senate committee when he continued to meet with NBG officials and to lobby senators on their behalf concerning proposed legislation, an inexcusable instance of peddling influence.[35] Finally, Lance secured a loan for himself from the First National

Bank of Chicago by putting up the NBG funds that he was originally supposed to divest. Carter played no role at all in the final two indiscretions, but his continued defense of the OMB chief only fed the perception that Carter was insensitive to the need to avoid even the appearance of impropriety, and it led some members of the press to believe that the new president had a blind spot for his old Georgia friends. The *New York Times* editorial argued that the affair was in part a "self-inflicted wound" related to Carter's standards of ethical conduct; *Time* magazine called Bert Lance a threat to the Carter administration's "whole aura of stern probity."[36]

In the end, the widening investigation of Lance proceeded along various fronts. The comptroller of the currency undertook an inquiry into allegations of overdrafts by Lance at the Calhoun Bank beginning in 1974. The IRS conducted its own internal investigation to determine whether the Treasury Department had handled earlier reviews of Lance objectively and whether individuals in Lance's office had failed to follow proper procedures. The Securities and Exchange Commission launched an investigation of its own. Until December 2, 1976, the Criminal Division of the Ford administration's Justice Department had also been investigating the Calhoun Bank's handling of overdrawn accounts maintained by Lance, with a special interest in the way these funds were used to support the Bert Lance for Governor Campaign Committee. Finally, as a result of that investigation's being closed on December 2, 1976, a few interested senators began their own inquiry into whether the US attorney's decision had been improperly influenced by Carter's transition team. Their suspicions were raised by the revelation that Lance's appointment as head of OMB had been announced barely twenty-four hours after the Department of Justice investigation was officially closed.[37]

Lance received some good news on August 18, 1977, when the comptroller of the currency issued his 394-page report: though Lance's various practices raised serious issues, there was no evidence of "indictable criminal conduct" per se.[38] President Carter tried to declare the matter over at a press conference held that exact same day.[39] Unfortunately for Carter and Lance, this reprieve was short-lived. The report had charged Lance with unsound banking practices. In a letter to President Carter dated September 3, 1977, Senators Ribicoff and Percy (R-Ill.), the chairman and the ranking Republican on the Government Affairs Committee respectively, requested that the matter be sent to the Justice Department for "investigation of the US Attorney's action and the possible need to reopen the case." They told Carter that there was information "which would appear to substantiate allegations that the Justice Department acted improperly in failing to fully investigate potential criminal violations of Federal banking law."[40] The two senators focused on the allegations arising from the use of bank loans in Lance's campaign for the governorship. Their committee elected to hold formal hearings on the issue on September 7 and 8, 1977. Meanwhile, the *New York Times* continued to charge Lance with not making full financial disclosures about his business interests.[41]

Perhaps the final straw for the White House came when it learned of the perks Lance had received that smelled of excessive special treatment. On July 9, 1975, the NBG had, pursuant to an oral agreement, purchased an airplane for Lance (then the bank's president) for $120,000. During and immediately after Jimmy Carter's campaign for the presidency a year later, the board of directors of NBG "encouraged Mr. Lance to use the aircraft in whatever way would benefit the bank in its promotion of state-wide agri-business development, increased correspondent bank relationships, and multi-bank holding company possibilities."[42] Lance used the plane in this way on numerous occasions beginning in July 1975 and continuing up through the 1976 presidential election and the transition period.

Soon after Jimmy Carter's election as president in November of 1976, Lance went from being an influential bank president in Georgia to being first a candidate and then later the nominee to head the OMB. Meanwhile, his use of the NBG aircraft continued up through January of 1977. Even after Lance's nomination to head the OMB on December 3, 1976, the list of travelers on the NBG plane included Secretary of State designate Cyrus Vance and various members of the presidential transition team. In fact, on January 3, 1977, Lance himself flew along with Congressman Jack Brooks (D-Tex.) down to Plains, Georgia, to discuss reorganization issues with the president elect. Others took the plane during the course of the campaign to get to debates or the conventions or to meet with Jimmy Carter near certain campaign events.[43] Many of these trips had only tenuous and indirect links to the business of the bank.

In August of 1977 the Office of the Comptroller of the Currency, in the process of completing its other inquiry into Lance's banking practices, assumed responsibility as well for investigating whether all the flights taken on the NBG plane were properly chargeable to the bank as deductible business expenses.[44] If not, both the bank and Lance would at least be required to amend their tax returns, and Lance would be required to pay a portion of the expenses back to NBG. But in early September, Comptroller Heimann determined that his office should refer the NBG airplane affair to the Justice Department as well. Instead of subsiding, the Lance affair was beginning to mushroom. Carter's White House counsel, Robert Lipshutz, warned the president that calls for a special prosecutor were imminent.[45]

That President Carter had been swept into some of these matters—he took several flights on the NBG plane while he was running for president in 1976 and he had intervened frequently in the Senate on Lance's behalf—made dismissing Lance a necessity. Lance testified before the Senate committee on the morning of September 15, 1977, accusing the committee of violating his rights. Though public opinion appeared to be shifting in his favor, White House officials including Chief of Staff Hamilton Jordan and Press Secretary Jody Powell, along with Vice President Walter Mondale, urged President Carter to force Lance's resignation to avoid further embarrassment to the administration. When Senate Majority Leader Robert Byrd joined in their judgment, Carter reluctantly acquiesced.[46]

On September 21, 1977, Lance formally resigned as director of the Office of Management and Budget. Questions abound concerning how he had made it as far as he had—he had served nine months as director before the problems became insurmountable. All of the charges concerned activities predating his tenure at the OMB. So why had the Senate Banking Committee been so willing to accept Lance's excuses, rather than aggressively investigating him *before* he began to serve? Evidently a Senate committee not quite up to its job gave far too much deference to the Democratic president's nominees.

Leaving the administration did not end Lance's troubles, however. The comptroller's investigation was referred to the Justice Department, which continued its investigation until 1979. Early on, the Justice Department used a three-lawyer special team to conduct the inquiry, which included a special computerized analysis of all of Lance's financial transactions.[47] By late 1978, however, Griffin Bell's close relationships with both the president and Lance had become a source of concern among congressional leaders from both sides of the aisle. Responding to the outcry, in March of 1979 Bell named a special counsel, Paul Jerome Curran, to address the issue on behalf of the Justice Department. Curran began under a grant of limited authority, needing the deputy attorney general's approval to file charges against targeted individuals. But when congressional Republicans continued to complain, Bell expanded Curran's province to include prosecutorial authority; he thus became a "special prosecutor" with the same powers enjoyed by Cox and Jaworski. Nearly seven months later, on October 16, 1979, Curran formally cleared Lance of diverting National Bank of Georgia funds to the Carter campaign.[48]

In 1981 Lance returned to the Calhoun National Bank, this time as its chairman. If any members of Congress were still wondering whether a revamped special prosecutors law was still necessary three years after Nixon's resignation, the Lance affair served as the latest exhibit in the case made by proponents of the new law. Of course those same proponents were hard-pressed to complain about Curran's investigation, which included a review of 80,000 documents, and interviews with numerous high-level witnesses, including a four-hour meeting with President Carter himself.

Dr. Peter Bourne: The War on Drugs Begins at Home

The first case of executive branch wrongdoing for which the new independent counsel provisions of the newly passed Ethics in Government Act of 1978 seemed made to order involved Dr. Peter G. Bourne, the first person to hold the title of "drug czar," or, more formally, of "director of national drug control policy." Bourne was yet another on the long list of Carter's transplanted friends from Georgia, although their relationship did not date back to Carter's boyhood. Born in England, Bourne attended medical school at Emory University, where he graduated in 1962. After serving as a captain in the US Army and doing a stint in Vietnam, Bourne returned to Georgia in 1971, at which point he became active in Democratic politics. After helping to set up Georgia's first state-wide drug treatment program during the administration of Governor Carter, he was named deputy campaign director for Carter's successful presidential run in 1976. Given Bourne's experience and high-level connections, it came as little surprise when President Carter named him his special assistant on health issues, and then later, the nation's first official drug czar.

The drug czar's problems began on July 19, 1978, when the *Washington Post* reported the arrest of a Washington, DC, woman who had attempted to buy the drug Quaalude with an allegedly illegal prescription written by Bourne.[49] Bourne's response to law enforcement officials—that he had written the prescription to a fictitious person to avoid embarrassing the patient for whom the drug was intended—provided little reassurance to his critics, given his position as the administration's point man in the drug wars. The problems for Bourne only increased when syndicated columnist Jack Anderson reported that Bourne had snorted cocaine at a party sponsored by the National Organization for the Reform of Marijuana Laws (known as NORML) in a DC suburb in December of 1977.

Bourne took leave from his White House duties to combat the various charges.[50] Virginia authorities investigated the cocaine incident and found no hard evidence that Bourne had violated the law, though the Georgia Board of Medicine did issue a reprimand against him several months later.[51] Because Bourne had admitted to writing the false prescription, that issue became a more serious matter for him, and ultimately for the White House as well. Bourne's claim that he was neither legally nor morally wrong, because he acted for a real patient and in her best interests, was beside the point. Certainly writing false prescriptions is a clear violation of state laws and the DC code, but prosecutors generally don't prosecute doctors who engage in such actions in the interest of the patient, so long as the doctor is not a repeat offender. Of course Bourne's status as the drug czar tended to render all these conventions moot in the current political environment. Even incidents of such relatively minor wrongdoing might benefit occasionally from the perspective of an independent counsel, not just to ensure that no person is above the law, but also to ensure that no offense is below it, either.

In truth, Bourne's days as a highly visible Carter administration official were numbered from the outset; no one could survive the political fallout of being a drug czar suspected of actively taking illegal drugs and violating the rules for prescribing legal ones. In mid-August 1978, both Virginia and US prosecutors announced they would not charge Bourne for writing a false name on a prescription.[52] Though Bourne was free from the law, questions remained about whether he had benefited from special treatment. The reprimand of the Georgia State Medical Board only fueled the perception that he had. The *Christian Science Monitor* opined that precisely because Bourne was the drug czar, his case had "become symbolic of lapsed integrity at the top . . . the nation needs a sense that the full legal process has been pursued."[53] In 1979 Bourne resigned as drug czar to become an assistant secretary-general at the United Nations.

A Mission to Niger Goes Awry: Valerie Plame and the Yellowcake Uranium Forgery Allegations

In late 2002 and early 2003, the Bush administration was engaged in a prolonged public relations effort to persuade Congress and leaders of foreign countries that Saddam Hussein was procuring nuclear material for the purpose of creating weapons of mass destruction, all in defiance of United Nations sanctions against Iraq. Pursuant to this effort, in testimony before the Senate Foreign Relations Committee, CIA Director George Tenet and Secretary of State Colin Powell both cited Iraq's attempted purchase of yellowcake uranium from Niger. President Bush repeated the charge in his 2003 State of the Union address, citing intelligence sources from Great Britain.

Almost a year earlier, in February 2002, during a period when Niger was steadfastly denying the charges, the CIA had sent former American diplomat Joseph Wilson to that country to investigate the claims himself. After meeting with various government officials and examining the evidence, Wilson concluded that it was in fact highly doubtful for both practical and political reasons that any such transaction ever took place. Apparently, CIA officials who had met with Wilson had kept his report in the CIA's counter proliferation department without passing it on to Tenet. Meanwhile, Wilson grew increasingly frustrated when the administration continued to cite the yellowcake purchases. Thus in July 2003, more than four months after the war in Iraq was launched, Wilson went public with his findings. In an op-ed piece in the *New York Times* under the headline "What I Didn't Find in Iraq," Wilson stated his position that the Bush administration had manipulated intelligence about Saddam Hussein's nuclear program to justify its invasion of Iraq.[54]

A bipartisan Senate committee would later conclude that Tenet in fact had not seen the report earlier. Thus in December 2002, he continued to believe that the case against Hussein for building weapons of mass destruction was a "slam dunk." Once he learned of the report, Tenet asked Deputy National Security Advisor Stephen Hadley to remove the reference to the yellowcake purchases from President Bush's speeches. (Those requests were ignored). On March 7, 2003, the International Atomic Energy Agency reported to the United Nations its finding that documents released by Italian intelligence sources that originally appeared to confirm Hussein's purchase of yellowcake uranium were in fact forged.[55] Who forged the documents? In a 2003 article in the *New Yorker*, Seymour Hersh argued that the forgery might have been a deliberate entrapment by current and former CIA officers to settle a score against Vice President Dick Cheney and other neoconservatives.[56] Others placed blame on Michael Ledeen, a former National Security Council consultant; for his part, Ledeen denied all such charges.

The monumental stakes in such a controversy might well have justified taxpayer expense for numerous investigations. Yet Jay Rockefeller (D-W.Va.), vice chairman of the Senate Select Committee on Intelligence, recognized the difficult issues inherent in trying to investigate Italian intelligence sources. He declined calls for a Senate inquiry, opting instead to defer to an FBI investigation. Fears that the findings of the investigation might influence the 2004 presidential election also demanded caution, and Rockefeller's own committee (run by the Republicans) was not likely or willing to carry the ball amid such controversy. As expected, the FBI's conclusions were vague and subject to heavy qualifications. On December 3, 2005, the *Los Angeles Times* reported that the FBI's initial investigation had to that point found no evidence of foreign government involvement in the forgeries. But the bureau did not interview Italian military intelligence official Rocco Martino, who was a central figure in a parallel drama unfolding in Rome.

Rather than steadily pursuing the source of the forgeries, media attention in the fall of 2003 shifted to allegations that White House aides had leaked CIA undercover agent Valerie Plame's name to the media as a means of exacting revenge against Wilson (Plame's husband) for going public with accusations that Bush had twisted the evidence of yellowcake uranium for his own purposes.

Attorney General John Ashcroft was the first to head up the investigation into who leaked Plame's name to the press. His formal inquiry began on September 26, 2003, in response to CIA requests for such an investigation. In this instance, only an outside prosecutor would have the leverage to demand that top White House aides fully cooperate. Ashcroft's prior relationship with Karl Rove (the attorney general had hired Rove to assist him in three political campaigns in Missouri) raised red flags for officials working under the attorney general. Finally, after Ashcroft recused himself entirely, Deputy Attorney General James B. Comey on December 30, 2003, appointed the US attorney for the Northern District of Illinois, Patrick Fitzgerald, as special counsel under Department of Justice Regulation 28 C.F.R. Part 600. Through this provision, Fitzgerald was delegated "all the authority of the attorney general."

Once in place, Fitzgerald was able to take actions in the course of the investigation that would have been impossible in the course of a more routine prosecution. For example, he subpoenaed the telephone records of Air Force One, and interviewed both Vice President Cheney and President Bush (although not separately and not under oath) to get their testimony. Some of Fitzgerald's legal filings in 2004 also contained pages blanked out for security reasons, which implied to some observers that he had investigated just how far national security had actually been compromised by the release of Plame's name to the public. Finally, Fitzgerald was willing to hold media members in contempt of court—even when doing so brought some sympathy to their plight—while simultaneously bringing prolonged attention to the investigation and heightening the embarrassment it might cause for White House officials.

Fitzgerald's investigation resulted in the conviction of Lewis Libby, Vice President Cheney's chief of staff, on counts of perjury, obstruction of justice, and making false statements to federal investigators. On July 2, 2007, President Bush granted a measure of clemency to Libby by commuting his sentence. Meanwhile, Rove was never indicted in the CIA leak scandal. Clearly no attorney general could have escaped suspicion of rampant bias had the decision not to indict Rove—an extremely controversial figure who played some role in the scandal—remained a strictly internal affair. In this instance the Republican-controlled Congress was not in a frame of mind to push the envelope or, alternatively, to complain to the executive branch about its malaise-filled approach to investigating the scandal.

chapter 6:

What's a Little Prosecution among Friends?

A Framework for Political Analysis

On April 7, 1995, Independent Counsel Joseph DiGenova filed his final report in the case of Elizabeth Tamposi and the passport search scandal. DiGenova had spent more than two years investigating allegations that Bush administration officials had encouraged State Department officials to conduct an illegal search of Bill Clinton's passport file during the 1992 general election campaign. DiGenova's report included several strong statements criticizing the State Department's mishandling of the passport matter at "virtually every step," though in the final analysis he concluded that no criminal acts had actually been committed by State Department personnel or anyone else involved.[1] As significant as DiGenova's specific findings in the passport files case were, however, what drew the most attention was his overall commentary on the use of the independent counsel law in this and other cases where the alleged crimes seemed minor: "A substantial case can be made that had the . . . investigation been conducted in a more deliberate fashion, with greater attention to the facts developed, no referral to the Department of Justice would have been made, and no independent counsel would have been sought or appointed."[2]

DiGenova's analysis of the circumstances that led to his own appointment, which was critical of the reasons for resorting to an independent counsel, was strikingly candid. Most independent counsels seek to justify their role in the process by following every lead—no matter how small—and by conveniently ignoring significant considerations (such as the dollar cost of the investigation or the political costs already borne by the targets) that under normal circumstances would militate against continued aggressive investigation of charges by prosecutors with limited resources. Yet DiGenova stunningly did just the opposite, albeit after his office had spent $2.2 million in taxpayer money to reach his unusual conclusion.

DiGenova's criticism of the earlier phases of the investigation focused on the mostly chaotic efforts of State Department Inspector General Sherman Funk to meet an arbitrary investigation deadline imposed by statute. Funk's struggles resulted in premature calls for the appointment of an independent counsel. Indeed, DiGenova's investigation, which convinced him that his own appointment had been unnecessary, helped lay the groundwork for more widespread criticism of the process nearly a decade later, during congressional hearings that preceded Congress's decision to allow the statute to lapse in June 1999. The Office of the Attorney General and other internal investigators expressed frustrations similar to DiGenova's over the haphazard conduct of preliminary investigations that had preceded the appointment of other independent or special prosecutors.

Since Watergate, the threat of a special prosecutor seems to lurk around every corner of the political system. An outer circle attorney general offers the best hope of effectively distinguishing between the unusual cases that require a special prosecutor and the vast majority of other cases that do not. The downside of appointing an outer circle attorney general is that the head of the Justice Department may be forced to render decisions that make the White House and its allies uncomfortable. Such decisions may in turn make the attorney general an outcast within his own administration, unable to influence policymaking, judicial appointments, or other areas of public interest. Yet our current system, which relies so heavily on the special prosecutor mechanism as a backstop to gain public confidence, requires that administrations make that tradeoff.

In Search of Due Process

In *Due Process of Law: A Brief History*, scholar John Orth draws upon English common law and the law of ancient Rome to establish a fundamental proposition of due process: that no one may be the judge of his or her own affairs.[3] According to Orth, judicial review in America was a natural outgrowth of this principle. Yet the focus on judicial review ignores other critically important decisions that prosecutors make before any form of judicial review even arises: (1) whether to launch a preliminary investigation in the first place, (2) whether to seek a formal indictment against a suspect, and (3) how to frame the charges against a defendant. In a case of alleged political corruption, the decision by a prosecutor to name someone publicly as a suspect, or to launch the investigative process against such a person, may well ruin the target's career, regardless of how the case concludes. At a minimum it makes life exceedingly difficult for an official whose legitimacy in office depends largely on maintaining continued public support.

Professor Katy Harriger's comprehensive treatment of special prosecutors offers yet another basis on which to assess the fairness of the investigative process: its capacity to avoid conflicts of interest. In her book *The Special Prosecutor in American Politics*, Harriger posits that in "[concentrating] law enforcement and all other legal functions in one Department of Justice," the United States, unlike many other free nations, puts undue pressure on the person who must preside as attorney general, as he or she must wrestle with and address political conflicts on a frequent basis.[4] Can the Justice Department continue to play a significant role in public corruption cases when even the appearance of a conflict can raise the public's ire?

Whether the greatest threat to due process arises through lack of impartiality or through conflicts of interest or other improprieties, the media and the public will view the sight of an attorney general investigating his or her own appointing president's administration as a new wart on whatever scandal is in progress. John Mitchell, Edwin Meese, and Alberto Gonzales are only the most recent attorneys general whose actions (or lack of them) have undermined the due process of law. In ordinary circumstances, career prosecutors and long-term Justice Department officials acting with only limited interference from above are in the best position to ensure executive branch officials' being treated like any other suspects or defendants. These career prosecutors and lower-level officials establish the department's law enforcement philosophy and the unwritten guidelines that define the "routine" or "normal" procedures governing its application.

By contrast, elevating political corruption to its own special place in law enforcement—a place that requires outside prosecutors for support—ensures that there will be no principle guiding the department's prosecution of these special cases. Due process of law is threatened not only when the executive branch is forced to investigate itself, but also when systematic and routine processes are replaced with fly-by-the-seat-of-your-pants justice exercised by a prosecutor who works outside the normal rules of accountability. To ensure that similar cases are treated similarly, criminal law enforcement requires referring to the current administration's past cases and precedents. The attorney general who was responsible for them in the first place is thus far better equipped than anyone else to ensure that an adequate level of due process is maintained.

Indeed, critical decision-making in public corruption cases begins with the attorney general, who must make a series of important decisions before an outside counsel ever gets named, and who must lead the way in (1) applying for an independent counsel (usually to a three-judge panel under the now-defunct statute), (2) appointing a special prosecutor who has the autonomy to investigate and prosecute without undue interference from the White House or elsewhere, or (3) electing not to apply for any form of outside counsel.

Pres. Richard Nixon's administration defined the problem of executive branch wrongdoing and Justice Department corruption for a generation of reformers to come—the Watergate cover-up became the symbol of executive corruption against which all transgressions would be measured and understood for the foreseeable future. In Nixon's case, a plague of corruption spread throughout the White House, and it eventually affected the former attorney general, John Mitchell, to such a degree that the administration became paralyzed. The appointment of special prosecutor Archibald Cox on May 19, 1973, at the urging of new Attorney General Elliot Richardson and the Congress, was the immediate result. President Nixon's decision to fire Cox five months later brought renewed attention to the administration's inability to engage in an honest investigation of Watergate.

The first independent counsel law enacted in 1978, the reauthorization acts of 1982 and 1987, and the revisions to the law enacted in 1994 all addressed this model of corruption by providing a statutory means of turning to outsiders for discretionary powers of investigation and prosecution. The Ethics in Government Act of 1978 specified that a special prosecutor need follow Department of Justice guidelines only "to the extent that the special prosecutor deems appropriate."[5] In other words, the guidelines were completely discretionary. The attorney general was vested with the sole power to request the appointment of an independent counsel under the 1978 act; similarly, he or she alone was authorized to remove a special prosecutor, and only for "extraordinary impropriety."[6] This last provision was aimed directly at the White House's decision to remove Archibald Cox during Watergate. Even under such an extreme circumstance as that envisioned under the act, the attorney general could still not remove a special prosecutor without submitting a report on the reasons why to congressional committees and to the three-judge panel that had appointed him. Finally, under the 1978 legislation, judicial review of the removal would also be available to an aggrieved special prosecutor.

The Independent Counsel Reauthorization Act of 1987 further limited the discretion of the attorney general to initiate a preliminary investigation determining whether a special prosecutor was even necessary—the attorney general would thereafter be required to launch such an inquiry whenever he or she received information that an official "[might] have violated" a federal criminal law.[7] Notably, however, the 1987 legislation had no impact whatsoever on the discretionary powers of the special prosecutor or independent counsel named under the act. In fact, it confirmed that the Justice Department was required to respond to requests from the independent counsel for assistance and for access to and use of any resources and personnel necessary to perform independent counsel duties.

Finally, the 1994 reauthorization retained the attorney general's ultimate authority to launch preliminary investigations and to make the final decision as to whether to apply for an independent counsel. At the same time, it imposed new cost constraints on the independent counsel, mandating that the comptroller audit the independent counsel's financial statements and report the results to Congress. Most important, the 1994 legislation mandated a level of consultation between the Justice Department and the independent counsel; under the new provisions, administrative personnel and even some prosecutors may be reassigned to assist the independent counsel in criminal matters.

None of these various adjustments to the act address the larger question of how best to protect the Justice Department against threats to its legitimacy and independence so that it can conduct its own inquiries in the vast majority of cases and also conduct more effective preliminary investigations in the cases that warrant them. The attorney general will not always be a source of problems and may in some cases offer the best hope for resolving them. Yet that is possible only by maintaining a proper distance from the White House. But when the Attorney General emerges from the White House itself, threats to the integrity of the Department of Justice are inevitable. Edwin Meese and Alberto Gonzales arrived at the Justice Department after serving immediately beforehand as White House counselors. Meese had maintained a close friendship with Reagan and Gonzales had maintained one with Bush over a period of several years. Could anyone be surprised when, in the course of serving as attorney general, neither could completely abandon his role as a loyal supporter of White House policies in favor of becoming a more neutral and independent arbiter, capable of confronting and challenging the president as necessary?

Many others who have headed the Justice Department during the past century—Herbert Brownell during the Eisenhower administration, and more recently Edward Levi, Janet Reno, and Michael Mukasey—rose to their positions not on the basis of any close past association with the president, but due to their unique experiences and qualifications. In fact, none of these people had ever before served the sitting president in any professional capacity, and thus each of them was in a position to offer truly independent leadership to the Justice Department. Unlike the other cabinet officials, the attorney general is obligated as the federal government's chief law enforcement officer to make decisions that may conflict with the interests of the administration as a whole and the White House in particular. Is the Justice Department up to this particular challenge? The question is an interesting one, since the Senate Judiciary Committee, which is the first body to weigh in on each attorney general appointment, has only rarely inquired into the personal connections between the nominee and the president—and even then its members would not consider any such association, no matter how close, as essentially disqualifying.

Attorneys General and the Decision to Prosecute

Not all inner circle attorneys general perform badly or end up in disgrace. Just thirty-five years before Watergate, Attorney General Robert Jackson worshipped his political mentor, Franklin Delano Roosevelt. Jackson's short tenure at the Justice Department proved successful enough to win him a nomination to the US Supreme Court and easy confirmation. And Attorney General Robert F. Kennedy was willing to brazenly use the Justice Department's authority in a way that was politically problematic for his brother's administration, such as when he pursued corrupt southern electoral officials who had strong ties to the Democratic Party base, and when he aggressively investigated and prosecuted a number of unsavory persons associated with the vice president. RFK's close connections to the White House rendered him fearless, rather than beholden to his bosses. Administrations would not so easily escape the pitfalls of such a dangerous arrangement in contemporary times.

The single most important factor in predicting success or failure is the attorney general's connections within the executive branch—does he or she hail from the president's "outer" or "inner" circle? Or can the attorney general be classified as an "Oval Office attorney general" who served the current president in a close, advisory role? Fortunately, this is also the factor over which the president enjoys the most control; only a handful of nominees to head the Justice Department have ever been rejected outright by the Senate. All told, that demonstrates a remarkable degree of Senate deference to the president's selection of attorney general.

Moreover, when the Senate has occasionally offered some amount of resistance to a candidate, close personal or professional connections to the chief executive have rarely been the obstacle. Senators complained about nominee Robert Kennedy's inexperience in 1961; they complained about Edwin Meese's "questionable personal ethics"; and those who opposed Alberto Gonzales's nomination in early 2005 complained about the White House counselor's controversial interpretations of the Geneva Convention and its rules about torture, which he had offered in the service of Pres. George W. Bush during the administration's first term. All three of those nominees were eventually confirmed.

A president can of course forego his power to name an intimate as attorney general, choosing instead one with whom he has no prior connections whatsoever. In doing so, he takes an important first step toward empowering the Justice Department to act boldly and forcefully to investigate allegations of public corruption without constantly resorting to special prosecutors. In truth, the political environment surrounding an administration as it addresses serious allegations of executive branch wrongdoing shifts dramatically depending on the connections the chosen attorney general has within the executive branch.

In an era when the decision to name special prosecutors or independent counsels has become a regular function of US attorneys general, a president who risks appointing an outer circle attorney general offers the most effective means of fulfilling that function. While the president may privately want an ally at the Justice Department, a tainted or compromised head of Justice can invite serious trouble for the White House with decisions that are second-guessed, publicly criticized, and in some cases undermined outright. The White House may rightfully expect *more* special prosecutors to be appointed when an inner circle attorney general is unable to declare his opposition to such appointments with credibility. Edward Levi's outsider status offered President Ford crucial protection from critics as his administration attempted to rebuild the Justice Department after Watergate; and when Levi was forced in late 1976 to make two critical decisions about resorting to special prosecutors, he did so in both cases without bending to political pressures. Janet Reno's decisions over the course of her eight years as attorney general made enemies of both Republicans and Democrats; by the time her tenure was over, the power of her office to render independent decisions about such appointments remained intact, though the lapsing of the independent counsel statute meant that subsequent attorneys

Scenario 1. The Outer Circle Attorney General: Insulated from Threats to Autonomy

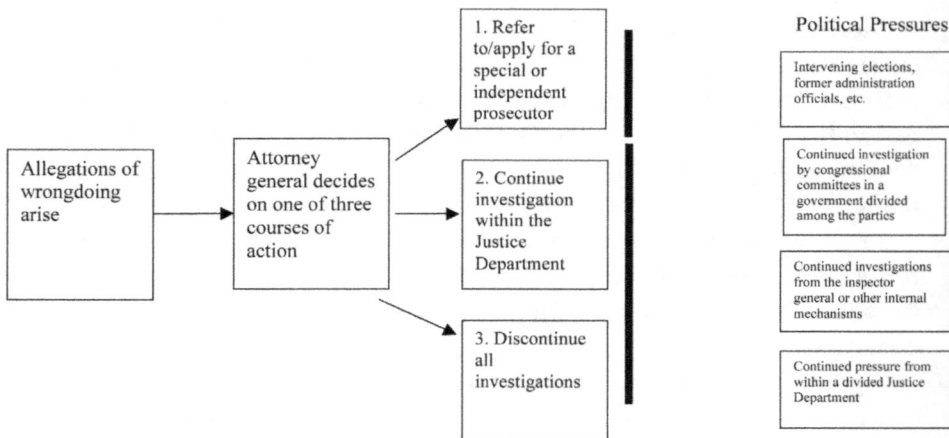

general would be naming nonstatutory special prosecutors for the foreseeable future. Finally, only outer circle attorneys general like Richard Thornburgh (during the Reagan administration) and Michael Mukasey have been in a position to clean up political messes caused by predecessors too close to the president.

Scenario 1 depicts the barrier that exists between an outer circle attorney general and the political pressures that might otherwise threaten his or her autonomy to make decisions consistent with due process. Regardless of what decisions the attorney general ultimately makes, he or she sits in a strong position to defend them on the basis of objective criteria discussed in chapters 3 through 5, including these:

- Whether the president, the vice president, or White House family members are under investigation
- Whether Justice Department officials are under investigation or involved in the wrongdoing
- Whether the official under investigation is a current official or a past official
- Whether the investigation will occur during politically sensitive times, such as when a presidential election is approaching
- Whether divided party government is in place

And there are other criteria as well. Because friends and enemies of the White House may attempt to politicize high-profile cases of misconduct, criticism of the attorney general's decision is likely to emerge from an assortment of different fronts: the opposition party in Congress, other investigators, and perhaps even frustrated constituencies within the Department of Justice. Thus while Janet Reno's decision to appoint a special prosecutor in the Henry Cisneros case pleased the FBI, which had been undermined by Cisneros, her decision not to appoint one in the 1996 campaign finance cases angered that same institution and its outspoken director, Louis Freeh.

Criticisms such as these—even those that may be bubbling up out of the attorney general's own agency—are inevitable in a democracy. Yet in the case of outer circle attorney generals, as Scenario 1 demonstrates, criticism does not tend to translate into more troubling developments that might threaten the Justice Department's role in the decision-making apparatus. Attorney General Edward Levi's decision to forego a special prosecutor in the Clarence Kelley case or the Martin Luther King surveillance scandal may have angered Jesse Jackson and other critics of the administration. It may have even bolstered the arguments made by supporters of a more comprehensive independent counsel regime prior to the enactment of one in 1978. But those reforms were directed not at the inadequacies of the attorney general or its Office of Professional

Political Pressures

Allegations of wrongdoing arise

Attorney general committed to separate the White House from the Justice Department decides on a course of action

1. Refers to a special or independent prosecutor — Continued pressure from congressional committees within a divided government

2. Continues investigations within the Justice Department — Continued investigations from the inspector general and other internal mechanisms

3. Discontinues all investigations — Continued pressure from within a divided Justice Department

Attorney general *not committed* to separate the White House from the Justice Department decides on a course of action

1. Refers to a special or independent prosecutor — Intervening elections, etc.

2. Continues investigations within the Justice Department — Pressure from congressional committees within a divided government

3. Discontinues all investigations — Investigations from the inspector general and other internal mechanisms

Pressure from within a divided Justice Department

1. Calls for a new attorney general?

2. Calls for new special prosecutor law?

3. Calls for reduced attorney general autonomy?

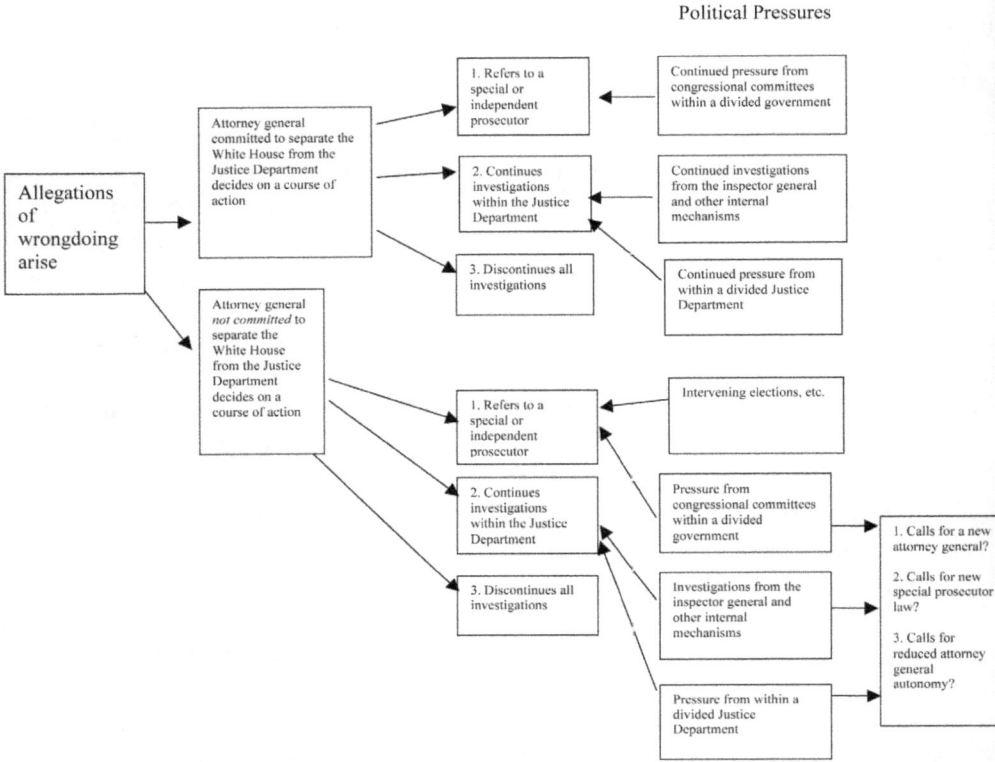

Responsibility. Janet Reno's status as an outsider attorney general allowed her to maintain credibility as an ardent opponent of the special prosecutor laws; it also allowed her to weather criticism of her decisions.

By contrast, in the case of the inner circle attorney general, as Scenario 2 shows, more serious outside pressures on autonomy and decision-making processes are invited, threatening whatever neutrality the attorney general may have brought to his or her position at the outset.

So long as strong political checks are in place, an inner circle attorney general is more likely to arrive at fair and just decisions, both within and outside the administration. While the inner circle attorney general may be committed to structure his or her agency to preclude (or at least reduce) the potential for too close a relationship between the White House and the Justice Department, that may not be enough to ensure a proper degree of independence in judgment. Thus an inner circle attorney general benefits indirectly from opposition party control in Congress, which supports scrutiny of the executive branch. Other

Allegations of wrongdoing arise → Attorney general is compromised from the outset regardless of the course of action he or she chooses →

1. Refers to a special or independent prosecutor → Potential for overreliance on special prosecutors

2. Continues investigations within the Justice Department

3. Discontinues all investigations

→ Justice Department is investigated →

1. Calls for a new attorney general?

2. Calls for new special prosecutor law?

3. Calls for reduced attorney general autonomy?

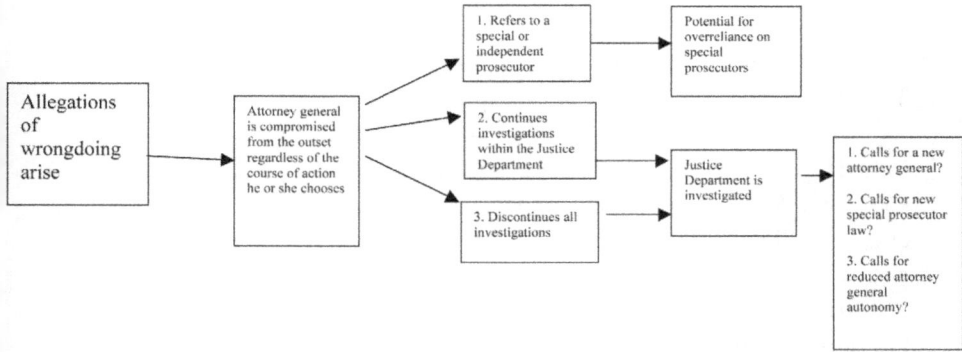

political checks arise from the nature of the wrongdoing: the administration may benefit politically if it arises from the acts of officials identified primarily with past administrations, or if it has been committed against the administration itself. The inner circle attorney general can survive charges of cronyism and favoritism if he or she is astute politically and willing to confront the president under appropriate circumstances. William French Smith was able to thrive in this capacity; John Mitchell, by contrast, proved too loyal for his own (and the administration's) good.

Finally, Scenario 3 describes a no-win situation for the administration, and perhaps for the White House as a whole. No matter what Oval Office attorneys general decide, they cast a dark shadow across their own agency because of the conflict inherent in their past and present positions that makes reviewing suspected administrative misconduct nearly impossible. If the attorney general tries to keep investigations within the agency, or to discontinue them altogether, the Justice Department must defend this decision publicly, and without much credibility to do so. Was there any type of misconduct that Attorneys General Edwin Meese or Alberto Gonzales could have investigated that would *not* have raised questions about their respective motives and agendas?

Internal Investigations in the Modern Era

It is impossible to know with any real certainty whether executive branch corruption is on the rise. Regardless, the modern presidency spends a considerable portion of its time on the defensive, answering to the public for every action it takes, or does not take, to address allegations of wrongdoing directed its way. Complicating this issue are the new realities that affect decision-making for those charged with investigating or prosecuting executive branch officials in the modern era.

1. Real Time Coverage of Legal Developments

The number of news media venues that now provide instantaneous coverage of news events has grown too large to count. CNN and MSNBC have been joined by Court TV and Fox News, as well as the countless traditional media-sponsored Web sites that are updated to reflect ongoing events continuously, and the millions of individuals who comprise the blogocracy that effectively ended Dan Rather's career at CBS. All law enforcement decisions, no matter how trivial, are made under this intense public glare, with the Internet media providing minute-by-minute commentary. A prosecutor must be increasingly sensitive to this new media environment.

2. Job Security for Attorneys General

A series of unbroken Supreme Court precedents beginning with *Myers v. United States* (1926) establishes the absolute and unqualified right of presidents to terminate purely executive officers without congressional approval. Attorneys general will always maintain a level of dependence on the chief executive who appointed them. At the same time, the intense media attention paid to every decision made by attorneys general affords them an unprecedented level of discretion. Practically speaking, can a dissatisfied president actually dismiss an attorney general for what he views as an inappropriate decision in the investigation or prosecution of executive branch wrongdoing? Only if that same president is willing to suffer a devastating political blow back in the court of public opinion. If the president persists despite all obstacles, history makes clear that the resulting public outrage may well embolden Congress to demand that any subsequent attorney general appoint a special prosecutor or some other outside counsel to investigate the original issue even more aggressively. Pres. Richard Nixon must have realized his error shortly after he forced the dismissal of Attorney General Elliot Richardson. Pres. Bill Clinton well understood the ramifications of dismissing Attorney General Janet Reno for affording too much investigative authority to Kenneth Starr. Firing Reno under those circumstances would have created a public relations fiasco nearly as dangerous to his presidency as Starr himself.

3. Protection from Unwarranted Dismissals for Special Prosecutors

The modern-day attorney general is not the only official in a position of unprecedented job security vis-à-vis the president. Although there is currently no statutory protection from dismissal, special or outside prosecutors are virtually immune from dismissal on the basis of their prosecutorial decisions. Any such dismissal would be interpreted as a cover-up in the news media, whether or not the prosecutorial decision itself could actually be justified objectively.

4. The Proliferation of Codes, Statutes, and Other Provisions against Public Corruption

Scandals and charges of executive branch wrongdoing arise more frequently now than they did in the past, in part because there are so many more ethics codes, conflict-of-interest statutes, and executive orders touching on public corruption. Whereas past attorneys general could go years without facing difficult questions on how to handle charges of wrongdoing in the executive ranks, such scandals have become part and parcel—on a continuous basis—of the modern-day attorney general's job responsibilities. The attorney general must be prepared to address these matters routinely and often, and without prolonged consultation.

5. The Proliferation of Agencies and Offices That Investigate Public Corruption

In the nineteenth and early twentieth centuries, when serious allegations of executive branch wrongdoing went public, they normally resulted in a congressional investigation and perhaps spurred some civil suits, but little more. Given the limited resources available to both branches of government, investigations often proceeded through a sort of horse trading between the Congress and the White House, with resignations, public admissions, and the like as the usual outcome. By contrast, today there is no shortage of government bodies dedicated to investigating allegations of executive branch wrongdoing. Inspectors general inside and outside the department where the wrongdoing occurs offer an initial line of defense. The Department of Justice maintains offices specifically charged with addressing public corruption; these include the Office of Professional Responsibility (which investigates lawyers) and the Office of Public Integrity.

All this points to a fundamental rule of modern-day Washington: given the never-ending parade of wrongdoing and the investigators ready to address it, executive branch officials and the administration they serve must have a simple and streamlined plan for addressing allegations from the first moments they arise. More than three decades after Watergate, it remains the case that officials get into more hot water ducking allegations than they do attempting to meet them head on. With the independent counsel statute now in remission, that truth has never been more apt. After all, an onslaught of "prosecutions among friends" offers no guarantee of anything beyond the busywork of executive branch officials investigating other executive branch officials.

Some Suggestions for Reform

In a *New York Times* essay published in March 2011, Rutgers University historian David Greenberg complained that so many books on social problems finish "with an obligatory prescription that is utopian, banal, unhelpful, or out of tune with the rest of the book."[8] I hope this book will not appear to join the ranks of those guilty of that offense: although I am going to conclude it by suggesting limited reforms to correct some of the worst executive branch excesses examined in earlier chapters, I believe these are reforms that are both reasonable in scope and entirely possible to achieve.

The keys to effective investigations and prosecutions are (1) a confident and neutral outer circle attorney general, (2) a Justice Department that abides by and supports neutral decision making by that same attorney general, and (3) a process of appointing special prosecutors that is quick, efficient, and likely to secure the public's trust from the outset. I offer these modest reforms to nudge the political system toward each of those three goals:

1. Increased Senate Scrutiny of Attorney General Nominees
During the past century, presidents have with little fanfare succeeded in appointing family members, poker-playing companions, former law firm colleagues, and other insiders to the post of attorney general. Given the serious nature of executive branch corruption and the increasingly important role an attorney general must play to combat it, the selection of the attorney general should undergo at least as much Senate scrutiny as that of a Supreme Court nominee, and perhaps more. How can that be accomplished? The Senate Judiciary Committee cannot continue to treat the appointment of the attorney general as a largely perfunctory event offering little more than a forum in which to criticize past Justice Department decisions. The attorney generalship requires a level of independence that is not usually required of other cabinet-level positions, and the confirmation process must reflect the consequent need for relatively stricter scrutiny. The following procedures would take a long stride in the direction of more intense Senate scrutiny:

- *Courtesy calls.* Like nominees to the Supreme Court, attorney general nominees should be willing to visit Senate Judiciary Committee members in their legislative chambers for more in-depth, behind-closed-doors discussions about their backgrounds, experiences, etc.

- *Witnesses at hearings.* Most confirmation hearings for cabinet-level positions do not include extensive witness lists—lists of individuals called to testify on behalf of or against the nominee. Officials who may have observed an attorney general nominee in past official capacities could shed important light on the nominee's ability to take independent positions in the face of counterpressures.
- *Proposed lists of special prosecutors.* When the Senate considered Elliot Richardson's appointment as attorney general in May of 1973, Richardson not only committed in advance to appointing Archibald Cox as Watergate special prosecutor, but on the fifth day of hearings actually appeared with Cox alongside him to answer questions about how he and the Justice Department planned to divide powers and responsibilities. The Senate Judiciary Committee should press nominees to submit a list of at least four or five possible special prosecutors that they would be willing to call on, depending on the circumstances. (Such a reform is possible only in the post–independent counsel act world, where the attorney general alone has the power to make this appointment.) Only by addressing the protocols for approaching public corruption in advance can senators be certain that the nominee has seriously thought about possible special prosecutors. This also allows the Senate to judge the nominee in part by the friends (in this case, in the form of outside prosecutors) that he or she keeps.

2. Bipartisan Staffing at the Justice Department

The missions and objectives of many agencies may alter course significantly with the arrival of a new president. By contrast, the basic functions of investigating and prosecuting executive branch misconduct should not vary widely from administration to administration. Just as Congress requires that the Federal Election Commission be divided between the major political parties (no more than three of six FEC commissioners can hail from the same party), Justice Department positions at the level of deputy attorney general, assistant attorney general, and division heads should also be divided between the two parties. This could help ensure that decisions about pursuing public corruption and executive wrongdoing are not made without first airing different political perspectives within the agency itself. Short of creating a brand new statutory regime of dubious constitutionality, the most effective way to accomplish this would be to require that the president elect submit his nominations for attorney general, deputy attorney general, and perhaps a handful of assistant attorneys general to the US Senate for confirmation—*at the exact same time.* The Senate Judiciary Committee sits in a strong enough position to insist that the president send what amounts to a slate of candidates who hail from different partisan affiliations; it can refuse to consider the attorney general nominee until those other names have been submitted, on the ground that a strong nominee from one party demands guarantees that the other side of the aisle be heard as well during internal decision-making processes. Accordingly, the confirmation hearings could thus be held in succession. Regardless, the need for a sufficiently independent Justice Department requires that the executive and the Senate treat appointments to that agency in a new and fundamentally different way.

3. Permanent Outside Counsels to Be Held on Retainer

The suggestion that attorney general nominees submit lists of names of possible special prosecutors at the time of their appointment would not be binding to any significant degree. Yet if the misconduct in question directly implicates the president or members of the Justice Department, there may be compelling reasons for the attorney general to fall back on the preapproved list. The so-called "preapproval" of these outside attorneys for duty as special prosecutors might come from the president, but would more likely be the attorney general's own. Regardless, the attorney general—rather than wading into the great unknown by searching for a special prosecutor on the fly—could look to a preapproved list of up to five outside counsels that would have been determined at the outset of the administration, *before* any particular misconduct had been discovered. Such a process would also offer the opportunity for other political entities (interest groups, leading members of Congress, etc.) to weigh in publicly on a counsel's qualifications and connections without regard to any particular factual context.

Certainly there is no quick fix to the problem of finding independent-thinking attorneys general and placing them in a position to make decisions that have a measure of legitimacy with the public. But attorneys general should not be able to sidestep the checks so crucial to a political system in which separate institutions must share powers, yet remain fundamentally apart. Theirs are problems inherent in the system they serve—problems that have been faced over and over by attorneys general past, and that will continue to be faced by attorneys general to come.

Notes

Preface

1. 487 US 654 (1988).
2. 487 US at 729 (Scalia, J., dissenting).
3. 487 US at 728–29.
4. See Nancy Baker, *Conflicting Loyalties: Law & Politics in the Attorney General's Office, 1789–1990* (Lawrence: University Press of Kansas, 1992); and Cornell Clayton, *The Politics of Justice: The Attorney General and the Making of Legal Policy* (Armonk, N.Y.: Sharpe, 1992).

Chapter 1: "Where There Is Smoke"

1. While living in Switzerland in 1983, Rich was indicted by the US government on charges of illegally trading with Iran as well as tax evasion. Rich never returned to the United States and remained on international most-wanted lists until President Clinton formally pardoned him on January 20, 2001. The controversy surrounding Rich's pardon stemmed in part from the fact that his former wife had made large donations to the Democratic Party and to the Clinton library while President Clinton was still in office.
2. See, for example, Carrie Johnson, "Waterboarding Is Torture, Holder Tells Senators," *Washington Post*, January 16, 2009.
3. "Holder: W. H. should act 'within dictates of wiretap law,'" *CNN Online*, January 15, 2009, http://politicalticker.blogs.cnn.com/2009/01/15/holder-presidents-should-act-within-the-dictates-of-surveillance-law/.
4. Josh Meyer, "Eric Holder: Waterboarding Is Torture: Attorney General Nominee Vows Review of Bush Administration Practices," *Chicago Tribune*, January 16, 2009; and "Holder Says He Learned from Marc Rich Pardon," *Associated Press*, January 15, 2009.
5. *Nomination of Eric H. Holder, Jr., Nominee to Be Attorney General of the United States: Hearing Before the Senate Committee on the Judiciary*, 111th Cong., 1st sess. (Jan. 15-16, 2000), 101-102.
6. See 28 C.F.R. Part 600 et seq. Under 28 U.S.C. 510, the attorney general has the power to make such provisions as he considers appropriate authorizing any other officer, employee, or agency of the Department of Justice of to perform any function of the attorney general.

7. Devlin Barrett, "Sen. Leahy Proposes Truth Panel on Bush Era Abuses," *Associated Press*, February 9, 2009.
8. Bobby Ghosh and Michael Scherer, "Obama: Still Opposed to Truth Commission," *Time*, May 21, 2009, http://www.time.com/time/nation/article/0,8559,1900035,00.html.
9. See, for example, the memo from the Office of the Assistant Attorney General to Alberto Gonzales: "Standards for Conduct of Interrogation," August 1, 2002, http://news.findlaw.com/wp/docs/doj/bybee80102mem.pdf.
10. 18 U.S.C. §§ 2340 et seq. implements in part the obligations of the United States under the Convention against Torture and Other Cruel, Inhuman and Degrading Treatment or Punishment. The most controversial of the Office of Legal Counsel memos (drafted in 2002) concluded that even though an act may be considered "cruel, inhuman, or degrading," it does not necessarily inflict the level of pain that 18 U.S.C. 2340 prohibits, and thus does not subject an interrogator to criminal prosecution. Additionally, it states that a defense of "necessity or self-defense may justify interrogation methods" that would otherwise violate 18 U.S.C. 2340.
11. Carrie Johnson and Joby Warrick, "Bush Anti-Terror Policies Get Reluctant Revisit," *Washington Post*, September 13, 2009.
12. 50 U.S.C. §§ 413 et seq. (1947 and as amended through 2004).
13. Jennifer Rubin, "Eric Holder's Justice Department: It's All Politics, All the Time," *Weekly Standard*, August 10, 2009, 22.
14. Carrie Johnson, "A Split at Justice on DC Voting Bill," *Washington Post*, April 1, 2009.
15. The two most notable examples were (1) Watergate special prosecutor Archibald Cox, who was terminated in October 1973 and (2) Whitewater special prosecutor Robert Fisk, terminated by the Special Division of the DC Circuit in 1994.
16. Benjamin Ginsburg and Martin Shefter, *Politics by Other Means* (New York: Norton, 1999), 163.
17. Carrie Johnson, "Prosecutor to Probe CIA Interrogations," *Washington Post*, August 25, 2009.
18. 28 U.S.C. §§ 595 et seq. (1994). The act actually lapsed for the first time in 1992, but was then reauthorized by an act of Congress on June 30, 1994.
19. 28 U.S.C. § 596 (as amended, 1996).
20. *The Future of the Independent Counsel Act: Hearings Before the Senate Committee on Government Affairs*, 106th Cong., 1st sess. (Feb. 24–Apr. 14, 1999).
21. 50 U.S.C. §§ 413 et seq. (1947 and as amended through 2004).
22. 42 U.S.C. Ch. 103, § 9601 et seq. (1980).

23. Statement of John Dingell, FG 22, WHORM Subject File, Ronald Reagan Presidential Library (cited hereafter as RRPL).

24. Ronnie Dugger, *On Reagan: The Man and His Presidency* (New York: McGraw-Hill, 1983), 75.

25. Haynes Johnson, *Sleepwalking through History: America in the Reagan Years* (New York: Anchor, 1992), 171.

26. Philip Shabecoff, "Rita Lavelle Gets 6-Month Term and Is Fined $10,000 for Perjury," *New York Times*, January 10, 1984.

27. Final Report of the Independent Counsel in re Henry G. Cisneros (August 13,1994), IV-6–IV-11.

28. Ibid., IV-110.

29. Ibid.

30. Ibid., IV-175.

31. Guy Gugliotta, "HUD Secretary Cisneros Sued for $256,000 by Former Lover," *Washington Post*, July 30, 1994.

32. Final Report of the Independent Counsel in re Henry G. Cisneros, V-28.

33. Ibid., V-29.

34. Ibid., V-64.

35. Ibid., V-69.

36. Brock Brower, "Bud McFarlane: Semper Fi," *New York Times*, January 22, 1989.

37. John Ehrman, *The Eighties: America in the Age of Reagan* (New Haven: Yale University Press, 2005), 140.

38. President Reagan's initial statement to the Tower Commission, which Reagan established on November 26, 1986, to investigate the Iran-Contra affair, confirmed that he had approved the shipment. Later, Reagan said he "didn't remember" when asked about approving it. See John Tower, Edmund S. Muskie, and Brent Snowcroft, *The Tower Commission Report: The Full Text of the President's Special Review Board* (New York: Bantam, 1987). See also *Final Report of the Independent Counsel for Iran/Contra Matters*, vol. 1 (August 4, 1983).

39. Final Report of the Independent Counsel on Iran-Contra Matters, vol. 1, Investigations and Prosecutions (August 4, 1993).

40. Ibid., ch. 1 ("U.S. v. Robert C. McFarlane"), 79–80.

41. Bob Schieffer and Gary Paul Gates, *The Acting President* (New York: Plume, 1990), 265.

42. Ibid., 283.

43. Ann Wroe, *Lives, Lies and the Iran-Contra Affair* (Taurus, 1992), 216.

44. Schieffer, *Acting President*, 289.

45. Final Report of the Independent Counsel for Iran/Contra Matters, vol. 1, Investigations and Prosecutions (August 4, 1993), 76–77.

46. Wroe, *Lives, Lies*, 219.

47. House Select Committee to Investigate Covert Arms Transactions with Iran, Report of the Congressional Committees Investigating the Iran-Contra Affair, with Supplemental, Minority and Additional Views, H.R. Rep. No. 100-433 (1987); see also Wroe, *Lives, Lies*, 38.

48. Wroe, *Lives, Lies*, 40–41.

49. Ibid., 41.

50. Ibid., 223.

51. Ibid., 227.

52. Final Report of the Independent Counsel for Iran-Contra Matters, vol. 1, 25.

53. Ehrman, *The Eighties*, 140.

54. Schieffer, *Acting President*, 290.

55. Ibid.

56. See, most notably, Katy Harriger, *Independent Justice: The Federal Special Prosecutor in American Politics* (Lawrence: University Press of Kansas, 1992).

57. 28 U.S.C. § 594(d)(1) (1996).

58. 28 U.S.R. pt. 600.5 (1999).

59. 28 C.F.R. pt. 607(b) (1999).

60. 28 C.F.R. pt. 607(d) (1999).

61. Lawrence Walsh, appointed in 1986 as independent counsel to investigate the Iran-Contra scandal, offered that exceedingly rare combination of extensive law enforcement experience with partisan neutrality. A former federal judge and high-level Justice Department official during the Eisenhower administration, Walsh was nevertheless considered the quintessential "Democrat who served Republicans," and thus provided limited passion for either side. See Ronald Ostrow, "Ex-Jurist to Head Iran-Contra," *Los Angeles Times*, May 20, 1990).

62. Maeva Marcus, *Truman and the Steel Seizure Case: The Limits of Presidential Power* (Durham: Duke University Press, 1994), 187.

63. Jack Goldsmith, *The Terror Presidency: Law and Judgment inside the Bush Administration* (New York: Norton, 2007).

64. Katy Harriger, *The Special Prosecutor in American Politics* (Lawrence: University Press of Kansas, 2000), 235.

65. 487 US 654 (1988).

66. 487 US 728–29 (Scalia, J., dissenting).

67. Benjamin Ginsberg and Matthew Crenson, *Downsizing Democracy* (Baltimore: Johns Hopkins University Press, 2002), 94.

68. Although an indictment or information theoretically precedes the decision to go to trial, prosecutors alone enjoy the power to decide that they will in fact present information to a grand jury, and in almost every instance the grand jury defers to the prosecution's requests.

69. Frank W. Miller and Frank J. Remington, *Prosecution: The Decision to Charge a Suspect with a Crime* (Boston: Little, Brown, 1969), 4.

70. John V. Orth, *Due Process of Law: A Brief History* (Lawrence: University Press of Kansas, 2003), 31.

71. Otto Kirchheimer, *Political Justice: The Use of Legal Procedures for Political Ends* (Princeton: Princeton University Press, 1961), 193–94.

72. The alternative may produce prejudice that cuts in one of two ways. Justice Department officials, as noted in the text, may be hesitant to conduct criminal investigations that prove embarrassing to the administrations they serve. Those same officials may also unduly target one official to make a public statement that the Justice Department does not condone government corruption. Under the latter scenario, the individual may actually become a victim, rather than a beneficiary of his or her political connections.

73. For a discussion of the short tenure of executive branch officials during the 1970s and earlier, see Hugh Heclo, *A Government of Strangers: Executive Politics in Washington* (Washington, DC: Brookings Institution Press, 1977).

74. See David Johnston, "Charge in Weinberger Case That Caused Furor before Election Is Thrown Out," *New York Times*, December 12, 1992.

75. George C. Benson, *Political Corruption in America* (Lexington, Mass:. Heath, 1978), 242.

76. Robert E. Stake, "Qualitative Case Studies," in Norman Denzin and Yvonna Lincoln, *The Sage Handbook of Qualitative Research*, 3rd ed. (Thousand Oaks, Calif.: Sage, 2005), 451.

77. John Gerring, *Case Study Research: Principles and Practices* (New York: Cambridge University Press, 2007), 96.

78. Stake, "Qualitative Case Studies," 451.

79. Ibid. See also M. Q. Patton, *Qualitative Evaluation and Research Methods*, 2nd ed. (Newbury Park, Calif.: Sage, 1990).

Chapter 2: Legal Regimes, Attorneys General, and Executive Accountability

1. In *Myers v. United States*, 272 US 52 (1926), the Supreme Court ruled that the president enjoys the exclusive power to remove executive branch officials without the approval of the Senate. The attorney general's role as chief lawyer of the US government leaves little doubt of the position's unambiguous status as an executive branch official.

2. See generally Timothy Rives, "Grant Babcock and the Whiskey Ring," *Prologue: Quarterly of the National Archives and Records Administration* 32, no. 3 (2000).

3. Burl Niggle, *Teapot Dome: Oil and Politics in the 1920s* (Baton Rouge: Louisiana State University Press, 1962), 115.

4. Leslie E. Bennett, "One Lesson from History: Appointment of Special Counsel and the Investigation of the Teapot Dome Scandal" (1999), Brookings Institution, http://www.brookings.edu/gs/ic/TeapotDome/teapotdome.htm.

5. See *Nomination of Elliot L. Richardson to Be Attorney General: Hearings Before the Committee on the Judiciary*, 93rd Cong., 1st sess. (1973), 45; Ken Gormley, *Archibald Cox: Conscience of a Nation* (Reading, Mass.: Addison-Wesley, 1997), 233.

6. Gormley, *Archibald Cox*, 234.

7. President Nixon, immediately after Attorney General Elliot Richardson and Deputy Attorney General William Ruckelshaus resigned, ordered Solicitor General Robert Bork (the acting head of the Justice Department) to fire Cox.

8. Edward Levi to the president, memo, July 15, 1976, "Office of Special Prosecutor, Govt Crimes, etc." file, White House Central Files (cited hereafter as WHCF), Subject Files, Gerald R. Ford Presidential Library (cited hereafter as GRFPL).

9. Ibid.

10. Charles Johnson and Danette Brickman, *Independent Counsel* (Washington, DC: CQ Press, 2001), 7.

11. Jim McGee and Brian Duffy, *Main Justice* (New York: Touchstone, 1996), 30.

12. In fact, from 1975 until the present, just two people have held the leadership post at the OPR: Shaheen and his successor, H. Marshall Jarrett. Thanks to that stability, the OPR was able to able to fend off challenges to its authority when Congress over a decade later insisted that the Justice Department join much of the executive branch in establishing an inspector general's office to conduct investigations of the agency's employees and programs. The compromise eventually reached was to limit the Justice Department's inspector general's office to investigations only of *nonattorney* conduct; the OPR, meanwhile, would continue to conduct nearly all investigations of attorney employees. Levi's 1975 brainchild apparently had enough allies on Capitol Hill to withstand challenges to its central mission.

13. For example, in the early 1990s Shaheen conducted the investigation of FBI Director William Sessions, documenting numerous ethical lapses by him and his office.

14. Jimmy Carter Presidential Campaign Statement, "Jimmy Carter's Code of Ethics," March 1, 1976, DPS Eisenstat file, Justice, Department of—Independent Attorney General (OA 6318), Jimmy Carter Presidential Library (cited hereafter as JCPL).

15. Bell to the president, memo, "Proposals regarding Independent Attorney General," April 11, 1977, DPS Eisenstat file, Justice, Department of—Independent Attorney General (OA 6318), JCPL.

16. Lipshutz and McKenna to the president, memo, "Your campaign commitment to establish an independent attorney general," June 23, 1977, DPS Eisenstat file, Justice, Department of—Independent Attorney General (OA 6318), JCPL.

17. J. Harmon to the attorney general, memo, February 21, 1977, DPS Eisenstat, Justice, Department of—Inspectors General, JCPL.

18. Ibid.

19. Paul Light, *Monitoring Government* (Washington, DC: Brookings Institution Press, 1993), 66.

20. See 5 U.S.C. App. §§ 1 et seq. (1978).

21. 5 U.S.C. App. § 3 (1978); and Light, *Monitoring Government*, 68.

22. 28 U.S.C. § 591 (1978).

23. Johnson and Brickman, *Independent Counsel*, 111.

24. 28 U.S.C. § 592 (as amended, 1983).

25. 28 U.S.C. § 593(c) (as amended, 1987).

26. *Ethics in Government Act Amendments of 1982: Hearings on S. 2059 Before the Subcommittee on Oversight of Government Management of the Senate Committee on Governmental Affairs*, 97th Cong., 2nd sess. (1982), 64.

27. See various provisions of the USA Patriot Act, P.L. 107–56 (2001).

28. Cornell W. Clayton, *The Politics of Justice* (New York: Sharpe, 1992), 21–22.

29. Nancy Baker, *Conflicting Loyalties: Law & Politics in the Attorney General's Office, 1789–1990* (Lawrence: University Press of Kansas, 1992), 169.

30. According to Michael Gerhardt, while senatorial deference varies, the Senate has been more deferential to cabinet offices than it has been to lower court judicial nominees or Supreme Court nominees: "The Senate as a whole or in committee has formally rejected or forced the withdrawal of fewer than two hundred of the more than two million executive nominations made since 1932" (*The Federal Appointments Process: A Constitutional and Historical Analysis* [Durham: Duke University Press, 2003], xx-xxi).

31. Baker, *Conflicting Loyalties*, 126.

32. No US attorney general in history has been formally appointed (and confirmed) to serve in multiple nonconsecutive terms as head of the Justice Department. Andrew Johnson renominated Henry Stanberry to be attorney general several months after Stanberry had resigned in early 1868 to defend Johnson during the latter's impeachment trial (he was successful in his defense of Johnson, but failed to secure confirmation from the Senate for a second term). By comparison, at least one attorney general served in an acting or interim capacity before being formally appointed to the position several years later: Eric Holder. Holder was the acting attorney general for two weeks at the beginning of George W. Bush's first term as president, holding down the fort until John Ashcroft was formally confirmed on February 2, 2001.

33. Mary Anne Borrelli, *The President's Cabinet: Gender, Power and Representation* (Boulder, Colo.: Rienner, 2002), 178.

34. William B. Saxbe, *I've Seen the Elephant* (Kent, Ohio: Kent State University Press, 2000), 135.

35. Richard G. Zimmerman, *Plain Dealing* (Kent, Ohio: Kent State University Press, 2006), 71.

36. Later, when aides to Nixon repeatedly asked Saxbe to intervene with Watergate special prosecutor Leon Jaworski to prevent what they thought to be an "infringement of executive privilege," the attorney general did nothing (J. Anthony Lukas, *Nightmare: The Underside of the Nixon Years* [Athens: Ohio University Press, 1999], 482).

37. Nancy Baker, *General Ashcroft: Attorney at War* (Lawrence: University Press of Kansas, 2006), 35.

38. 462 US 476 (1983).

39. Baker, *General Ashcroft*, 35.

40. Ibid., 40.

41. *The Nomination of John Ashcroft to Be Attorney General of the United States: Hearing Before the Committee on the Judiciary*, 107th Cong., 1st sess. (Jan. 16, 2009), 107.

42. Ibid., 150.

43. Ibid., 122.

44. Jack Goldsmith, *The Terror Presidency: Law and Judgment inside the Bush Administration* (New York: Norton, 2007), 24.

45. Ibid.

46. *The Nomination of Michael Mukasey to Be Attorney General of the United States: Hearings Before the Senate Committee of the Judiciary*, 110th Cong., 1st sess. (October 17–18, 2007).

47. Baker, *Conflicting Loyalties*, 121.

48. Anthony Summers, *The Arrogance of Power* (New York: Penguin, 2001), 311.

49. Baker, *Conflicting Loyalties*, 121.

50. Ibid., 122.

51. This was the view of the lifelong Democrat who ran the solicitor general's office during that period, Erwin Griswold. See Jeffrey Rosen, *The Strong Man: John Mitchell and the Secrets of Watergate* (New York: Doubleday, 2008), 75.

52. Ibid., 76.

53. Ibid., 67–68.

54. *The Nomination of Elliot L. Richardson to Be Attorney General: Hearings Before the Senate Committee on the Judiciary*, 93rd Cong., 1st sess. (May 9–22, 1973), 13–19 passim (testimony of Elliot L. Richardson).

55. Ibid., 49.

56. Baker, *Conflicting Loyalties*, 151–52.

57. Betty Glad, *Jimmy Carter: In Search of the Great White House* (New York: Norton, 1980), 73.

58. Victor Lasky, *Jimmy Carter* (New York: Marek, 1979), 331.

59. Glad, *Jimmy Carter*, 414.

60. James Reston, "Carter's First Mistake," cited in Mark J. Rozell, *The Press and the Carter Presidency* (Westview Press, 1989), 31.

61. *Time* magazine's coverage of Carter's appointment was straightforward: "Bell is something of a crony of Carter's. . . . But Carter had seemed to promise more than a comfortable ally in such a crucial post" ("The Transition: Mr. Outside Opts for 'Ins,'" *Time*, January 3, 1977, http://www.time.com/time/magazine/article/0,9171,947796,00.html.

62. Deborah Hart Strober and Gerald S. Strober, *The Reagan Presidency: An Oral History of the Era* (Washington, DC: Potomac Books, 2003), 68.

63. Other moves contributed to that perception as well, including Thornburgh's decision to reduce the size and scope of the attorney general's annual public report, and his implementation of new procedures for approving press interviews with department officials.

64. Ryan J. Barilleaux and Mark J. Rozell, *Power and Prudence* (College Station: Texas A&M University Press, 2004), 110.

65. Edwin Meese III, *With Reagan: The Inside Story* (Washington, DC: Regnery: 1992), 78.

66. Ibid., 80.

67. *Confirmation of Edwin Meese III: Hearings Before the Senate Committee on the Judiciary*, 99th Cong., 1st sess. (January 29–31, 2005) (testimony of Senator Joseph Biden, Senator Patrick Leahy).

68. Bob Schieffer and Gary Paul Gates, *The Acting President* (New York: Plume, 1990), 203.

69. Leslie M. Werner, "Senate Approves Meese to Become Attorney General," *New York Times*, February 24, 1985.

70. *Confirmation of Edwin Meese III: Hearings Before the Senate Committee on the Judiciary* (January 29), 108.

71. Ibid.

72. John Ehrman, *The Eighties: America in the Age of Reagan* (New Haven: Yale University Press, 2005), 143.

73. Schieffer and Gates, *Acting President*, 308.

74. Haynes Johnson, *Sleepwalking through History: America in the Reagan Years* (New York: Anchor, 1992), 185.

75. Ibid.

76. Bill Minutaglio, *The President's Counselor: The Rise to Power of Alberto Gonzales* (New York: HarperCollins, 2006).

77. *The Nomination of Alberto Gonzales to Be Attorney General of the United States:*

Hearing Before the Senate Committee on the Judiciary, 109th Cong., 1st sess. (January 6, 2005), 136.
78. Ibid., 117.

Chapter 3: When All Bets Are Off

1. Ch. 150, 16 Stat. 162 (1870).
2. Benjamin Wittes, *Starr: A Reassessment* (New Haven: Yale University Press, 2002), 36.
3. Ibid, 37.
4. Ibid.
5. Francis Clines, "Spiro T. Agnew, Point Man for Nixon Who Resigned Vice Presidency, Dies at 77," *New York Times*, September 19, 1996.
6. Elliott Richardson to the file, memo, August 14, 1973, Agnew Case: Dept Docs and Memoranda File, Attorney General Subject File, Papers of Elliott Richardson, Library of Congress (cited hereafter as LOC), Washington, DC.
7. Ibid.
8. Richard M. Cohen and Jules Witcover, *A Heartbeat Away: The Investigation and Resignation of Vice President Spiro T. Agnew* (New York: Viking, 1974), 118.
9. Ibid., 119.
10. Ibid., 123.
11. Ibid., 124.
12. FBI file on Spiro T. Agnew (2003), accessed via PURL from the FBI website at http://foia.fbi.gov/foiainndex/agnew.htm.
13. Cohen and Witcover, *A Heartbeat Away*, 131.
14. Ibid., 132–33.
15. Jonathan Aitken, *Nixon: A Life* (New York: Regnery, 1996), 503.
16. Elliott Richardson to the file, memo.
17. J. Anthony Lukas, *Nightmare: The Underside of the Nixon Years* (Athens: Ohio University Press, 1999), 404.
18. Ibid.
19. Nixon admitted as much many years later, telling one writer, "I think he deserved some condemnation, but I do not believe that he deserved the almost hysteria that went on in the US Attorney's Office and everywhere else that he had committed the crime of century. It had happened before to governors in Illinois and I'm sure it happened in a lot of other states . . . but with the problems I had at that particular time there was nothing I could do for him. I only wish I'd been stronger. If I had been I would have stopped him from going" (Aitken, *Nixon*, 503–04).
20. Lukas, *Nightmare*, 407.

21. Investigation Status Report filed in the US Attorneys' records on Spiro T. Agnew, Precedent Case Files, 1933–1973, Record Group 118: Records of US Attorneys, National Archives and Records Administration, Philadelphia, Pa.

22. Lukas, *Nightmare*, 322, 408.

23. K. Clawson to all subcabinet level personnel, memo, October 10, 1973, FBI file on Spiro T. Agnew (2003), accessed via PURL from the FBI website at http://foia.fbi.gov/foiainndex/agnew.htm.

24. Lukas, *Nightmare*, 412.

25. The details of the written plan are laid out in the "Final Report of the U.S. Senate Select Committee to Study Governmental Operations with Respect to Intelligence Activities," April 23, 1976, http://www.icdc.com/~paulwolf/cointelpro/churchfinalreportIIIm.htm.

26. Fred Emery, *Watergate: The Corruption of American Politics and the Fall of Richard Nixon* (New York: Times Books, 1994), 47.

27. Felt, nicknamed "Deep Throat" as an informant on "deep background" for *Washington Post* reporters Bob Woodward and Carl Bernstein, later confessed to this role in a *Vanity Fair* magazine article in 2005 (John D. O'Connor, "I'm the Guy They Called Deep Throat," *Vanity Fair*, July 2005).

28. Ronald Kessler, *The FBI: Inside the World's Most Powerful Law Enforcement Agency* (New York: Pocket Books, 1993), 269.

29. Melvin Small, *The Presidency of Richard Nixon* (Lawrence: University Press of Kansas, 2003), 277.

30. Lukas, *Nightmare*, 242.

31. Ibid.

32. White House tapes gave evidence of a deliberate attempt by Nixon and his aides to stress the "national security thing" in their responses to inquiries about Watergate. See, for example, Stanley I. Kutler, *Abuse of Power: The New Nixon Tapes* (New York: Simon and Schuster, 1998), 539.

33. Lukas, *Nightmare*, 248.

34. Stanley Kutler, *The Wars of Watergate: The Last Crisis of Richard Nixon* (New York: Knopf, 1990), 189.

35. Ken Gormley, *Archibald Cox: Conscience of a Nation* (Reading, Mass.: Addison-Wesley, 1997), 256.

36. Lukas, *Nightmare*, 417.

37. *Nomination of Elliot L. Richardson to be Attorney General: Hearings Before the Senate Committee on the Judiciary*, 93rd Cong., 1st sess. (May 9–22, 1973) (testimony of Elliot Richardson, Secretary of Defense), 47; and Terry Eastland, *Ethics, Politics and the Independent Counsel* (New York: University Press of America, 1989), 18.

38. Eliot Richardson to the file, memo, "Special Prosecutor—First Cut," May 9,

1973, Watergate Special Prosecutor Files, AG Subject Files, Box 231, Elliot Richardson Papers, LOC.

39. Ibid.

40. Memo, Leon Jaworski File, Watergate Special Prosecutor Search (Candidates "I-J"), AG Subject Files, Box 230, Elliot Richardson papers, LOC.

41. Cox himself suspected that Richardson's nomination as attorney general "hung, perhaps, on his naming a special prosecutor" who was suitable to the president as well as to Congress (Gormley, *Archibald Cox*, 233).

42. Katy Harriger, *The Special Prosecutor in American Politics* (Lawrence: University Press of Kansas, 2000), 16.

43. Gormley, *Archibald Cox*, 238.

44. Ibid.

45. Ibid., 281–82.

46. "Duties and Responsibilities of the Special Prosecutor," memo, May 19, 1973, "Watergate Special Prosecutor: Congressional Inquiry into Dismissal of Cox" file, Attorney General Subject File, Papers of Elliot Richardson, LOC.

47. See *United States v. Nixon*, 506 US 224 (1974).

48. To FBI director, memo, "William 'Billy' Carter," Foreign Agents Registration Act, Libya, May 4, 1979, accessed via PURL from FBI website at http://foia.fbi.gov/foiainndex/carter_b.htm.

49. Burton Kaufman, *The Presidency of James Earl Carter* (Lawrence: University Press of Kansas, 2006), 137.

50. Mark J. Rozell, *The Press and the Carter Presidency* (Westview Press, 1989), 168.

51. Kaufman, *Presidency of James Earl Carter*, 190.

52. Ibid.

53. Charles Babcock, "Civiletti and Justice Find Themselves on the Defense," *Washington Post*, September 2, 1979.

54. Charles Babcock and Edward Walsh, "Civiletti Admits He Talked with President about Billy," *Washington Post*, July 26, 1980.

55. Mark J. Rozell, *The Press and the Carter Presidency* (Westview Press, 1989), 170.

56. See Final Report of the Independent Counsel (in re Madison Guaranty Savings & Loan Association) of Matters Related to the White House Travel Office, June 30, 2000.

57. Wittes, *Starr: A Reassessment*, 127.

58. Final Report of the Independent Counsel in re William David Watkins and in re Hillary Rodham Clinton, October 18, 2000, 12–13, http://www.gpoaccess.gov/icreport/watkins/orders.pdf.

59. See Reno's testimony at *Nomination of Janet Reno to be Attorney General of the United States, Hearings Before the Committee on the Judiciary*, 103rd Cong., 1st sess. (March 9–10, 1993), 67.

60. See Reno's testimony at *The Independent Counsel Statute: Hearings Before the Senate Governmental Affairs Committee*, 106th Cong., 1st sess, March 17, 1999.

61. Final Report of the Independent Counsel in re Madison Guaranty Savings & Loan Association, January 5, 2001.

62. Jeff Gerth, "Clintons Joined S & L Operator in an Ozark Real-Estate Venture," *New York Times*, March 8, 1992.

63. See Final Report of the Independent Counsel in re Madison Guaranty Savings & Loan Association, App.4 (Chronology), January 5, 2001.

64. Ibid.

65. James B. Stewart, *Blood Sport: The President and His Adversaries* (New York: Simon & Schuster, 1996), 398.

66. Kent Gormley, *The Death of American Virtue* (New York: Random House, 2010), 111–112.

67. Ibid., 111.

68. Wittes, *Starr: A Reassessment*, 184.

69. David Johnston, "Committee Told of Beijing Cash for Democrats," *New York Times*, May 12, 1999.

70. See Committee on Governmental Affairs, "Investigation of Illegal or Improper Activities in Connection with 1996 Federal Election campaigns," S. Report No. 105-167.

71. John F. Harris and Charles R. Babcock, "Documents Detail Gore's Calls for DNC," *Washington Post*, August 27, 1997.

72. Nathan Abse, "A Look at the 94 Who Aren't Talking," *Washington Post*, June 9, 1998; George Lardner Jr., "Panel Sputters; Immunity Vote Fails," *Washington Post*, May 14, 1998; and remarks of Chairman Fred Thompson (R-Tenn.) before the Senate Governmental Affairs Committee, October 7, 1997, reported in "Mr. President . . . This Is Your Campaign," *Washington Post*, October 8, 1997.

73. Neil Lewis, "Freeh Says Reno Clearly Misread Prosecutor Law," *New York Times*, July 16, 1998.

74. Bob Woodward, *Shadow* (New York: Simon & Schuster, 2000), 450; and Pierre Thomas, "Reno Aide Recommends Independent Campaign Finance Probe," *CNN.com*, July 23, 1998, http://www.cnn.com/ALLPOLITICS/1998/07/23/labella/.

75. *Clinton v. Jones*, 520 US 681 (1997).

76. Text of Attorney General Janet Reno's application to the Special Division of the appeals court to expand Kenneth Starr's authority, released by the Justice Department on January 29, 1998.

77. 28 US § 592(a)(2)(A).

78. See 28 U.S.C. § 593(c)(2)(c); United States v. Wade, 83 F.3d 196, 198 (8th Cir. 1996).

79. 28 U.S.C. § 592(a)(1).

80. Associated Press, December 3, 2004.

Chapter 4: A Bit *Too* Familiar

1. David J. Garrow, *The FBI and Martin Luther King Jr.: From Solo to Memphis* (New York: Norton, 1981), 89.

2. Jesse Jackson to Gerald Ford, Mailgram letter, May 9, 1976, Jesse Jackson file, WHCF Name Files, GRFPL. Jackson was most likely referring to William Sullivan in his statement. In fact Sullivan was now the director of the newly created Office of National Narcotics Intelligence and thus was no longer working in the FBI per se.

3. Ibid.

4. Philip Buchen to Jesse Jackson, letter, May 27, 1976, Jesse Jackson file, WHCF Name Files, Gerald Ford Presidential Library (cited hereafter as GFPL).

5. Garrow, *The FBI and Martin Luther King*, 224.

6. Long-time columnist Robert Novak suspected that Sullivan had been murdered and alluded to that possibility in his memoir, *The Prince of Darkness* (New York: Random House, 2007), 210–11.

7. Edward Levi to President Ford, memo, September 2, 1976, Justice-FBI Allegations against Clarence Kelley—General (1) file, General Subject Files, Philip Buchen files, GFPL.

8. Philip Buchen to President Ford, memo, June 26, 1976, Justice-FBI—General (2) file, General Subject Files, Philip Buchen files, GFPL.

9. Department of Justice press release, September 4, 1976, Justice-FBI Allegations against Clarence Kelley—Public Correspondence (2) file, General Subject Files, Phil Buchen files, GFPL.

10. Levi to Ford, memo, September 2, 1976, Justice-FBI Allegations against Clarence Kelley—General (1) file, General Subject Files, Phil Buchen files, GRFPL. Thus, for example, Kelley's personal automobile had been brought to the bureau's garage for repair by his driver, apparently without the director's knowledge.

11. Ibid.

12. *Facts on File Yearbook*, September 11, 1976, 664.

13. Haynes Johnson, *Sleepwalking through History: America in the Reagan Years* (New York: Anchor, 1992), 170.

14. Brand to Perry, letter, February 10, 1983, Shredders File (OA 14717), Office of the Council to the President: Investigations, RRPL, Simi Valley, California; and Gorsuch to Schmults, letter, February 14, 1983, Shredders File (OA 14717), Office of the Council to the President: Investigations, RRPL, Simi Valley, California.

15. Mark J. Rozell, *Executive Privilege: The Dilemma of Secrecy and Accountability* (Baltimore: Johns Hopkins University Press, 1994), 118.

16. Olson's controversial testimony was referred to in *Morrison v. Olson*, 487 US 654, and in the predecessor case at the Court of Appeals, in re Olson, 818 F.2d 24 (DC Cir. 1987).

17. Report of the Attorney General Pursuant to 28 U.S.C. § 592(c)(1) regarding Allegations against Department of Justice Officials in United States House Judiciary Committee, cited in in re Olson, 818 F.2d 34, 36; and Charles Johnson and Danette Brickman, *Independent Counsel: The Law and the Investigations* (Washington, DC: CQ Press, 2001), 157.

18. Johnson and Brickman, *Independent Counsel*, 157.

19. Johnson, *Sleepwalking*, 174.

20. Report of Independent Counsel in re Edwin Meese III, July 5, 1988, 134.

21. Ibid., 170–172.

22. Johnson, *Sleepwalking*, 174.

23. Ibid., 175.

24. Report of Independent Counsel in re Edwin Meese III, 259–260.

25. Ibid., 240–255.

26. 2 U.S.C. § 1602 (1978).

27. Report of Independent Counsel in re Edwin Meese III, 73–99.

28. Ibid., 100.

29. CBS News Report, May 31, 1989, Headline: Congress/Investigation (Record No. 568778).

30. Letter, Congressional Black Caucus to President George Bush, June 6, 1989, Doc. ID #042558, FG017, WHORM Subject Files—general, Bush Presidential records, George Bush Presidential Library (cited hereafter as GBL), College Station, Texas.

31. CBS News Report, June 2, 1989, Headline: Gray Investigation/Ethics (Record No. 327519); video available at http://tvnews.vanderbilt.edu/program. pl?ID=327519.

32. Letter, Stephen Saltzburg to Vicki Miles-LaGrange, July 14, 1989, Doc. ID #047587, FG017, WHORM Subject Files—general, Bush Presidential records, GBL, College Station, Texas.

33. David M. Johnson, "Thornburgh Took Polygraph Test in Leak Inquiry," *New York Times*, May 26, 1990.

34. Ibid.

35. Ronald J. Ostrow, "Aide Says Thornburgh Meddled in Leak Probe," *Los Angeles Times*, May 20, 1990.

36. Johnson, "Thornburgh Took Polygraph Test."

37. Judiciary Committee, H.R. Report No. 102–857, "The INSLAW Affair" (September 10, 1992).
38. Ibid.
39. "Justice Department Is Held in Contempt in a Bankruptcy," *New York Times*, June 14, 1987.
40. Judiciary Committee, H.R. Report No. 102–857.
41. Elliot Richardson, "A High-Tech Watergate," *New York Times*, October 21, 1991.
42. Richard Fricker, "The INSLAW Octopus," *Wired* (online version), March/April 1993, 7, http://www.wired.com/wired/archive/1.01/inslaw.html.
43. Jeffrey A. Frank, "The INSLAW File," *Washington Post Magazine*, June 14, 1992, 31.
44. Ibid., 32.
45. Richardson, "High-Tech Watergate."
46. Judiciary Committee, H.R. Report No. 102–857, "The INSLAW Affair" (September 10, 1992).
47. B. Drummond Ayres, "As U.S. Battles Computer Company, Writer Takes Vision of Evil to Grave," *New York Times*, September 3, 1991.
48. Heather Dewar, "Jury's Out on Performance of U.S. Attorney Lehtinen," *Miami Herald*, November 14, 1989.
49. Letter, Donna Stevenson to George Bush, January 28, 1990, folder on Dexter Lehtinen, Lee Lieberman Misc. file, CFO 266, Bush Presidential Office: Counsel's Office, GBL, College Station, Texas.
50. Jeff Leen, "Bar Report 'Exonerates' Me, Lehtinen Tells Senate Panel," *Miami Herald*, May 27, 1990.
51. "White House Press Secretary Blasts Lawyers," *South Florida Sun-Sentinel*, February 24, 1990.
52. Larry Rohter, "Miami Prosecutor's Stormy Passage," *New York Times*, September 6, 1991.
53. Ibid.
54. 50 U.S.C. Ch. 36, § 1566 (1978).
55. James Risen and Eric Lichtblau, "Bush Lets U.S. Spy on Callers without Courts," *New York Times*, December 16, 2005.
56. Attorney General Alberto Gonzales, testimony before the Senate Judiciary Committee, July 24, 2007.
57 *Questions for the Record for Attorney General Alberto Gonzales, Department of Justice Oversight: Hearing Before the Committee on the Judiciary*, 109th Cong. (July 18, 2006).
58. David Johnston, "Bush Intervened in Dispute over N.S.A. Eavesdropping," *New York Times*, May 16, 2007.

59. Many of these details are also described in Jack Goldsmith, *Terror Presidency: Law and Judgment inside the Bush Administration* (New York: Norton, 2007).

60. Eric Lichtblau, *The Remaking of American Justice* (New York: Pantheon Books, 2008), 179–182.

61. Renee Montagne, "Context: How U.S. Attorneys Are Hired and Fired: Interview with David Burnham," *Morning Edition*, National Public Radio, March 14, 2007.

62. Congressional Research Service (CRS) Report for Congress: U.S. Attorneys Who Have Served Less Than Full Four-Year Terms, 1981–2006 (February 22, 2007). The two US attorneys so identified were (1) William Kennedy (S.D. Calif.), dismissed in 1982 by President Reagan for accusing the Justice Department of blocking his attempt to prosecute a key CIA informant, and (2) J. William Petro (N.D. Ohio), dismissed in 1984 by President Reagan after allegedly disclosing information about an indictment pending from an undercover operation. (Petro was later convicted of the charges.)

63. Letter, Sen. Feinstein and Sen. Leahy to A. Gonzales, January 9, 2007, http://feinstein.senate.gov/

64. 28 US § 546(c), (as revised on March 9, 2006).

65. See a summary of the bill at http://dpc.senate.gov/.

66. See *Department of Justice Oversight: Hearings Before the Senate Committee on the Judiciary*, 110th Cong., 1st sess. (January 18, 2007).

67. Unnamed GOP sources were cited, for example, in Jane Ann Morrison, "Bush Administration's Ouster of U.S. Attorneys an Insulting Injustice," *Las Vegas Review-Journal*, January 18, 2007.

68. *Preserving Prosecutorial Independence: Is the Department of Justice Politicizing the Hiring and Firing of U.S. Attorneys? Hearings Before the Senate Committee on the Judiciary*, 110th Cong., 1st sess. (February 6, 2007).

69. Murray Waas, "Administration Withheld E-mails about Rove," *National Journal*, May 10, 2007.

70. Senator Gordon Smith (R-Ore.) was among the first Republican senators to call for the resignation of Gonzales—he did so in a public statement on March 15, 2007.

71. *Department of Justice Oversight: Hearings Before the Senate Committee on the Judiciary*, 110th Cong., 1st sess. (April 19, 2007).

72. See 18 U.S.C. § 7321 et seq. (as amended in 1993).

73. *Continuing Investigation into the U.S. Attorneys Controversy and Related Matters (Part 1): Hearing Before the House Committee on the Judiciary* (May 23, 2007) (testimony of Justice Department official Monica Goodling).

74. Letter, G. Fine to Sen. P. Leahy re: investigation of former Attorney General Alberto Gonzales's sworn testimony before the Senate Judiciary Committee,

August 30, 2007, http://judiciary.senate.gov/resources/documents/110thCongress.cfm.

75. US Department of Justice, "An Investigation of Allegations of Politicized Hiring by Monica Goodling and Other Staff in the Office of the Attorney General," Special Report, Office of the Inspector General, July 28, 2008.

76. Ibid.

Chapter 5: More Political Considerations

1. For a discussion of the short tenure of executive branch officials during the 1970s and earlier, see Hugh Heclo, *A Government of Strangers: Executive Politics in Washington* (Washington, DC: Brookings Institution Press, 1977).

2. For a complete list of all individuals covered under the act, see the now-defunct provisions of the Ethics in Government Act of 1978, as amended: 28 U.S.C. § 591.

3. Edward Levi to the president, memo, July 15, 1976, "Office of Special Prosecutor, Govt Crimes, etc." file, WHCF Subject Files. GRFPL.

4. Jay French to Philip Areeda, memo, December 6, 1974, EEOC-Powell (1)-(2) file, Jay French files, GRFPL.

5. Ibid.

6. Philip Areeda to the EEOC file, memo, January 29, 1975, Justice-General (2) file, General Subject File, Philip Buchen files, GRFPL.

7., Ibid., Powell, John (3 of 3) file, Philip Buchen files, GRFPL.

8. Ibid.

9. Ibid.

10. Dudley Chapman to Roderick Hills, memo, May 20, 1975, Chron files–Chapman (7/1/75–8/31/75), Dudley Chapman Papers, GRFPL.

11. Nicholas M. Horrock, "Possible Covert Union Gifts to Ford from '64 to '74 Called Target of Inquiry by Watergate Prosecution," *New York Times*, September 26, 1976.

12. "The Campaign: Ford's Toughest Week," *Time*, October 18, 1976, http://www.time.com.

13. Bob Woodward and Carl Bernstein, "Levi, Top Aides Initiated Probe of Ford Funds," *Washington Post*, October 1, 1976.

14. Ibid.

15. Nicholas Horrock, "Prosecutor Reports No Violation by Ford on Political Funds," *New York Times*, October 15, 1976.

16. See, for example, Mike Curtin, "GOP Attack on Clinton May Backfire," *Columbus Dispatch*, August 19, 1992. This attack on Clinton as an Oxford Rhodes scholar scheming to avoid the draft was heard throughout the general election campaign.

17. Final Report of the Independent Counsel in re Janet G. Mullins, November 30, 1995, 2.
18. Ibid.
19. In re *Janet G. Mullins*, 84 F.3d 1429, 1440 (DC Cir. 1996).
20. Final Report of the Independent Counsel in re Janet G. Mullins, 2–3.
21. Ibid.
22. Ibid., 3.
23. Robert Pear, "Many Questions Linger Following State Dept. Inquiry," *New York Times*, November 20, 1992. Tamposi later told investigators that the expedited search had been approved by a top State Department official, Undersecretary of State for Management John F. W. Rogers, and had been initiated by DePlacido at Rogers' request. For his part, Rogers denied that he had approved the search in any way, although he did report the search to Eagleburger on October 1, a day after it began. At that point Rogers could have halted the search through Clinton's files, but he did not do so.
24. During the week of October 5, news reports on the passport files case appeared in the *Wall Street Journal*, the *New York Times*, and the *Washington Post*. According to the *Washington Post*, State Department officials were "privately suggesting" that they might not have much in the passports to investigate, and that the requests for access probably should have been denied because of federal Privacy Act provisions. See Jackson Diehl, "U.S. Aides Won't Clarify Clinton Passport Story; Mention of FBI Fuels Partisan Suspicions," *Washington Post*, October 6, 1992.
25. Political affiliation sometimes plays a role in the naming of inspectors general as well. Consider as an example the appointment of Republican Janet Rehnquist, the eldest daughter of conservative Chief Justice William Rehnquist. The jurist's daughter was appointed inspector general for the US Department of Health and Human Services in 2001. She resigned just two years later when it became known that she had granted delays to a draft audit of Florida's pension program that might have proven embarrassing to Governor Jeb Bush and, indirectly, to President Bush as he was seeking reelection in 2004. (The federal audit focused on whether the state had properly accounted for US contributions to the state's pension program.)
26. Final Report of the Independent Counsel in re Janet G. Mullins, 4–6.
27. Robert Pear, "Many Questions Still Linger Following State Department Inquiry," *New York Times*, November 20, 1992.
28. Michael Posner, "Rifling Clinton Passport File Deemed 'Stupid,' Not Illegal," *Chicago Sun-Times*, December 1, 1995.
29. Kenneth Morris, *Jimmy Carter: American Moralist* (Athens: University of Georgia Press, 1997), 258.
30. William Safire, "Carter's Broken Lance," *New York Times*, July 21, 1977

31. Jimmy Carter, *Keeping Faith* (Fayetteville: University of Arkansas Press, 1995), 127–28.

32. Mark J. Rozell, *The Press and the Carter Presidency* (Westview Press, 1989), 56.

33. Document entitled "Committee Efforts to Date," OCP Box 31, Lance, Bert— Comptroller's Internal Investigation, 9/77, Lipschutz files, JCPL.

34. Burton Kaufman, *The Presidency of James Earl Carter* (Lawrence: University Press of Kansas, 2006), 60.

35. Ibid.

36. Rozell, *Press and the Carter Presidency*, 57.

37. "Committee Efforts to Date" (see n. 33).

38. Betty Glad, *Jimmy Carter: In Search of the Great White House* (New York: Norton, 1980), 439.

39. Woodward, *Shadow*, 58.

40. Kaufman, *Presidency of James Earl Carter*, 62.

41. Ibid., 61.

42. Lipshutz to Powell, memo, September 7, 1977, Lipshutz files, Lance, Bert, Airplane, 8/77–1/79 file, JCPL.

43. Ibid.

44. Document entitled "Re: Bert Lance Matter, September 7, 1977, Lipshutz files, Lance, Bert, Airplane, 8/77–1/79 file, JCPL.

45. Kaufman, *Presidency of James Earl Carter*, 62.

46. Ibid., 62–63.

47. Nancy Lewis, "Lance Probe to Last Another 8–12 Weeks," *Atlanta Constitution*, May 26, 1978.

48. Edward Pound, "Carter's Business Cleared in Inquiry on Campaign Funds," *New York Times*, October 17, 1979.

49. Lawrence Mayer and Alfred E. Lewis, "Carter Aide Signed Fake Quaalude Prescription," *Washington Post*, July 19, 1978.

50. Some controversy ensued from this decision as well: though "on leave," Bourne continued to collect his $51,000 a year government salary (Lasky, *Jimmy Carter*, 369).

51. Letter from Hamilton Jordan to Cong. William Dickinson, October 9, 1979, WHCF Name Files (Bourne, Peter), JCPL.

52. Victor Lasky, *Jimmy Carter* (New York: Marek, 1979), 373.

53. Ibid.

54. Joseph Wilson IV, "What I Didn't Find in Iraq," *New York Times*, July 6, 2003.

55. "Transcript of ElBaradei's U.N. Presentation," *CNN.com*, March 7, 2003, http://www.cnn.com/2003/US/03/07/sprj.irq.un.transcript.elbaradei/.

56. Seymour M. Hersh, "How Conflicts between the Bush Administration and the Intelligence Community Marred the Reporting on Iraq's Weapons," *New Yorker*,

October 27, 2003 (http://www.newyorker.com/archive/2003/10/27/031027fa_fact).

Chapter 6: What's a Little Prosecution among Friends?

1. Final Report of the Independent Counsel in re Janet G. Mullins, November 30, 1995, 377.
2. Ibid. See also Charles Johnson and Danette Brickman, *Independent Counsel: The Law and the Investigations* (Washington, DC: CQ Press, 2001).
3. John V. Orth, *Due Process of Law: A Brief History* (Lawrence: University Press of Kansas, 2003), 19.
4. Katy Harriger, *The Special Prosecutor in American Politics* (Lawrence: University Press of Kansas, 2000), 122.
5. 28 U.S.C. pt. 2, ch. 40, § 594 (1978).
6. 28 U.S.C. pt. 2, ch. 40, § 596 (1978).
7. "Independent Counsel Reauthorization Act of 1987," Report of the Senate Committee on Governmental Affairs, Report No. 100-123, 100th Cong, 1st Sess. (1987)."
8. David Greenberg, "No Exit," *New York Times Book Review*, March 20, 2011.

Select Bibliography

This bibliography includes major works and sources consulted in writing this book. To that limited end, it is not exhaustive of all relevant material on the subject of the investigation and prosecution of federal officials.

Archival Collections

George Bush Presidential Library, College Station, Texas
  George H. W. Bush Personal Records Collection
  C. Boyden Gray Files
  Michael P. Jackson Files
  White House Office of Records Management Collection
  White House Subject Files
Jimmy Carter Presidential Library, Atlanta, Georgia
  Peter Bourne Files
  Chief of Staff Files
  Lloyd Cutler Files
  DPS Eisenstat Files
  Richard Harden Files
  Robert Lipshutz Files
  OCP-McKenna Files.
  White House Central Files
  White House Office Central Files
Gerald Ford Presidential Library, Ann Arbor, Michigan
  Philip Buchen Files
  Dudley Chapman Papers
  Dorothy Downton Files
  Jay French Files
  David Gergen Files
  Kenneth Lazarus Files
  Ron Nessen Papers
  Presidential Handwriting Files
  John Robson Files
  Edward C. Schmults Files
  White House Central Files
Library of Congress, Washington, DC
  Gerhard Gesell Files

Elliot Richardson Papers
Ronald Reagan Presidential Library, Simi Valley, California
  Sherrie Cooksey Files
  Counsel to the President: Investigations Collection
  Counselor to the President: Records Collection
  Bryce Harlow Files
  Richard Hauser Files
  Nancy Hodapp Files
  James E. Jenkins Files
  Robert Kruger Files
  Peter Rusthoven Files
  David B. Waller Files
  White House Office of Records Management: Subject Files Collection

Government Reports and Other Public Documents

House Committee on Government Reform. *The Justice Department's Imple-
  mentation of the Independent Counsel Act, Hearing Before the Committee on
  Government Affairs.* 106th Cong., 2d sess., 2000.
House Committee on Government Reform and Oversight. *The Current
  Implementation of the Independent Counsel Act, Volume 1, Hearings Before
  the Committee on Government Reform and Oversight.* 105th Cong., 1st
  sess., 1997.
———. *The Current Implementation of the Independent Counsel Act, Volume 2,
  Hearings Before the Committee on Government Reform and Oversight.* 105th
  Cong., 1st sess., 1997.
House Committee on the Judiciary. *Continuing Investigation into the U.S.
  Attorneys Controversy and Related Matters, Part 1, Hearing Before the Sub-
  committee on Commercial and Administrative Law of the Committee on the
  Judiciary.* 110th Cong., 1st sess., 2007.
———. *Impeachment Inquiry: William Jefferson Clinton, President of the United
  States, Consideration of Articles of Impeachment: Hearings Before the House
  Committee on the Judiciary.* 105th Cong., 2nd sess., 1998.
———. *Independent Counsel Amendments Act of 1987, Hearings Before the
  Subcommittee on Administrative Law and Governmental Relations.* 100th
  Cong., 1st sess., 1987.
———. *Reauthorization of the Independent Counsel Statute, Part I, Hearings
  Before the Subcommittee on Commercial and Administrative Law.* 106th
  Cong., 1st sess., 1999.
———. *Report No. 102-857, The INSLAW Affair.* 102nd Cong., 2nd sess.,
  September 10, 1992.

———. *Report on the Investigation of the Role of Department of Justice in the Withholding of Environmental Protection Agency Documents from Congress in 1982–1983*. 98th Cong., 1st sess., 1985.

Long Report for Congress *98-283*. Independent Counsel Provisions: An Overview of the Operation of the Law. March 20, 1998.

Report of Independent Counsel David Barrett. In re Henry G. Cisneros. August 13, 1994.

Report of Independent Counsel Arthur Christy. Alleged Possession of Cocaine by Hamilton Jordan in Violation of 21 U.S.C. § 844(a). May 28, 1980.

Report of Independent Counsel Joseph DiGenova. Final report of the Independent Counsel in re Janet Mullins. November 30, 1995.

Report of Independent Counsel James C. McKay. Appendix to Report of Independent Counsel in re Franklyn C. Nofziger, Edwin Meese III, Before the US Court of Appeals for the DC Circuit, Division No. 87-1. July 18, 1988.

———. Report of Independent Counsel in re Edwin Meese III, Before the US Court of Appeals for the DC Circuit, Division No. 87-1, July 5, 1988.

Report of Independent Counsel Alexia Morrison in re Theodore B. Olson and Robert Perry: Report of the Independent Counsel. December 27, 1988.

Report of Independent Counsel Robert W. Ray. Final report in re Madison Guaranty Savings & Loan Association. 5 vols. 2002.

———. Final Report, in re William David Watkins and in re Hillary Rodham Clinton. 2000.

Report of Independent Counsel Kenneth Starr. Report on the Death of Vincent W. Foster, Jr., by the Office of Independent Counsel in re Madison Guaranty Savings & Loan Association, Before the US Court of Appeals for the DC Circuit, Division No. 94-1. October 10, 1997.

Report of Independent Counsel Jacob Stein. Report of the Independent Counsel Concerning Edwin Meese III. September 20, 1984.

Report of Independent Counsel Lawrence E. Walsh. Iran-Contra: The Final Report, Before the US Court of Appeals for the DC Circuit. August 4, 1993.

Senate Committee on Governmental Affairs. The Ethics in Government Act of 1978, Senate Report 95-170. 95th Cong., 2nd sess., 1978.

———. *Ethics in Government Act Amendments of 1982, Hearings Before the Subcommittee on Oversight of Government Management*. 97th Cong., 2nd sess., 1982.

———. *The Future of the Independent Counsel Act, Hearings Before the Committee on Governmental Affairs*. 106th Cong., 1st sess., 1999.

——. Independent Counsel Reauthorization Act of 1987: Report of the Committee on Governmental Affairs. 100th Cong., 1st sess., 1987.

Senate Committee on the Judiciary. *Confirmation Hearing on the Nomination of John Ashcroft to be Attorney General of the United States, Hearing Before the Committee on the Judiciary.* 107th Cong., 1st sess., 2001.

——. *Confirmation Hearing on the Nomination of Alberto R. Gonzales to be Attorney General of the United States.* 109th Cong., 1st sess., 2005.

——. *Confirmation of Edwin Meese III, Hearings Before the Committee on the Judiciary.* 99th Cong., 1st sess., 1985.

——. *Department of Justice Oversight, Hearings Before the Committee on the Judiciary.* 110th Cong., 1st sess., 2007.

——. *Nomination of Michael Mukasey to be Attorney General of the United States.* 110th Cong., 1st sess., 2007.

——. *Nomination of Janet Reno to be Attorney General of the United States.* 103rd Cong., 1st sess., 1993.

——. *Nomination of Elliot L. Richardson to be Attorney General, Hearings Before the Committee on the Judiciary.* 93rd Cong., 1st sess., 1973.

——. *Nomination of William B. Saxbe to be Attorney General.* 93rd Cong., 1st sess., 1973.

——. *Preserving Prosecutorial Independence: Is the Department of Justice Politicizing the Hiring and Firing of U.S. Attorneys? Hearings Before the Committee on the Judiciary.* 110th Cong., 1st sess., 2007.

Select Books and Articles

Federal Investigations, Prosecutors, and Ethics—General Theory and Practice

Anechiarico, Frank and James P. Jacob. *The Pursuit of Absolute Integrity: How Corruption Control Makes Government Ineffective.* Chicago: University of Chicago Press, 1996.

Baker, Nancy. *Conflicting Loyalties: Law and Politics in the Attorney General's Office, 1879–1990.* Lawrence: University Press of Kansas, 1992.

Berg, Larry L., Harlan Hahn, and John R. Schmidhauser. *Corruption in the American Political System.* Morristown, N.J.: General Learning Press, 1976.

Borelli, Mary Anne. *The President's Cabinet: Gender, Power and Representation.* Boulder, Colo.: Lynne Rienner, 2002.

Carter, Stephen L. "The Independent Counsel Mess." *Harvard Law Review* 102 (1988): 105–41.

Cass, Ronald A. *The Rule of Law in America.* Baltimore: Johns Hopkins University Press, 2001.

Clayton, Cornell. *The Politics of Justice: The Attorney General and the Making of Legal Policy*. New York: Sharpe, 1992.

——,ed. *Government Lawyers: The Federal Legal Bureaucracy and Presidential Politics*. Lawrence: University Press of Kansas, 1995.

Cox, Archibald. "Curbing Special Counsels." *New York Times*, December 12, 1996.

DeLeon, Peter. *Thinking About Political Corruption*. Armonk, N.Y.: Sharpe, 1993.

Eastland, Terry. *Ethics, Politics and the Independent Counsel*. Washington, DC: National Legal Center for the Public Interest, 1989.

Eisenstein, James. *Counsel for the United States: U.S. Attorneys in the Political and Legal Systems*. Baltimore: Johns Hopkins University Press, 1978.

Ginsberg, Benjamin, and Martin Shefter. *Politics by Other Means*. New York: Norton, 1999.

Grossman, Eugene. "A Symposium on Special Prosecutors and the Role of the Independent Counsel: Introduction." *Hofstra Law Review* 16 (Fall 1987): 1–9.

Harriger, Katy J. *Independent Justice: The Federal Special Prosecutor in American Politics*. Lawrence: University Press of Kansas, 1992.

——. *The Special Prosecutor in American Politics*. 2nd ed., rev. Lawrence: University Press of Kansas, 2000.

Heclo, Hugh. *A Government of Strangers: Executive Politics in Washington*. Washington, DC: Brookings Institution Press, 1977.

Johnson, Charles A., and Dannette Brickman. *Independent Counsel: The Law and the Investigations*. Washington, DC: CQ Press, 2001.

Johnson, James N. "The Influence of Politics upon the Office of the American Prosecutor." *American Journal of Criminal Law* 2 (1973): 187–215.

Kessler, Ronald. *The FBI: Inside the World's Most Powerful Law Enforcement Agency—by the Award-Winning Journalist Whose Investigation Brought Down FBI Director William S. Sessions*. New York: Pocket Books, 1993.

Kirchheimer, Otto. *Political Justice: The Use of Legal Procedures for Political Ends*. Princeton, N.J.: Princeton University Press, 1961.

Lichtblau, Eric. *The Remaking of American Justice*. New York: Pantheon Books, 2008.

Light, Paul Charles. *Monitoring Government: Inspectors General and the Search for Accountability*. Washington, DC: Brookings Institution, 1993.

Mackenzie, G. Calvin. *Scandal Proof: Do Ethics Laws Make Government Ethical?* Washington, DC: Brookings Institution, 2002.

McDonald, William F., ed. *The Prosecutor*. Beverly Hills, Calif.: Sage, 1979.

McGee, Jim, and Brian Duffy. *Main Justice*. New York: Simon & Schuster, 1996.

Miller, Frank. *Prosecution*. Boston: Little, Brown, 1969.

Moore, Mark H., and Margaret Jane Gates. *Social Research Perspectives: Inspectors General, Junkyard Dogs or Man's Best Friend*. New York: Russell Sage Foundation, 1986.

Orth, John. *Due Process of Law*. Lawrence: University Press of Kansas, 2003.

Roberts, Robert. *White House Ethics*. Westport, Conn.: Greenwood Press, 1988.

Rozell, Mark J. *Executive Privilege: The Dilemma of Secrecy and Accountability*. Baltimore: Johns Hopkins University, 1994.

Schultz, Jeffrey D. *Presidential Scandals*. Washington, DC: CQ Press, 1999.

Thompson, Dennis F. *Political Ethics and Public Office*. Cambridge, Mass.: Harvard University Press, 1987.

Turkheimer, Frank M. "The Executive Investigates Itself." *California Law Review* 65 (1977): 597–635.

Scandals and Corruption—Thoughout History and in Multiple Administrations

Andrew, Christopher. *For the President's Eyes Only: Secret Intelligence and the American Presidency*. New York: Harper Collins, 1995.

Eisenstadt, Abraham S., et al. *Before Watergate: Problems of Corruption in American Society*. New York: Brooklyn College Press, 1978.

Frank, Jeffrey. "The INSLAW File." *Washington Post Magazine*, June 14, 1992, 14.

Garment, Suzanne. *Scandal: The Culture of Mistrust in American Politics*. New York: Anchor Books, 1992.

Mitchell, Jack. *Executive Privilege: Two Centuries of White House Scandals*. New York: Hippocrene, 1992.

Noggle, Burl. *Teapot Dome: Oil and Politics in the 1920s*. Baton Rouge: Louisiana State University Press, 1962.

Richardson, Elliot L. "A High-Tech Watergate." *New York Times*, October 21, 1991.

Ross, Shelley. *Fall From Grace: Sex, Scandal and Corruption in American Politics from 1702 to the Present*. New York: Ballantine, 1988.

Sorenson, Theodore. *Watchmen in the Night: Presidential Accountability after Watergate*. Cambridge, Mass.: MIT Press, 1975.

Woodward, Bob. *Shadow: Five Presidents and the Legacy of Watergate*. New York: Simon & Schuster, 1999.

Scandals and Corruption—Nixon Administration

Agnew, Spiro T. *Go Quietly . . . or Else*. New York: Morrow, 1980.

Aitken, Jonathan. *Nixon: A Life*. New York: Regnery, 1996.

Ben-Veniste, Richard, and George Frampton Jr. *Stonewall: The Real Story of the Watergate Prosecution*. New York: Simon & Schuster, 1979.

Bernstein, Carl, and Bob Woodward. *All the President's Men*. New York: Simon & Schuster, 1974.

Cohen, Richard M., and Jules Witcover. *A Heartbeat Away: The Investigation and Resignation of Vice President Spiro T. Agnew*. New York: Viking, 1974.

Dash, Samuel. *Chief Counsel: Inside the Ervin Committee—the Untold Story of Watergate*. New York: Random House, 1976.

Doyle, James. *Not Above the Law: The Battles of Watergate Prosecutors Cox and Jaworski*. New York: William Morrow, 1977.

Emery, Fred. *Watergate: The Corruption of American Politics and the Fall of Richard Nixon*. New York: Random House, 1994.

Ervin, Samuel. *The Whole Truth: The Watergate Conspiracy*. New York: Random House, 1980.

Federal Bureau of Investigation. *Spiro T. Agnew: An Electronic Resource*. Washington, DC: FBI, 2003.

———. *Watergate: An Electronic Resource*. Washington, DC: FBI, 2000.

Gormley, Ken. *Archibald Cox: Conscience of a Nation*. Boston: Addison-Wesley, 1997.

Harris, John F. *The Survivor: Bill Clinton in the White House*. New York: Random House, 2005.

Jaworski, Leon. *The Right and the Power: The Prosecution of Watergate*. New York: Reader's Digest Press, 1976.

Jenness, Linda and Andrew Pulley. *Watergate: The View from the Left*. New York: Pathfinder, 1973.

Kutler, Stanley I. *Abuse of Power: The New Nixon Tapes*. New York: Free Press, 1997.

———. *The Wars of Watergate: The Last Crisis of Richard Nixon*. New York: Alfred A. Knopf, 1990.

Lukas, J. Anthony. *Nightmare: The Underside of the Nixon Years*. New York: Viking, 1976.

Mosher, Frederick C. *Watergate: Implications for Responsible Government*. New York: Basic Books, 1974.

Richardson, Elliot. "The Saturday Night Massacre." *Atlantic Monthly*, March 1976, 40-44.

Rosen, James. *The Strong Man: John Mitchell and the Secrets of Watergate*. New York: Doubleday, 2008.

Saxbe, William B. *I've Seen the Elephant*. Kent, Ohio: Kent State University Press, 2000.

Schudson, Michael. *Watergate in American Memory: How We Remember, Forget, and Reconstruct the Past*. New York: Oxford University Press, 1980.

Sirica, John. *To Set the Record Straight: The Break-in, the Tapes, and the Pardon*. New York: Norton, 1979.

Small, Melvin. *The Presidency of Richard Nixon*. Lawrence: University Press of Kansas, 1999.

Summers, Anthony. *The Arrogance of Power*. New York: Viking, 2000.

Thompson, Fred D. *At That Point in Time: The Inside Story of the Senate Watergate Committee*. New York: Quadrangle, 1975.

Witcover, Jules. *White Knight: The Rise of Spiro Agnew*. New York: Random House, 1972.

Scandals and Corruption—Ford Administration

Ford, Gerald. *A Time to Heal: The Autobiography of Gerald R. Ford*. New York: Harper and Row, 1979.

Molenhoff, Clark R. *The Man Who Pardoned Nixon*. New York: St. Martin's, 1976.

Schapsmeier, Edward L. *Gerald Ford's Date with Destiny: A Political Biography*. New York: Lang, 1989.

Scandals and Corruption—Carter Administration

Babcock, Charles R. "Civiletti and Justice Staff Find Themselves on the Defense." *Washington Post*, September 2, 1979.

Babcock, Charles R., and Edward Walsh." Civiletti admits he talked with President about Billy," *Washington Post*, July 20, 1980.

Bell, Griffin B., with Ronald J. Ostrow. *Taking Care of the Law*. New York: William Morrow, 1982.

Dumbrell, John. *The Carter Presidency: A Re-evaluation*. New York: St. Martin's, 1993.

Glad, Betty. *Jimmy Carter: In Search of the Great White House*. New York: Norton, 1980.

Jordan, Hamilton. *Crisis: The Last Year of the Carter Presidency*. New York: Putnam, 1982.

Kaufman, Burton. *The Presidency of James Earl Carter, Jr.* Lawrence: University Press of Kansas, 1993.

Lance, Bert. *The Truth of the Matter: My Life In and Out of Politics*. New York: Summit, 1991.

Lasky, Victor. *Jimmy Carter: The Man and the Myth*. New York: Richard Marek, 1979.

Mollenhoff, Clark R. *The President Who Failed: Carter Out of Control*. New York: MacMillan, 1980.

Pound, Edward. "Carter's Business Cleared in Inquiry of Campaign Funds." *New York Times*, October 17, 1979.

Rozell, Mark. *The Press and the Carter Presidency*. Westport, Conn: Westview, 1989.

Safire, William. "The Lance Cover-Up." *New York Times*, August 1, 1977.

Stapleton, Ruth. *Brother Billy*. New York: Harper and Row, 1978.

Scandals and Corruption—Reagan Administration

Draper, Theodore. "How Not to Deal with the Iran-Contra Crimes." *New York Review of Books*, June 14, 1990, 39–44.

———."Rewriting the Iran-Contra Story." *New York Review of Books*, January 19, 1989, 38–45.

———. *A Very Thin Line: The Iran-Contra Affairs*. New York: Hill and Wang, 1991.

Dugger, Ronnie. *On Reagan: The Man and His Presidency*. New York: McGraw Hill, 1985.

Ehrman, John. *The Eighties: America in the Age of Reagan*. New Haven: Yale University Press, 2005.

Johnson, Haynes. *Sleepwalking through History: America in the Reagan Years*. New York: Norton, 1991.

Kmiec, Douglas W. *The Attorney General's Lawyer: Inside the Meese Justice Department*. New York: Praeger, 1992.

Marshall, Jonathan, et al. *The Iran-Contra Connection: Secret Teams and Covert Operations in the Reagan Era*. Boston: South End Press, 1987.

Meese, Edwin. *With Reagan: The Inside Story*. Washington, DC: Regnery, 1992.

Schieffer, Bob, and Gary Paul Gates. *The Acting President*. New York: Plume, 1990.

Smith, William French. *Law and Justice in the Reagan Administration: The Memoirs of an Attorney General*. Stanford: Hoover Institution Press, 1991.

Strober, Deborah Hart, and Gerald S. Strober. *The Reagan Presidency: An Oral History of This Era*. Washington, DC: Potomac Books, 2003.

Timbers, Edwin. "Legal and Institutional Aspects of the Iran-Contra Affair." *Presidential Studies Quarterly* 20 (Winter 1990): 31–41.

Traub, James. *Too Good to Be True: The Outlandish Story of Wedtech*. New York: Doubleday, 1990.

Walsh, Lawrence. *Firewall: The Iran-Contra Conspiracy and Cover-up*. New York: Norton, 1997.

Welfield, Irving. *HUD Scandals: Howling Headlines and Silent Fiascoes*. New Brunswick: Transaction Publishers, 1992.

Wills, Garry. *Reagan's America: Innocents at Home*. Garden City, N.Y.: Doubleday, 1987.

Wroe, Ann. *Lives Lies, and the Iran-Contra Affair*. London: Taurus, 1992.

Scandals and Corruption — George H. W. Bush Administration

Barilleaux, Ryan J. and Mark J. Rozell. *Power and Prudence: The Presidency of George H. W. Bush*. College Station: Texas A&M University Press, 2004.

Barilleaux, Ryan J., and Mary E. Stuckey, eds. *Leadership and the Bush Presidency*. Westport, Conn.: Praeger, 1992.

Berry, Steven K. "Senate Republicans Hire Official Cited in Clinton Passport Search." *New York Times*, January 19, 1993.

Campbell, Colin, and Bert A. Rockman, eds. *The Bush Presidency: First Appraisals*. Chatham, N.J.: Chatham House, 1991.

Glaberson, William. "Thornburgh Policy Leads to a Sharp Ethics Battle." *New York Times*, March 1, 1991.

Mervin, David. *George Bush and the Guardianship Presidency*. New York: St. Martin's, 1996.

Pincus, Walter. "Tamposi Implicates Superiors in Passport Search Scandal." *Washington Post*, November 17, 1992.

Rohter, Larry. "Miami Prosecutor's Stormy Passage." *New York Times*, September 6, 1991.

Seib, Gerald. "On a Slow Road Towards Justice." *The Wall Street Journal*, April 6, 1994.

Scandals and Corruption — Clinton Administration

Baker, Peter. The Breach: Inside the Impeachment and Trial of William Jefferson Clinton. New York: Simon & Schuster, 2000.

Blumenthal, Sidney. The Clinton Wars. New York: Farrar, Straus and Giroux, 2003.

Brinkley, Alan. "Kenneth Starr's Page in the History Books." New York Times, February 7, 1999.

Carpozi, George, Jr. Clinton Confidential. Del Mar, Calif: Dalton, 1995.

Goldberg, Jeffrey. "What is Janet Reno Thinking?" New York Times Magazine, July 6, 1997.

Gormley, Ken. The Death of American Virtue: Clinton v. Starr. New York: Crown, 2010.

——. "Monica Lewinsky, Impeachment, and the Death of the Independent

Counsel Law: What Congress Can Salvage from the Wreckage—a Minimalist View." Maryland Law Review, 60 (2001): 97–148.

Johnson, David. "Reno Rejects a Prosecutor on Clinton and Gore Calls: Bitter G.O.P. Vows to Fight." New York Times, December 3, 1997.

Labaton, Stephen. "At issue: Intent of Prosecutor Law." New York Times, December 3, 1997.

McDougal, James, and Curtis Wilkie. Arkansas Mischief. New York: Henry Holt, 1998.

Rosen, Jeffrey. "Low Crimes and Misdemeanors: Is Kenneth Starr Really a Rogue or Just Part of a Trend?" New Yorker, November 16, 1998, 41–47.

———. "Kenneth Starr, Trapped." New York Times Magazine, June 1, 1997, 42.

Rozell, Mark, and Clyde Wilcox, eds. The Clinton Scandal and the Future of American Government. Washington, DC: Georgetown University Press, 2000.

Ruddy, Christopher. The Strange Death of Vincent Foster: An Investigation. New York: Free Press, 1997.

Stephanopoulos, George. All Too Human. Boston: Little, Brown, 1999.

Stewart, James B. Blood Sport: The President and His Adversaries. New York: Simon & Schuster, 1996.

Toobin, Jeffrey. "Starr Can't Help It." New Yorker, May 18, 1998, 32–38.

———. A Vast Conspiracy: The Real Story of the Sex Scandal That Nearly Brought Down a President. New York: Random House, 1999.

Winerip, Michael. "Ken Starr Would Not Be Denied." New York Times Magazine, September 6, 1998, 36.

Wittes, Benjamin. Starr: A Reassessment. New Haven: Yale University Press, 2002.

———. "Starr Search: The Man Who Placed Truth over Justice." New Republic, April 3, 2000.

Scandals and Corruption—George W. Bush Administration

Baker, Nancy V. *General Ashcroft: Attorney at War.* Lawrence: University Press of Kansas, 2006.

Draper, Robert. *Dead Certain: The Presidency of George W. Bush.* New York: Free Press, 2007.

Goldsmith, Jack. *The Terror Presidency: Law and Judgment inside the Bush Administration.* New York: Norton, 2007.

Hersch, Seymour M. "How Conflicts between the Bush Administration and the Intelligence Community Marred the Reporting on Iraq's Weapons." *New Yorker*, October 27, 2003.

Johnson, Carrie. "Probe of Alleged Torture Weighed." *Washington Post*, July 12, 2009.

———. "Prosecutor to Probe CIA Interrogations." *Washington Post*, August 25, 2009.

Kane, Paul, "House Will Investigate CIA's Handling of Canceled Program." *Washington Post*, July 20, 2009.

Mayer, Jane. "Counterfactual: A Curious History of the CIA's Interrogation Program." *New Yorker*, March 29, 2010.

Minutaglio, Bill. *The President's Counselor: The Rise to Power of Alberto Gonzales.* New York: Harper-Collins, 2006.

Index

The letter *t* following a page number denotes a table.

Bennett, Leslie, 35
Bentsen, Lloyd, 44
Bernstein, Carl, 159*n*27
Berry, Steven K., 122–23
Bert Lance for Governor Campaign
  Committee, 127
Biden, Joseph, 64
Bob Jones University, 50
Boland Amendment, 14, 17
Borelli, Mary Anne, 45
Bork, Robert H., 22; and the firing of
  Cox, 74, 154*n*7
Bourne, Peter G., 130–31, 168*n*50
Braniff (airline), 118
Brewer, C. Madison, 101
Brian, Earl W., 102
Bristow, Benjamin, 43
Brooks, Jack B., 38, 102, 128
Broward County (Florida) Sheriff's
  Office, 106
Brownell, Herbert, 138
Bua, Nicholas, 103
Buchen, Philip, 88, 116
Burns, Arnold, 97
Burr, Aaron, 63
Burton, Danny Lee (Dan), 82
Bush, George H. W., 30, 104, 107;
  and the Clinton passport scandal,
  122, 124, 134; and INSLAW, 100,
  103; and Iran-Contra scandal,
  14–15, 17, 19; and Thornburgh,
  48, 56
Bush, George W., 1, 2, 4, 44, 45,
  167*n*25; administration of, xi, 1, 5,
  32, 105; and Ashcroft, 45, 49–51;
  and dismissal of US attorneys, 110,
  111; and enhanced interrogation,
  1, 3–5, 6; and Gonzales, 2, 44,
  50–51, 59–60, 139; and Holder,
  155*n*32; and Mukasey, 51; and Olson, 93; and the Plame revelation,
  133; speeches of, 131, 132; and

warrantless surveillance program,
  1, 4–6, 51, 106, 109; and weapons
  of mass destruction, 131
Bush, John Ellis (Jeb), 104, 167*n*25
Bush-Quayle Campaign, 124
Buzhardt, Fred, 66
Bybee, Jay, 50
Byrd, Robert, 129

CAB. *See* Civil Aeronautics Board
  (CAB)
Calhoun (Georgia) First National
  Bank, 126, 127, 129
Capital City Club (Atlanta), 55
Capital Management Services (CMS),
  79
Card, Andrew, 109
Carter administration, 38, 88
Carter, Jimmy, 38, 41, 102; and Bell,
  44, 54–55, 157*n*61; and the Billy
  Carter affair, 74–76; and Bourne,
  130–31; and the Kelley investiga-
  tion, 92; and the Lance investiga-
  tion, 125–30
Carter, Rosalynn, 75
Carter, William (Billy), 74–76
Casey, Paula, 79
Casey, William, 14–15, 17
Casolaro, Danny, 103–104
CBS, 144; News, 98–99
Central Intelligence Agency. *See* CIA
  (Central Intelligence Agency)
Cernuda, Ramon, 105
Chappaquiddick scandal, 70
Cheney, Richard (Dick), 64, 132–33
Chicago Seven, 53
Christian Science Monitor, 131
Chung, Johnny, 81, 82
Church Committee. *See* US Senate:
  Select Committee to Study Gov-
  ernmental Activities with Respect
  to Intelligence Activities

CIA (Central Intelligence Agency), 18, 113; and congressional oversight, 5–6; and electronic surveillance program, 4–5, 6, 69; and informants, 165*n*62; and Iran-Contra, 18; and interrogation/torture of Guantanamo detainees, 4–6; and the Niger uranium scandal, 131–33; and Vice President Cheney, 132; and the Watergate scandal, 69–71, 113
    directors of: Casey, 14–15, 17; Panetta, 4, 12; Tenet, 4, 131–32
Cisneros, Henry G., 11–13; and misconduct, 18, 19, 33, 141
Civil Aeronautics Board (CAB), 118–23
Civil Service, 117
Civiletti, Benjamin, 75–76, 97; as inner circle attorney general, 47*t*2.2, 55
Clayton, Cornell, xi
Clinger, William, 76
Clinton, Bill, 1, 6, 30, 41, 110; and the appointment of independent counsel, 8, 21; choice for attorney general, 48–49; and the Cisneros payoff scandal, 11–13; and citizenship issues, 122, 166*n*16; and Fiske, 21; and fundraising irregularities, 81–83; and Holder, x, 1; impeachment of, 83, 85; and the INSLAW scandal, 100, 103; and passport search, 122–24, 134, 167*nn*23, 24; and Reno, 12, 44, 49, 80, 144 *(see also main entry);* and the Rich pardon, x, 1, 149*n*1; and the Starr investigations, 6, 44, 83–85; and the Travel Office investigation, 76–78; Whitewater investigation of, 78–80
Clinton, Hillary: and the Travel Office investigation, 77–78; and the

Whitewater investigation, 79–80
CMS. *See* Capital Management Services
CNN, 144
Coburn, Tom A., 111
Code of Official Conduct (Congressional), 121
Coelho, Anthony (Tony), 98
Colfax, Schuyler, 63
Colson, Charles, 69
Comey, James, B., 108–13, 133
Committee to Reelect the President (CREEP), 53, 54, 70
Comprehensive Environmental Response, Compensation, and Liability Act (CERCLA), 9
Comptroller of the Currency, 128
conflict(s) of interest, 61, 145; and the attorney general, 6, 19, 86; avoidance of, 136; and Carter's standards, 126; and the Clintons, 79; conditions that require a response, 19–20, 29, 114; in the executive branch, 34, 145; and Freeh, 82–83; and Meese, 15, 57, 97; and O'Melia, 119; and a special prosecutor, 21; and Starr, 84; and the three-judge panel, ix
Congressional Black Caucus, 98
Congressional Research Service, 165*n*62
Connally, John B., Jr., 64
Constitution of the United States, vii, xii, 38–39; Fourth Amendment, 108; Fifth Amendment, xii, 82; Fourteenth Amendment, xii; Twenty-fifth Amendment, 63
Contras (Nicaraguan guerilla fighters), 14, 15, 17
Convention against Torture and Other Cruel, Inhuman and Degrading Treatment or Punishment, 150*n*10

independent prosecutorial judgment, 22, 41, 166n2; violation of, 96. *See also* independent and special prosecutor(s)
Evans, Donald L., 59
Everglades, 104, 107
executive privilege: and Barr, 56; and the EPA, 93–95; and Nixon, 73, 156n36

Fall, Albert, 35
FBI (Federal Bureau of Investigation): background checks, 11–13, 33, 119; circumvention of, 69; and the Clinton citizenship/passport issue, 123, 124; and the Clinton Travel Office, 76, 78; and the Cisneros payoffs, 11–13, 19, 141; Domestic Intelligence Division of, 87; and Iran-Contra scandal, 16, 18, 56; and the John Powell/EEOC investigation 116–17, 119; and Lehtinen investigation, 106; misappropriation of funds by, 89–92; oversight of, 37, 76, 78, 88; Recreation Association, 89, 92; and uranium forgery allegations, 132; and the Watergate investigation, 30, 70–71; and Whitewater/Madison Guaranty investigation, 76, 79; and the William Gray leak, 98; unauthorized surveillance of King, 87–89 *directors of:* Freeh, 12, 13, 82, 83, 141; Kelley (*see under main entry*); Mueller, 109; Sessions, 154n13; Webster, 16–17
Federal Bureau of Investigation. *See* FBI
Federal Election Commission, 147
Federal Intelligence Surveillance Act (FISA), 107–108
Feingold, Russell, 59–60

Feinstein, Dianne, 50, 51, 110
Felt, W. Mark, 70; as "Deep Throat," 159n27
Fielding, Fred, 71
Fielding, Lewis J., 69, 73
Fifth Amendment *See* Constitution of the United States: Fifth Amendment
Fine, Glenn, 112
First National Bank of Chicago, 126–27
FISA. *See* Federal Intelligence Surveillance Act (FISA)
Fiske, Robert (Bob), Jr., 21, 76, 78, 80, 150n15
Fitzgerald, Patrick, 133
Fitzwater, Marlin, 105
Florida (state of): Dade County (state attorney's office), 49
Florida Wildlife Federation, 104
Ford, Gerald R., vii; alleged campaign irregularities of, 38, 120–21; appointment as Vice President, 63; and the CAB investigation, 118–19; and investigation of FBI director Kelly, 91; and the John Powell/EEOC investigation 116–17, 119; and Levi 36–37, 48, 92, 140; and the Nixon pardon, viii, 26; and Saxbe, 47; and the surveillance of King, 87–88
Foster, Vincent, 76, 78, 80
Fountain, Lawrence, 38
Fourteenth Amendment. *See* Constitution of the United States: Fourteenth Amendment
Fourth Amendment. *See* Constitution of the United States: Fourth Amendment
Fox News, 144
Freedom of Information Act (FOIA), 122, 123, 124

Justice Department (*cont.*)
  Intelligence, 162*n*2; Professional
  Responsibility (OPR) *(see under
  main entry* Office of Professional
  Responsibility); Public Information, 56; Public Integrity (OPI),
  12, 37, 38, 94, 145
  solicitors general: Bork, 22, 74,
  154*n*7; Griswold, 53, 156*n*51;
  Starr *(see main entry)*

Kaufman, Burton, 75
Kauper, Thomas E., 53
Kean, Thomas, 9
Keating, Frank, 105
Keating, William J., 47
Keeney, John C. (Jack), 94, 117
Kelley, Clarence, 89–92, 141,
  162*n*10; and the Ford investiga-
  tion, 120, 121
Kennedy, Edward M. (Ted), 50, 70,
  118–19
Kennedy, John F., 43, 54, 87
Kennedy, Robert F., 43, 44, 87, 139
Kennedy, Ted. *See* Kennedy,
  Edward M. (Ted)
Kennedy, William, 165*n*62
Kent County (Michigan) Republican
  Committee, 121
King, Martin Luther, Jr., 87–89, 141
Kirchheimer, Otto, 26
Kissinger, Henry, 68, 69
Kleindienst, Richard, 36; as inner cir-
  cle attorney general, 47*t*2.2, 52–54;
  and the ITT investigation, 119; and
  Mitchell, 53, 71; resignation of, 43,
  72; and Watergate, 71, 72
Kohl, Herbert H. (Herb), 2
Krogh, Egil (Bud), 69

LaBella, Charles, 83
Lance, Bert, 125–29

Lavelle Superfund scandal. *See* Superfund scandal. *See also* Lavelle, Rita
Lavelle, Rita: and congressional investigations, 92–94; and a divided
  government, 33; at EPA, 9–11, 19;
  and the Justice Department, 19
Leahy, Patrick, 3, 109–10
Ledeen, Michael, 132
LeGrand, Ronald, 103
Lehtinen, Dexter, 104–107
Levi, Edward H.: and the appointment of special prosecutors, 36–38,
  140–41; and the CAB investiga-
  tion, 118; and Ford campaign
  irregularities, 38, 120–22; and
  investigation of FBI director Kel-
  ley, 89–92, 141; as outer circle
  attorney general, 46, 47*t*2.2, 91,
  92, 140; qualifications of, 138; and
  support of OPR, 37, 48, 86–88,
  97, 154*n*12; and surveillance of
  King, 87–88, 90
Levitas, Elliott, 93
Lewinsky, Monica, 73, 83–85
Libby, Lewis, 133
Liddy, G. Gordon, 54, 69, 70, 71
Lipshutz, Robert, 38, 128
Los Angeles Times, 132
Love Canal disaster, 9
Lukas, J. Anthony, 66, 67
Lumbard, J. Edward, 72

Mack, Connie, 107
Madison Guaranty Savings & Loan,
  79–80
Magruder, Jeb Stuart, 71
Mahoney, George P., 64
Martinez, Raul, 106
Martino, Rocco, 132
Maryland State Roads Commission,
  64
Mathias, Charles, 58

McCord, James W., 70–72

McDougal, Jim, 79

McDougal, Susan, 79

McFarlane, Robert (Bud), 13; and Cooper, 15–17; as envoy in arms sales to Iran, 14–15; and misconduct, 18; resignation of, 19

McGrath, J. Howard, 43

McKay, James, 97

McKean, John, 57

McLarty, Mac, 78

McNulty, Paul, 111

Medas, James, 9

Medlar, Linda, 11–13

Meese, Edwin, 23; and appointment of independent counsel, 94–95; confirmation of, 44, 57, 139; and due process of law, 136; and the INSLAW scandal, 101, 102, 103; and the Iran-Contra scandal, 14–18, 19, 95; and Lehtinen, 104; as oval office attorney general, 44, 47t2.2, 48, 52, 57–59, 87, 95, 143; and Reagan, 14–15, 44, 138; resignation of, 48, 97; and Superfund, 9, 11, 94–95; and Wedtech, 95–97

Meet the Press, 51

Miers, Harriet, 112

Mitchell, John, 23, 55, 137; confirmation of, 44; and due process, 136; as inner circle attorney general, 28, 47t2.2, 52–53, 143; and the Watergate scandal, 26, 69, 71, 120

Mondale, Walter, 129

Monroe (James) administration, 49

Morrison v. Olson, ix, x, 23, 30, 31

Morrison, Alexia J., 11, 94

Morrison, Jane Ann, 165n67

Mountain Bell (telephone company), 93

MSNBC, 144

Mueller, Robert, 109

Mukasey, Michael: and the appointment of a special prosecutor, 112–13: as outer circle attorney general, 46, 47t2.2, 51, 141; qualifications of, 138

Mullins, Janet G., 122, 124

Myers v. United States, 38, 144, 153n1

National Bank of Georgia (NBG), 126–28, 129

National Marine Engineers Beneficial Association, 120–25

National Organization for the Reform of Marijuana Laws (NORML), 130

National Security Agency (NSA), 18, 51, 107–109

National Security Council. *See* US National Security Council

Navarro, Nick, 106

Negroponte, John, 109

New Jersey Supreme Court, 72

New York Times, 55, 69, 78, 100, 132, 146; and the Bert Lance scandal, 125, 127, 128; and Clinton passport search, 167n24

New Yorker, 132

Nicaraguan Democratic Resistance Forces, 16

Niger, 131

Nixon, Donald, 74

Nixon, Richard M., xi, 110; and the Agnew investigation, 63–68, 158n19; and the appointment of a special prosecutor, 72–74; calls for his impeachment, 22, 67; and EEOC, 116, 119; executive misconduct of, 137; and the firing of Cox, viii, 22, 36, 47, 54, 73–74, 137, 154n7; and Kelley, 91; and Kleindienst, 54–55; and

www.ingramcontent.com/pod-product-compliance
Lightning Source LLC
Chambersburg PA
CBHW021903020426
42334CB00013B/462